IN QUEST OF EXCELLENCE

Success is to be measured not so much by the position that one has reached in life, as by the obstacles which he has overcome while trying to succeed.

—Brooker T. Washington

IN QUEST OF EXCELLENCE...

Benjamin Franklin

Marcus Aurelius

Napoleon Bonaparte

Ralph Waldo Emerson

Mother Teresa

By

S.M. Bijli

ANMOL PUBLICATIONS PVT. LTD.

NEW DELHI - 110 002 (INDIA)

ANMOL PUBLICATIONS PVT. LTD.
4374/4B, Ansari Road, Daryaganj
New Delhi - 110 002
Ph.: 23261597, 23278000
Visit us at: www.anmolpublications.com

In Quest of Excellence

First Published, 2004

ISBN 81-261-1795-8

PRINTED IN INDIA

Published by J.L. Kumar for Anmol Publications Pvt. Ltd., New Delhi - 110 002 and Printed at Mehra Offset Press, Delhi.

Dedication

In loving memory of my beloved wife
Ittiyanath Madhavi Bijli
M.A. Econ, B.Sc. Physics

(November 27, 1932–August 5, 1976)

(D/o The Late Mr. P. Krishna Menon)
B.A., B.L.

on whom
God in His Mercy had
bestowed
the triple qualities of
tolerance, patience, and endurance
and
who cherished the ambition
'never to give pain to another'

I am surprised at her image which remains impressed in my eye, though constantly washed (with tears)
Such tears I shed, that as they coursed in my eye, everyone paused to ask:
"which (new) river is this?"

Contents

Preface

The desire to sketch the portraits of some of the great men and women who touched the heights of excellence, owe to a conversation I had with some university students who happen to travel with me in the train from Madras to Delhi, and who were expressing their regrets for not knowing and learning about some of the great men and women the world has produced. I, therefore, felt imperative to draw a simple introductory sketch of some of the philosophers, statesmen, men and women of courage, wisdom and compassion, to en noble rather than to destroy life and civilization. In fact, it is the duty of the teachers and the parents to make their children know about the great men of the past (provided they themselves know!) which may rouse them into great rage at stories of human wrong and suffuse their eyes with moisture on recitals of heroic deeds of unselfishness and courage. It may create a spark of the divine fire, which may enter noble souls and carry themselves in the pursuit of a generous cause. It may rekindle a spirit and a sense of pride in the greatness of our ancestors and their achievements. An urge to appreciate and to tread in the footsteps of the heroes may help to display in their lives, the love of learning and persistent search for truth, for which these great men were distinguished.

With this aim in view I desired to paint the images of a few personalities who have left their footprints "on the sands of time". Starting with Benjamin Franklin in the first chapter, I took up the philosopher King of Rome Marcus Aurelius in the second chapter followed by Emperor Napoleon Bonaparte and American Philosopher Emerson in the third and fourth chapters. The fifth chapter is a tribute to Mother Teresa.

I am confident, young men and women will develop an interest and appreciate the depth of their commitment, which may perhaps help to shape their personalities.

Perhaps, this is finally to say that only that literature is worth studying which provides us with the richest opportunities for examining our own minds.

Aligarh
August 5, 2001

—S.M. Bijli

Acknowledgements

It was my father the late Mr. K.M. Bijli—humanist and educationist, who first inspired me with the sayings of Franklin, and later about the character and personality of Napoleon. On observing my interest, he gave me a book on the life of Napoleon Bonaparte by Abbott to read. Although it was a very voluminous one with minute print, I enjoyed reading the same, and dragged my mother the late Ms. Bashir-un-Nisa Bibi and my wife the late Madhavi, who were thrilled to hear about the courage and bravery of Napoleon, his humanism and his respect for talents and his appreciation by rewarding the noble deeds. They, however, were screaming on hearing of the treachery and the hypocrisy of the then British Cabinet by inviting Napoleon to England as guest and then arresting him and sending him to St. Helena as a prisoner and the subsequent humiliation and torture by Sir Hudson Lowe, the then Governor of St. Helena and treating him in an uncivilized way. While writing about Napoleon my thoughts naturally went back to those days, and I felt nostalgic.

My Dad used to quote Franklin whenever he found us careless in our duties, which had a profound influence on our character formation. For instance, if we fail to get up in the early hours of the morning, he will quote Franklin's famous saying: "*Early to bed, early to rise makes a man healthy, wealthy and wise*"; and that "*a sleeping fox catches no poultry*" and "*God gives all to industry*", that "*sloth like rust consumes faster than labour wears, while a used key is always bright*". These words made us get up and we started reading and writing. Hence I felt (on observing the lethargic nature of the present day youth) that one should be acquainted with the wise words of such great men of wisdom which would help to mould one's character and way of life. These sayings inspired me to search for such practical words of wisdom and I began reading a number of authors on morals, ethics and philosophy. One such work which attracted me was the philosophy of Emperor Marcus Aurelius— the Philosopher King of Rome. Aurelius believed in the God of love and brotherhood of man. According to him "*There is nothing good and nothing bad, but thinking makes it so. We suffer from our opinions, our inhibitions and our limited vision*". Aurelius preached contentment all his life. Hence, I thought, in this materialistic world I should enrich the minds of the young the philosophical thoughts in brief of Emperor Marcus Aurelius.

The American philosopher Emerson's life and speeches had its impact on me. Emerson says "*man is half in himself, the other half is his expression*". He further says "*Every man I meet, I consider him superior to me in some way*". How thoughtful of Emerson when he said this. His essays on the "*Nature*" and "*The conduct of life*" should be a guide to every young man.

For all these, I should thank my father for instilling in our minds the sayings of such great men of understanding and thought in the early years of our formation. He was Great indeed.

To bestir the youth, I also included in this book what I wrote on Mother Teresa at the time of her passing away, and about her concern for the poor and the unwanted. She conjured up an image of an angelic entity healing the wounds of humanity with the loud proclamation to everyone not to miss the kingdom of God within himself. Love and compassion are part of moral preparation to reflect within man the divinity of God, for, love resolves all differences between man and man, and that only through love, human soul realized the unity of God. The present day youth should know about her sacrifices and comforts and for giving a healing touch to the unwanted and helpless brethren of ours.

To those kind and good who understood me viz. Professor B. Sheik Ali-Former Vice Chancellor of Mangalore and Goa

Universities; Professor Abdur Rahim Kidwai, Director, Academic Staff College, Aligarh Muslim University, Professor G.R. Kamath (Goa), Mr. Aftab Ahmad Khan of AMIR NISHAN, Mr. M.S. Ravi Kumar, Mr. C.K. Thota and Mr. Kamlesh Hari Dwivedi, whose wisdom and affection I have depended on, I can only record, but never adequately express my gratitude.

My younger brother Mr. Amir Ahmad Bijli has been very kind in bearing all the expenses in connection with the preparation of this book. I am thankful to him and his understanding wife Shamim and pray to God for their good health and happiness.

The magnificent library of the Aligarh Muslim University from where I was able to draw a lot of information from the very rare books in the Reserve Section, has been a boon to me. I record my appreciation of the helpful nature of the very obliging staff of both the Reserve Section and the Research Division of this rich store house of knowledge—in particular, the Professionals Dr. Radhay Shyam, Mr. Baqar Ali Khan, Mr. Irtaza Hussain, and Mr. Mazhar Ali.

My devoted friend Mr. Mohd. Akram M.Sc. B.Lib. has been a source of great strength to me, and so is Mr. Jahangir Alam, and Mr. Mohd. Shakir who showered their kindness and love on me. The consistency of their conduct has been impressive.

It would be the "*most unkindest cut of all*" on my part if I do not thank my sister Raufunisa, my son Shariq, my daughters Shaheen and Shireen, and my sons-in-law Qayyum and Syed Ali—for encouraging me in my work of reading and writing; and to my grandsons Shadab, Shiraz, Shahbaz, Shoaib, and Shihab whose outrageous wit and humour cheered me up at moments of gloom; and to Munna Singh Yadav (my personal attendent) for attending to my needs; and to my secretary Mr. Rameshwar Dayal for typing the manuscript in a methodical way.

I also take this opportunity to thank the various authors of the books, journals, magazines, newspapers etc. from where I was able to draw a whole lot of information for the benefit of the present day youth of the country who have no time to go through such voluminous books.

And finally, my sincere feelings of gratefulness to Anmol Publications Pvt. Ltd., New Delhi for promptly agreeing to publish this book.

—S.M. Bijli

Introduction

Excellence implies a striving for the higher standards in every phase of life. As a person contemplates the word 'excellence', he reads into his own aspirations, his own conception of high standards, his hopes for a better world. He thinks not only of the greatness we might achieve but of the mediocrity we have fallen into.

The idea of excellence seem to be attractive to most people and inspiring to some. But taken alone, it is a fairly abstract notion. It is not universally powerful moving force that one might wish. We must ask ourselves what are the moving and meaningful ideas that will inspire and sustain people as they strive for excellence. The answer is, that, it is our well established ideal of individual fulfilment. The ideal is implicit in our conviction concerning the worth of an individual. It undergirds our belief in equality of opportunity. It is expressed in our conviction that every individual should be en nobled to achieve the best in him.

There are impressive opportunities for the able individual to rise to the top. But those who do not rise, are given wide latitude in writing the rules which hem him in when he gets there. When such rules are inspired by standards of fair play or by basic judgements as to what constitutes excellence, proponents of democracy can have no objection. For example, when we say "let the best man win", we must specify what we mean by 'best'. Most ruthless? Most brilliant? Most constructive? Most wily? This is something the whole society has a right to decide. But when the society as a whole devises rules which are calculated to inhibit excellence or stifle the person of superior gifts, then, all who pray for the continued vitality of democracy must protest.

But people may look excellence from different angles. Let us concern ourselves with the fate of excellence in our kind of society. There is the kind of intellectual activity that leads to a new machine. There is the mind that finds its most effective expression in teaching and the mind that is most at home in research. There is the mind that works best in quantitative terms and the mind that luxuriates in poetic imagery. And, there is excellence in art, in music, in craftsmanship, in human relations, in technical work, in leadership, in parental responsibilities. Some kind of excellence can be fostered by the educational system and others must be fostered outside the educational system. Some kinds–e.g. managerial–may lead to worldly success, and others (e.g.) compassion–may not.

Individual excellence in all its forms is needed–in every kind of creative endeavour, in political life, in education, in industry and in short, universally.

A society that does not believe in anything will never achieve excellence. As long as we are true to our deepest convictions as human beings, a concern for the individual will be a central theme of our consciousness. But concern for the individual is not enough. Free men must see their goals at two levels – the level of the individual and the level of the society.

Individual fulfilment on a wide scale can occur only in a society which is designed to cherish the individual, which has the strength to protect him, the richness and diversity to stimulate and develop him, and the system of values within which he can find himself – and lose himself! – as a person. Such societies do not simply grow by themselves. They will grow – and they will survive – only if free men give devoted attention to the welfare of their society. In this sense every free man lives for himself but also lives for his society. His goal must be not only individual fulfilment but the enrichment and strengthening of his society.

We fall into the error of thinking that happiness necessarily involves ease, diversion, tranquillity – a state in which all of one's wishes are satisfied. For most people, happiness is not to be found in this vegetative state but in striving towards meaningful goals. But the dedicated man has not achieved all of his goals. His life is the endless pursuit of goals, some of them unattainable. He may never have time to surround himself with luxuries. He may often be tense, worried, fatigued. He has little of the leisure one associates with the story book conception of happiness.

But he has found a more meaningful happiness. The truth is that, happiness in the sense of total gratification is not a state to which man can aspire. It is for the cows, possibly for the birds, but not for us.

We want meaning in our lives. When we raise our sights, strive for excellence, dedicate ourselves to the highest goals of our society, we are enrolling in an ancient and meaningful cause – the age-long struggle of man to realise the best that is in him. Man reaching toward the most exalted goals he can conceive, man striving impatiently and restlessly for excellence, has achieved great religious insights, created great work of art, penetrated secrets of the universe and set standards of conduct which give meaning to the phrase, "the dignity of man." Hazlitt said "Man is the only animal that laughs and weeps; for he is the only animal that is struck with the difference between what things are, and what they ought to be."

On the other hand, men without standards, men with eyes on the ground, have proved over and over again, in every society, and at every period of history–including the present–that human beings can be lower than the beasts, sink in ignorance, morally and ethically blind, living a life devoid of meaning. A concern for excellence, a devotion to standards, a respect for the human mind and spirit at its best, move us toward the former condition, and away from the latter condition.

At any given time in a particular society, the idea of what constitutes excellence tends to be limited–but the conception changes as we move from one society to another or one century to another. Taking the whole span of history and literature, the images of excellence are amply varied:

Emerson saying: 'everyman I meet is superior to me in some way.'

Lincoln writing the second inaugural
"with malice towards none"...

Leonides defending the pass at
Thermopylae...

Napoleon asserting that
'the spirit is greater than the sword.'

Spinoza saying:
'Our greatest victories are won not by arms, but by greatness of our soul.'

Jesus saying "Father forgive them, for
they know not what they do"...

Mozart composing his first oratorio at the age of eleven...

Franklin asserting many times that
'there is no such thing as a good war or a bad peace.'

Sir Syed Ahmad Khan fighting against ignorance and
obscurantism with his own Co-religionists...

Swami Vivekananda declaring that:
'I do not believe in a God or a religion that cannot
wipe the widow's tears or bring a piece of bread to
the orphan's mouth.'

Confucious teaching to the feudal lords
to govern wisely...

Alexander Pope penning the melancholy lines when he was twelve:

"Thus let me live unseen, unknown
Thus unlamented let me die
Steal from the world and not a stone
Tell where I lie."

Mother Teresa promoting peace in the most fundamental manner by her confirmation of the inviolability of human dignity.

The list is long and the variety great. Taken collectively, human societies have gone long way toward exploring the full range of human excellences.

With all those clavichord recitals at the age of seven, Mozart could not have had much time for exploration of his other gifts. Such one sided developments may be essential to the highest reaches of performance, and it might be foolish to try to prevent it in people of great talent. But anyone responsible for very gifted young people, would do well, to assist them in exploring the full range of their talents where possible, and to postpone at least for a time the tyrannical narrowing down.

Dedication

Of course, every line of behaviour has its pathology, and there is pathology of dedication. People sometimes commit themselves to vicious or criminal goals. Or their commitment to worthy goals become so fanatical that they destroy as much as they create. And there is the 'true believer' who surrenders himself to a mass movement or to dogmatic beliefs, in order to escape the responsibilities of freedom. A free society does not invite that kind of allegiance. It wants only one kind of devotion, the devotion of free, rational, responsible individuals.

We shall need such dedication. The years ahead will be fateful ones for all men. All of our wisdom, all of our talent and vitality, all of our steadfastness will be needed in this new century. The establishment of a durable peace, the preservation of a free society, the enrichment of the tradition on which freedom depends – these cannot be achieved by listless men.

The virtues which flower in any society are the virtues that the society nourishes. The qualities of mind and character which stamp a people are the qualities which that people honour, the qualities they celebrate, the qualities they recognise instantly, and respect profoundly.

Unfortunately, our society not only fails to ask for, or expect any depth of commitment from the individual, in a curious way it even discourages such commitment. Perhaps nothing is more effective in suppressing any spirit of endeavour on the part of the individual than the overpowering size and complexity of the giant enterprise in which we are all participants.

Competence

Today more than anything else we need Competent men if we want to build. In our society competence should be taken as an elementary duty. Men and women doing competently whatever job is theirs to do, tone up the whole society. And the man who does a slovenly job–whether he is a janitor or a judge, a surgeon or a technician–lowers the tone of the society. So do the chiselers of high and low degree, the sleight-of-hand artists who always know how to gain an advantage without honest work. They are regrettable burdens of a free society. Our society cannot achieve greatness unless individuals at many levels of ability accept the need for high standards of performance and strive to achieve those standards within the limits possible for them.

We cannot meet the challenge facing our society unless we can achieve and maintain a high level of morale and drive throughout the society. Men must have goals which in their eyes merit effort and commitment, and they must believe that their efforts will win their self respect and the respect for others. We can not have islands of excellence in a sea of slovenly indifference to standards. I am not saying that we can expect every man to be excellent. It would please me if this were possible. I am not one of those who believe that a goal is somehow unworthy if everyone can achieve it. But those who achieve excellence will be few at best. All too many lack the qualities of mind and spirit which would allow them to conceive excellence as a goal or to achieve it if they conceived it.

Socrates was offered his life on condition that he should renounce his search for truth. His answer deserves to be inscribed in the heart of every young man.

> "If you propose to acquit me on condition that I abandon my search for truth, I will say: I thank you O Athenians' but I will obey God–who as I believe set me this task–rather than you, and so long as I have breath and strength, I will never cease my occupation with philosophy. I will continue the practice of accosting whomever I meet and saying him:
>
> "Are you not ashamed of setting your heart on wealth and

honours, while you have no care for wisdom and truth and making your soul better. I know what death is – it may be a good thing, and I am not afraid of it, but I do not know that it is a bad thing to desert one's post, and I prefer what may be good to what I know to be bad."

Men of sterling character have the courage to speak the truth. They are bound to speak the truth in the love of it. It is the courageous man in fact who can best afford to be generous, or rather it is his nature to be so.

❖ ❖ ❖

King Leonides who perished with 300 Lacedemonians defending the defile of Thermopylae, remembered glory before all things, for glory is true wealth. Nothing degrades the soldier like love of money. He must care only for honour and reputation, but this reputation must be acquired in the midst of dangers. A battle gained without costing the conqueror any blood, is an inglorious success, while, the conquered cover themselves with glory by perishing with their arms in their hand. Among the 300 Lacedemonians, no one came back alive including the king. Though it was a technical defeat, it perhaps is the best example of their valour. After the war, the Spartans erected a memorial on the battlefield of Thermopylae saying only –**"Strangers, tell the Lacedemonians that we lie here in obedience to their orders."**

❖ ❖ ❖

By the same token, **Napolean's** life speaks of his courage and conviction. His thoughts, spirit and his courage continue to inspire succeeding generations. It is energy – the central element of which is the will – that produces miracles of enthusiasm in all ages. Napolean's self-confidence was colossal. His success was the consequence of his admirable foresight, of his calculations rapid as lightning, and of the conviction of his boldness is often the truest wisdom. When Napolean was told before the Battle of the Nations at Leipzig in 1814, he was outnumbered by three to one, he replied, **"I have fifty thousand men, add myself and you get one hundred**

and fifty thousand". Napolean asserted that the 'spirit is greater than the sword.' His personality, his sense of destiny, his energy and his soaring ambitions made even failure seem like success. His remarkable saying to the pupil of a school where he once visited. **"My young friend, every hour of time is a chance for misfortune for future life"** formed the rule of his own conduct. He said on another occasion, **"Victory belongs to the more persevering."**

❖ ❖ ❖

Like **Napolean, Beethoven** was always very sure of his greatness. When, as a youngman who had composed nothing of importance, he was rebuked for comparing himself with the great composer Hayden, he replied, "With men who do not believe in me because I am not famous, I can not associate." Ten years later he wrote to a prince, one of his kindest benefactors **"What you are, you are through accident of birth; what I am through my own efforts. There are princess and there will be thousands of princess more, but there is only one Beethoven."**

When Beethoven became deaf, he said "What a sorrowful life I must lead" and then rising above the first defeat he said "I will seize facts by the throat" and **wrote great music he could never hear.**

❖ ❖ ❖

When men have been struck a great bodily blow in their material fortune, they turn to the affairs of the mind. It is only through periodic illness that the world reflects, and it is only through periodic reflection that the world is worthy of survival. Philosophy therefore, thrives in the sick chamber of civilization. It was Plato's dream of a new ideal state to rise above the ruins of old. The ideal state was to be ruled by a philosopher king, and **Marcus Aurelius** might fulfil that. As **Aurelius donned the purple,** he gazed on the sadness of fate and the savagery of war. He said **"There is nothing good and nothing bad but thinking makes it so. We suffer from our opinions, from our limited vision.** It is possible to make us misfortune proof by adopting a simple formula. If unfulfilled desires are the bane of existence, let us limit our own desire to the scope of our ability to fulfil them. Since the material goods of life are so fleeting and rare, let us be content with our spiritual goods–a good mind and a good character. 'Call them positive virtues'. Even death, though it destroys the mind as well as the body, the good character as well as the good fortune, must be regarded as a negative event. **For, death may destroy the philosopher but not his philosophy.** It kills the mind of the individual, but it does not, disturb the Majesty of the world'. Learn, therefore, to be indifferent to your 'fate', for, all of us are subject to the same fate at the end. Live in accordance with the laws of Nature."

Justice to his fellowmen and indifference to his fate–this was the highest virtue in the philosophy of Marcus Aurelius. This, and fearlessness in the face of death. "Banish the fear of death by regarding it not with superstition or awe, but merely as one of the natural functions in the cycle of life, such as eating and drinking, sleep and sex."

He taught magnanimity to his fellow men and cherished the ambition never to give pain to another. With him reigned philosophy, through him the world was for one short moment guided by the last of the greatest man of the day. He apprehended the vanity of all joys, and full of gentle but deep seated disenchantment with regard to life, he had ceased to expect any satisfaction from power.

❖ ❖ ❖

Emerson preached the simplicity and energy of the Higher Law – the Oneness of mankind. He proclaimed the doctrine of individual liberty and universal tolerance–the new world principle of mutual collaboration between free men as against the old formula of mutual distrust between enslaved individuals and nations. He said **"Every man I meet is my superior in some way."** How noble was his thoughts. He placed the ethical code of humanity upon a practical American basis–**to live, let live, and help live.** He advocated a practical application of the Sermon of the Mount rather than the conventional adherence to the ceremonies of the church. Indeed, he forcefully objected to some of the ceremonies –

especially the one dealing with the sacrament of the Lord's Supper. He said **"the kingdom of God is not meat and drink, but righteousness and peace." "Surrender yourself to the power in you–not the power to enslave but the power to liberate, to help."** "Dare to become the master of your own fate and teach all and sundry to dare likewise. Know wherever you are, that the world exists for you. 'Dare to assert yourselves as accredited citizens of this great Republic of mankind and cast off the foolish artificial garments of servitude and sycophancy and humiliation.' Your birth in to this world has been no mistake. You are an invited guest to the banquet of life. Divine generosity is, hidden somewhere behind the mystery of creation."

Thomas Emerson came of a pioneer stock, poor, but self-reliant, had come to Concord in 1635–"had hard labour and spare diet and off wooden trenches, but they had peace and freedom. The light struggled in, through windows of oiled paper, but they read the word of God by it." **One of his ancestors had prayed every evening that none of his descendants might ever be rich but educated. Emerson** died a poorman but left behind a name in history.

❖ ❖ ❖

Abraham Lincoln–the saviour of the United States of America was born in a log cabin, the year which also saw the birth of Darwin, Tennyson and Gladstone. Descended from a Quacker family of English origin, has, for a long time represented not only the romance of Lincoln's career but also the chance of any little backwoods–boy to become the President of U.S... The phrase 'from log cabin to White House' has become the household name for Lincoln. The declaration of independence after the American revolution of 1776, brought Lincoln to the fore front of American Politics and the birth of Republican Party. There was much cruel and degrading about American slavery. Lincoln said **"If slavery is not wrong, nothing is wrong."** The declaration of independence began with very brave words.

"We hold these truths to be self-evident, – that all men are created equal; that they are endowed by the Creator with certain inalienable rights; that among these are: life, liberty and the pursuit of happiness."

He believed, slavery to be wrong and saw that he could have no common ground with those who believed it to be right. He also saw that a house divided against itself could not stand. And the U.S. could not for long remain half slave and half free. War broke out between North and South on the issue of slavery. Lincoln moved slowly and patiently. In honour of those who had fallen in the war the final words of Lincoln's speech at Gettysburg are unforgetable.

"It is for us here to be dedicated to the great task remaining before us – that from the honoured dead we take increased devotion to that cause for which they gave the last full measure of devotion; that we here highly resolve that these dead shall not have died in vain, that this nation, under God, shall have a new birth of freedom; and that **GOVERNMENT OF THE PEOPLE, BY THE PEOPLE, FOR THE PEOPLE** shall not perish from the earth."

"With malice towards none; with charity towards all, with firmness in the right, let us strive on to finish the works we are in; to build up the nation's wounds, to care for him who shall have borne the battle and for his widow and his orphan–to do all which may achieve and cherish a lasting peace among ourselves and with all nations." **"Emancipation of slaves followed, and on Lincoln's foundation, the greatness of America was built. He was a common man with a love for his fellows. 'God must have loved the common people' he once remarked and said "because he made so many of them."** He was great.

❖ ❖ ❖

"It is a disgrace to die rich." The man who wrote these words and gave away seventy million pounds because he believed them to be true, was Andrew Carnagie, the son of a Scottish weaver, born in a one room attic home more than a century ago. Started his life as a telegraphist in a private telegraph company, a businessman who visited the Telegraph Office frequently was attracted by the intelligence of this young operator and absorbed him in his business. With a gift of imagination, Carnagie saw in his mind, the great American rail roads swept by Sleeping Car Expresses, and he persuaded his company to build some of these cars, and Carnagie made a model car. Carnagie's ideas appealed to the company most, and they started building the sleeper cars. This proved to be a very great success and at the age of 30, he resigned after getting his hard earned fortune £ 10,000 from the Railway Company, and started the metal industry on the opening of the Prairies and Wild West, and with boundless enthusiasm, he became the iron master or Steel king. He said **"enjoy life–do not be a slave to work."**

When he retired, he wrote these words: **"It is a disgrace to die rich" and gave away seventy million pounds to establish a foundation for scientific research** and said it is ignorance which is the root of all evils.

Perhaps Carnagie was touched by **Luther's** comments on riches. Luther said "Riches are the smallest gift of God to man. What are they compared to God's word? What compared to His gifts of the body, beauty and health; what compared to understanding and wisdom? It is, therefore, that God gives riches to the merest donkeys to whom he gives nothing else."

Carnagie believed that a rich man's life should be divided into two parts, the first is making money and the second giving away. This task of giving money away he believed to be as difficult and as important as making it. Many laughed at him, but to all his critics he answered "Wait and see."

In 1900, Carnagie retired. He wrote down on a piece of paper the price he wanted for his business. The paper was taken to his fellow-millionaire Mr. Pierpont Morgan who looked at it and said "I accept". The price was £ 80,000,000–the biggest buying deal ever made. Then, for nearly 20 years Carnagie gave his money away. "After a time" he wrote to a friend "I shall become a wiser and more useful man." These were the brave words for an old man, and it is probably true that the last years of his long life were the happiest and most useful. He fought against ignorance, which he believed to be the root of all evil. He preferred to finance Scientific research rather than hospitals; libraries, universities and schools, rather than other forms of social work. **When the Carnagie Trust was formed he said: "Let my Trustees ask themselves from time to time, from age to age, how they can best help man in his glorious ascent onward and upward, and to this end devote this Fund."**

But the real greatness of Carnagie lies in his ideals. His "Gospel of wealth" has profoundly influenced the modern world. In a letter to him from a friend, this is plainly put:

"I estimate the value of your life not so much by the wealth you have attained, or even the distribution of it, as is the fact that the whole sentiment of mankind will be affected by the principles which you have laid down and which you are putting in to practice. **It seems to me that your position in the history of social development will be that of the man who first compelled wealth to recognize its duties, not merely as a matter of moral obligation, but of a decent self-respect on the part of men who control large fortunes."**

After Carnagie's example had staggered the business world, a great change took place in the attitude of many very rich businessman. We have only to think of Rockfeller, Lord Nuffield, Cycil Rhodes, Henry Ford and others, to realise how closely they have followed Carnagie in their desire to avoid the disgrace of dying rich.

❖ ❖ ❖

By the same token another great visionary who struggled to reform his own co-religionists, and fought against ignorance and obscurantism through the instrument of education was the great **Sir Syed Ahmad Khan** in the 19th century. Despite the staunch opposition by the Mullahs and Ulema, he carried on his mission of uplifting the Muslims of India from the shackles of ignorance and privation. Introduced western system of education based on science and philosophy, he founded the Mohamaden Anglo-Oriental College at Aligarh in 1877 which later blosomed in to the Aligarh Muslim University. The first modern institution of higher learning in India for Muslims, it became a centre of intellectual and cultural movement of the Muslims of this sub-continent. Future historians will discover in Aligarh one of the main sources which contributed to the evolution of modern India. Noble souls like **Sir Syed** are the gifts of God born once in centuries. But for his visionary zeal, the Muslims would have remained backward and illiterate. His far-sightedness, his sagacity, his patience and his capacity to endure the opposition from his own co-religionists who were strictly opposed to change due to ignorance and lethargy, is highly admirable indeed. Maulana Hali, in his elegy on Sir Syed Ahmad had this to say:

> "To be treated cruely by your brethren
> but to live for their good;
> To be pierced by the arrow
> and to remain fond of the arrow,
> To live anxious to serve your nation
> and to die with—that anxiety in your heart.
> You may aspire to be a Syed Ahmad
> if you can live up to his ideal life."

❖ ❖ ❖

The twentieth century brought into focus **Mother Teresa** – a great social reformer who conjured up an image of an angelic entity, healing the wounds of humanity with the loud proclamation to every one not to miss the Kingdom of God within himself. That Kingdom is of love, which manifests itself in the whole universe, for, the nature of God is love. Mother Teresa is love personified who drills in to every ear that **love is the manifestation of the Divine Absolute in our heart,** and only through love, human soul realises the Unity of God. In the words of Professor Sheik Ali, **"Others have spoken of the love, but the Mother became the crusading practitioner of this great concept, others were waiting to cover the journey, but she reached the goal and showed the world what must be done to make love bubble in soul."** The Mother's constant prayer was:

"Lord make us worthy to serve the poor around the world who live and die in poverty, hunger and disease."

In 1979 while awarding the Nobel Prize to Mother Teresa, the citation read as follows:

> "There would be no better way of describing the intentions that motivated the decision of the Norwegian Nobel Committee than the comment of the President of the World Bank, Robert Mc. Namara when he declared, "Mother Teresa deserves Nobel peace prize because, she promotes peace in the most fundamental manner by her confirmation of the **inviolability** of human dignity." May God grant her soul peace and Salvation, Amen.

❖ ❖ ❖

We have just had brief glimpses of excellence of a few personalities chosen at random who achieved something great. They had a mission and an ideal before them. Is it possible for people to achieve excellence if they do not believe in anything? Have we lost the sense of purpose and the drive which would make it possible for us to achieve excellence?

Excellence is a powerful word – a word which the people feel strongly and deeply. The readers may reflect on their personalities and their contribution. Many examples of such men and women who touched the height of 'excellence' can be cited. I have only cited a few who were my favourites.

In the *Asrare Khudi* (Secrets of the self) Sir Mohd. Iqbal says:

"Life cannot create any revolution in its environment unless it takes place first in the depths of its own being, and no new world can come into existence unless it is first framed in the minds and spirits of individual men and women."

The Quran says:

> "Verily God does not alter the fortunes of a nation until they bring about a change in their own Psychology." This is applicable with equal vitality to individual and collective life.

Man lives his life today in a patiently changing and dynamic world in which the stable and the precarious are in-extricably intertwined in which there are at every step 'plural possibilities' offering choice and discrimination to the individual in which experience is adventurous, on-going and progressive. This 'open' world demands the active, intelligent and resourceful cooperation of all individuals for its progressive development and fulfilment. Therefore, the most intellectual quality which individuals need in a world of this discipline is "creative intelligence", constantly exercising itself on the old as well as the new problems and situations which may arise in such environment.

As Professor Deway emphasised "All that the school can and need do for the pupils, so far as their minds are concerned, is to develop their ability to think." And, that is possible **when we provide that literature to study which may enable us with the richest opportunities to examine our own minds.**

1

Benjamin Franklin

Statesman

Benjamin Franklin

(1706–1790 A.D.)

"I made that man my enemy by doing him too much kindness. It is the honestest way of acquiring an enemy."

—Benjamin Franklin

In any age, in any place, Franklin would have been great. Mind and will, talent and art, strength and ease, wit and grace met in him as if nature had been lavish and happy when he was shaped. Nothing seems to have been left out except a passionate desire, as most men of genius, to be all ruler, all soldier, all saint, all poet, all scholar, all some one, gift or merit or success. **Franklin's Powers were from first to last in a flexible equilibrium.** Even his genius could not specialize him. He moved through his world in a humorous mastery of it. Kind as he was, there was perhaps a little contempt in his lack of exigency. He could not put so high a value as single minded men put on the things they have their lives for. Possessions were not worth that much, nor achievements. Comfortable as Franklin's possessions, and numerous as his achievements were, they were less than he was. "Whoever learn about his deeds, remembers longest the man who did them. And sometimes with his marvellous range, inspite of this personal tang, he seems to have been more than any singleman, harmonious human multitude."

In 1856 when a statue of Benjamin Franklin was unveiled in Boston, the principal speaker said:

> "Behold him, ye that are humblest
> and poorest in present condition
> or in future prospect – lift up
> your heads and look at the image
> of a man who rose from nothing, who
> owed nothing to parentage or patro-
> nage...but who lived to stand before Kings."

Born in Boston, Massachussets on January, 17, 1706 in a pious puritan household of a man who was a soap maker, candle maker and a skilful mechanic, Benjamin praised his mother as a 'discreet and virtuous women' who raised a family of 13 children and Benjamin happened to be the 10th, and complemented his father by saying that his 'great excellence' lay in a sound understanding and solid judgement. In honouring his parents and his affection for the New England ways, Franklin demonstrated the presence of his puritan heritage. He learned to read very early and had one year in grammar school and another under a private teacher, but his formal education ended when he was 10. At 12 he was apprenticed to his brother James, a Printer. His mastery of the printer's trade of which he was proud to the end of his life, was achieved between 1718 and 1723. **In the same period, he read tirelessly and taught himself to write effectively.** His first enthusiasm was for poetry and his father told him that:

"Verse makers were always beggars" and thereafter his interest in poetry was sporadic. Prose was another matter. Benjamin was pleased to read 'The Spectator' – a periodical of essays started by Joseph Addison and Richard Steele in England between 1711–12 and began imitating them by reading them and taking note of the idea of each sentence and thus improving the vocabulary. He, then founded a spectator like weekly newspaper under the caption 'New England Current' to which readers were invited to subscribe. Rejecting the calvinist theology of his father, Franklin opened himself to the more secular world view of Sir Isaac Newton and

John Locke and read the deist philosophers and gave allegiance to the Enlightenment. Thus, by the time he left home, his charm and attitude towards life had already a basic orientation.

The circumstances of his flight from home also reveal essential qualities. Denied a formal education by his family's poverty, Franklin became an apprentice to his brother James, Printer of a Boston newspaper. He began writing clever pieces signed 'Silence do good' satirizing the Boston establishment resulting in to imprisonment of the printer James (his brother) for his criticisms. Having thus learned to suffer his brother's petty tyrannies, he ran away to Philadelphia in 1723. Penniless and with out friends in the new city, Franklin soon demonstrated his enterprise and skill as a printer, gained employment. In 1724 he went to England where he quickly became a master printer and returned to Philadelphia and soon established his own press publishing a newspaper (the Pennsylvania Gazettee) – Poor Richard's Almanac. Through the columns of this 'Poor Richard' **he extolled hard work, thriftiness and honesty as the poor man's means of escaping the prison of want and explained how any man could develop an exemplary character with practice and perseverance.** Though the sayings like **'Sloth maketh all things difficult but industry easy'** do not amount to a profound philosophy of life (as Franklin knew perfectly well), **they do suggest useful steps for self-improvement.**

'Poor Richard' was soon the most successful almanac in America, selling more than 10,000 copies a year. The source of this success was not only the appeal of 'Poor Richard's' ingenuous personality. His almanac's pages were crowded with amusing verses, proverbs, and aphorisms. Franklin took many of these from earlier almanacs and from collection of epigrams and sayings. But he constantly improved upon previous anthologists, by sharpening, simplifying, balancing the epigrams that made "Poor Richard says" – a household phrase throughout colonial America. Here is a sample of Franklin's best efforts drawn from the twenty years during which he edited and wrote the Almanac.

Kings and Bears often worry their keepers.

He is a fool that makes his doctor his heir.

Beware of meat twice boil'd, and an old foe reconciled.

The poor have little, beggars none, the rich too much, enough not one.

After 3 days men grow weary, of a wench, a guest, and weather rainy.

Men and melons are hard to know.

Where there is marriage without love, there will be love without marriage.

Neither a fortress nor a maidenhead will hold out long after they begin to parley.

An egg today is better than a hen tomorrow.

He that waits upon fortune, is never sure of a dinner.

Marry your son when you will, but your daughter when you can.

Approve not of him who commands all you say.

Three may keep a secret, if two of them are dead.

Opportunity is the great Bawd.

Here comes the Orator with his flood of words and his drops of reason.

An old young man, will be a young old man.

Sally laughs at everything you say? why?

Because she has fine teeth.

Fish and visitors stink in 3 days.

He that lives upon hope, dies fasting.

Let thy maidservant be faithful, strong, and homely.

Admiration is the daughter of ignorance.

She that paints her face, thinks of her tail.

A countryman between 2 lawyers, is like a fish between two cats.

There are no ugly loves, nor handsome prisons.

Write with the learned, pronounce with the vulgar.

Keep your eyes wide open before marriage, half shut afterwards.

Thou can'st not joke an enemy in to friend; but though may'st a friend into enemy.

He that falls in love with himself, will have no rivals.

To bear other peoples afflictions, every one has courage enough and to spare.

Learn of the skilful. He that teaches himself, hath a fool for his master.

Epitaph on a scolding wife by her husband – "Here my poor Bridget's corpse doth lie, she is at rest–and so am I"

A ploughman on his legs is higher than a gentleman on his knees.

If your head is wax, don't walk in the sun.

You can bear your own faults, and why not a fault in your wife?

The golden age never was the present age.

Old boys have their play things as well as young ones, the difference is only in the price.

The proud hates pride – in others.

He that is of opinion that money will do everything may well be suspected of doing everything for money.

Love your neighbour; yet don't pull down your hedge.

Love your enemies, for they tell you your faults.

The huge circulation of both the sayings of "the Poor Richard" under the title "The way to wealth" led to the scathing assault from the miserly and small minded apostles of thrift. Franklin started operating a bookshop and entered into partnership with Printers of Nova Scotia to the West Indies. He had a comfortable income from his business. He then philosophised about his grand success and applied his understanding to civic enterprises.

As a Civic Leader

The first of his project of social improvement by collective effort was the Junto or leather Apron club organised in 1727 to debate questions on morals, politics and natural philosophy and to exchange knowledge of business affairs that might be valuable to the more enterprising members. Grasping the fact that by united efforts, a community may have amenities that only the wealthy few can get themselves, he established institutions that no one now takes for granted – a fire company, a library, an insurance company, an Academy of Philadelphia from which grew the University of Pennsylvania. He arranged for paving, cleaning and lighting the streets and for a night watch. So much successful Franklin was in promoting such public utility companies, that every one with a good cause in mind was likely to turn to him for help. These foundations were the first of their kind in North America.

He made friends with young men of his own age "All lovers of Reading." Inadvertently, he encouraged one of them James Rolph to become America's first professional writer. He also continued to aid the poorest members of his family especially his sister, and to the family of his wife. He also reared his illegitimate son Wilson, often his own father's companion who was appointed Governor of New Jersey and was later to be notable as a loyalist during the revolution.

Therefore, although, he worked and prospered, Franklin never list his interest in morality and religion, which he had inherited from puritan Boston. He created his own set of religious exercises, some of which he recited daily. He wanted to live without committing fault at any time. But at the same time his attention was taken up in guarding against one fault, he was surprised by another. Inclination was sometimes too strong for reason. For this purpose he contrived the following method:

> "In the various enumerations of the
> moral virtues I had met with in my
> reading, I found the catalogue more
> or less numerous, as different writers included more or
> fewer ideas under the same name.
> Temperance, for example, was by some
> confined to Eating and Drinking,
> while by others it was extended to
> mean the moderating every other pleasure.
> Appetite, inclination or passion, bodily
> or mental, even to our avarice and ambition.
> I proposed to myself, for the sake of
> clearness, to use rather more names with

fewer ideas annexed to each, than a few
names with more ideas; and I included
under thirteen names of virtues all
that at that time occurred to me
as necessary or desirable, and annexed to each a short precept,
which fully expressed the extent
I gave to its meaning.
These names of virtues with their
precepts were

1. **Temperance**

   Eat not to Dullness.
   Drink not to Elevation.

2. **Silence**

   Speak not but what may benefit
   other or yourself. Avoid trifling conversation.

3. **Order**

   Let all your things have their
   places. Let each part of your
   business have its time.

4. **Resolution**

   Resolve to perform what you ought.
   Perform without fail what you resolve.

5. **Frugality**

   Make no expence but to do good
   to others or yourself: i.e. Waste nothing.

6. **Industry**

   Loose no time. Be always employ'd
   in something useful.
   Cut off all unnecessary actions.

7. **Sincerity**

   Use no hurtful Deceit. Think innocently and justly; and, if you speak, speak accordingly.

8. **Justice**

   Wrong none by doing injuries or omitting the Benefits that are your duty.

9. **Moderation**

   Avoid extremes, forbear resenting injuries so much as you think they deserve.

10. **Cleanliness**

    Tolerate no uncleanness in body, cloths or habitation.

11. **Tranquillity**

    Be not be disturbed at trifles, or at accidents common or unavoidable.

12. **Chastity**

    Rarely use venery but for health or offspring; never to dullness, weakness, or the injury of your own or another's peace or reputation.

13. **Humility**

    Imitate Jesus and Socrates.

"I gave priority for 'Temperance' first, as it tends to procure that coolness and clearness of head, which is so necessary where constant vigilance was to be kept up, and guard maintained, against the unremitting

attraction of ancient habits, and
the force of perpetual temptations.
This being acquired and established,
silence would be more easy, and my
desire being to gain knowledge at the
same time that I improved in
virtue, and considering that in
conversation it was obtained rather by
the use of the ears than of the
tongue, and therefore wishing to
break a habit I was getting into of
prattling. Punning and joking, which
only made me acceptable to trifling
company, I gave silence the second
place. This, and the next, order,
I expected would allow me more time
for attending to my project and my
studies; RESOLUTION, once become
habitual, would keep me firm in my
endeavours to obtain all the
subsequent virtues; frugality and industry,
by freeing me from my remaining
debt, and producing affluence and
independence, would make more easy
the practice of sincerity and justice etc."

His respect and affection for his father and mother continued to be a factor in life even though he was a mature man. He was also a deeply paternal man. He converted almost every circle in which he moved into a kind of family with himself as a father.

In a letter to his sister on January 6, 1727 Franklin writes from Philadelphia: "Remember that, modesty, as it makes the most homely virgin amiable and charming, so the want of it infalliably renders the most perfect beauty disagreeable and odious. But when that brightest of female virtue shines among other perfections of body and mind in the same person, it makes the women more lovely than an angel."

His advise to young men both on kindness and in business and money matters is very appealing. **In 1763 he wrote "I made that man my enemy by doing him too much kindness. It is the honestest way of acquiring an enemy".** By the age of 42, Franklin was a distinctly successful man. His printing business was earning him well over two thousand pounds a year. Looking back on his experience, he wrote an essay that was reprinted numerous times in subsequent years. The raw young man (Franklin) who had arrived in Philadelphia with only a dollar and a few pennies in his pocket now spoke with the seasoned voice of success. Here under I quote Franklin's advice to young tradesman.

(July 21, 1748)

Advice to a young tradesman, written by an old one
To my friend A.B.
As you have desired it of me,
I write the following Hints, which
have been of service to me, and
may, if observed, but so to you.

Remember that **Time** is money.
He that can earn Ten Shillings a
day by his Labour, and goes abroad,
or sits idle one half of that Day
tho'he spends but Sixpence during
his Diversion or Idleness, ought
not to reckon that the only expense
he has really spent or rather thrown
away five Shillings besides.

Remember that **Credit** is money.
If a man lets his money lie in my
hands after it is due, he give me the
interest, or so much I can make of it
during that time. This amounts to a
considerable sum where a man has good and large Credit,

and makes good Use of it.
"Remember that money is of prolific generating Nature. Money can beget Money, and its offspring can beget more, and so on. Five Shillings turn'd, is Six: Turn'd again, 'ts seven and Three Pence; and so on till it becomes an Hundred Pound The more there is of it, the more it produces every Turning, so that the Profits rise quicker and quicker. He that kills a breeding cow, destroys all her offsprings to the thousandth generation. He that murders a crown destroys all it might have produc'd even scores of Pounds."

"Remember that Six Pounds a year is but a Groat a Day. For this little Sum (which may be daily wasted either in time expense unperceived) a man of Credit, may, on his own security have the constant possession and use of a hundred Pounds. So much in Stock briskly turn'd by an industrious man, produces great advantage".

"Remember this saying, that the good paymaster is Lord of another man's Purse. He that is known to pay punctually and exactly to the time he promises, may at any time, and on any Occasion, raise all the money his friends can spare. This is sometimes of great Use: Therefore, never keep borrow'd Money an hour beyond your friends purse forever."

"The most trifling actions that affect
a man's Credit, are to be regarded. The sound
of your hammer of five in the morning or nine
at night heard by a Creditor, makes his easy
Six Months longer. **But if he sees you at a
Billiard Table, or hears your voice in a
Tavern, when you should be at work, he sends
for his money the next day.** Finer cloths that
he or his wife wears, or greater expense in any
particular than he affords himself, shocks
pride, and he duns you to humble you.
Creditors are a kind of people, that have
the best memories of any in the world.

Good-natur'd Creditors (and such one would always choose to deal with if one could) feel pain when they are oblig'd to ask for money. Spare them that pain, and they will love you. When you receive a sum of money, divide it among them in proportion to your debts. Don't be asham'd of paying a small sum because you owe a greater. Money, more or less, is always welcome; and your creditor had rather be at the trouble of receiving ten pounds voluntarily brought to him, though at ten different times or payments, than be oblig'd to go ten times to demand it before he can receive it in a lump. It shows, besides, that you are mindful of what you owe; it makes you appear a careful as well as an honest man; and that still increases your credit.

Beware of thinking all your own that you possess, and of living accordingly. 'It is a mistake that many people who have credit fall into. To prevent this, keep an exact account for some time of both your expenses and your incomes. If you take the pains at first to mention particulars, it will have this good effect; you will discover how wonderfully small trifling expenses mount up to large sums, and will discern what might have been, and may for the future be saved; without occasioning any great inconvenience.

In short, the way to wealth, if you desire it, is as plain as the way to market. It depends chiefly on two words, **Industries and**

Frugality; i.e. waste neither time nor money, but make the best use of both. He that gets all he can honestly, and saves all he gets (necessary expenses excepted) will certainly become **Rich;** if that being who governs the world, to whom all should look for a blessing on their honest endeavours, doth not in his wise providence otherwise determine."

How true and practical his observations were:

Interest in Science

His contribution to comfort and safety of daily life is immense. He invented a stove to give more warmth than open fire places. He developed a great interest in the study of science.

Electricity was at this period more a curiosity than a science. It has attracted the attention of numerous learned men in Europe, but no one knew what it was and how it worked. Hence, his attention focused primarily on electricity and read the new treatise on the subject and acquired ingenious equipment. In his famous Kite experiment, proving that lightning is a form of electricity, he linked laboratory experiments with static electricity to the great universal force and made a previously mysterious and terrifying natural phenomenon understandable. Franklin's letters concerning his discoveries and theories about electricity to the Royal Society in London brought him fame. The invention of the lightning rod, which soon appeared on all buildings all over the world added to his stature.

The experiment that he suggested to prove the identity of lightning and electricity was first made in France before he is believed to have tried the simpler but dangerous experiment of flying a kite in a thunderstorm. He concluded alongwith his associates, that 'electric fire' was an element diffused among and attracted by other matter, particularly water and other metals. He wrote on Nov. 1, 1749 "Electrical fluid agrees with lightning in these particulars: 1. Giving light. 2. Colour of the light. 3. Crooked direction. 4. Swift motion. 5. Being conducted by metals. 6. Crack or noise in exploding. 7. Subsisting in water or ice. 8. Rending bodies it passes through. 9. Destroying animals. 10. Melting metals.

11. Firing inflammable substances. 12. Sulphurous smell. The electrical fluid is attracted by points. We do not know whether this property is in lightning. But since they agree in all the particulars wherein we can already compare them, is it not probable they agree likewise in this? Let the experiment be made."

By July 29, 1750, Franklin had worked out the details for an experiment to prove that lightning and electricity were the same.

When a body with an over quantity approached one with an underquantity, a discharge equalized the electric fire in the two. This "one fluid" theory accounted for more of the observable phenomena than had any previous hypothesis, and his suggestion that buildings might be protected by lightning by erecting pointed iron rods proved both practical and dramatic. He also invented many terms still used in discussing electricity (positive, negative, battery, conductor and so on) and he described the experiment with lucidity.

Franklin's fame spread rapidly. His scientific ingenuity, earning him election to the Royal Society in 1756, also found outlet in the theory of heat, charting the Gulf stream, ship design, meteorology and the **Invention of Bifocul Lenses** (biofocul eye glass) and a 'Harmonica' – a musical instrument made of glasses, filled with just the right amount of water before each performance; and providing enough glasses to give the instrument a decent range, created Harmonicas so large that it was possible to play them seated from a single position. It became extremely popular on the continent. Mozart, Beethovan and several other famous musicians compose music for the Harmonica. In a letter to his mother in April 1750 Franklin remarked that when he died, he would rather have it said:

"He lived usefully than he died rich"

Public Service

Politics and Diplomacy

Involving himself in politics, he was clerk in the Pennsylvania Legislature and Post Master of Philadelphia. He was given charge of organising a Militia for the defence of the colony against possible invasion by the French and the Spaniards. Franklin was sent to England and kept on as London Agent for Pennsylvania, and three other colonies relied on him to represent their interest – Georgia, New Jersey and Massachussetts.

On the voyage to England, Franklin prepared the text for 'Poor Richard' of 1758. With plenty of time on his hands, he went through all his previous volumes, and wrote an introductory essay, **'The Way to Wealth',** which has to become one of his most famous compositions–with a very unfortunate effect on his reputation. Poor Richard's advice, on, how to get rich achieved wide fame in Franklin's life time and was reprinted repeatedly in the hundred years after his death. It made Franklin's name synonymous with saving, and even with penny–pinching–an ironic fate for a man who abandoned what he called "the pursuit of wealth to no purpose" at the age of forty-two. Franklin did pinch his pennies as a young man starting out in business with heavy debts. But, as his letters have already demonstrated, once he achieved financial security, he was generous and open handed. The essay, in which Franklin created another of his memorable characters, wise old **Father Abraham**, was really more of an intellectual exercise. The tone is highly ironic and at times is even close to parody. Franklin was actual laughing just a little at himself and 'Poor Richard' and the whole nation of persuading men to save money – while, simultaneously working in to the text a maximum number of quotations from his previous almanacs. Perhaps it was the last Benjamin Franklin himself wrote.

Poor Richard, 1758

> "...a great number of people were collected at a Vendue (auction) of merchant goods. The hour of sale not being come, they were conversing on the badness of the times, and one of the company call'd to a plain clean old man, with white locks, pray **Father Abraham**, what think you of the times? Won't these heavy taxes quite ruin the country? How shall we be ever able to pay them? What would you advise us to? – Father Abraham stood up, and reply'd, if you'd have my advice, I'll give it you in short, **for a word to the wise is enough,** and

many words won't fill a bushel, as Poor Richard says. They join'd in desiring him to speak his mind, and gathering round him, he proceeded as follows:

"Friends, says he, and neighbours, the taxes are indeed very heavy, and if those laid on by the Government were the only ones we had to pay, we might more easily discharge them; but we have many others, and much more grievous to some of us. **We are taxed twice as much by our idleness, three times as much by our pride, and four times as much by our folly**, and from these taxes the commissioner cannot ease or deliver us by allowing an abatement. However, let us hearken to good advice, and something may be done for us: **God helps them that help themselves**, as Poor Richard says, in his Almanac of 1733.

It would be thought, a hard Government that should tax its people one-tenth part of their times, to be employed in its service. **But idleness taxes many of us much more, if we reckon all that is spent in absolute sloth, or doing of nothing, with that which is spent in idle employments or amusements that amount to nothing. Sloth, by bringing on diseases, absolutely shortens life. Sloth, like rust, consumes faster than labour wears, while the used key is always bright,** as poor Richard says. **But dost thou love life, then do not squander time, for that's the stuff life is made of, as Poor Richard says. How much more than is necessary do we spend in sleep! Forgetting that the sleeping fox catches no poultry, and there will be sleeping enough in the grave,** as Poor Richard says. If time be of all things the most precious, wasting time must be, as Poor Richard says, the greatest prodigality, since as he elsewhere tells us, **lost time is never found again:** and **what we call time-enough, always proves little enough:** Let us then be up and be doing, and doing to the purpose: So by diligence shall we do more with less perplexity. **Sloth makes all things difficult, but industry all easy,** as Poor Richard says: **and**

he that riseth late, must trot all day, and shall scarce over taken his business at night. While laziness travels so slowly, that poverty soon overtakes him, as we read in Poor Richard, who adds, drive thy business, let not that drive thee: **and early to bed, and early to rise, makes a man healthy, wealthy and wise.**

So what signifies wishing and hoping for better times. We may make these times better if we bestow ourselves. Industry need not wish, as Poor Richard says, And he that lives upon hope will die fasting. There are no gains, without pains: Then help hands, for I have no lands, or if I have, they are smartly taxed. And, as Poor Richard likewise observe, he that hath a trade hath an estate, and he that hath a calling hath an office of profit and honour; but then the trade must be worked at, and the calling well followed, or neither the estate, nor the office, will enable us to pay our taxes. If we are industrious we shall never starve: for, as Poor Richard says, At the working man's house hunger looks in, but dares not enter. Nor will the bailief nor the constable enter, for industry pays debts, while despair increaseth them says Poor Richard. What though you have found no treasure, nor has any rich relation left you a legacy, **diligence is the mother of good luck,** as Poor Richard says, **And God gives all things to industry.** Then plough deep, while sluggards sleep, and you shall have corn to sell and to keep, says Poor Dick. Work while it is called today, for you know not how much you may be hindered tomorrow, which makes Poor Richard say, One today is worth two tomorrow; and further, have you somewhat to do tomorrow do it today. If you were a servant, would you not be ashamed that a good master should catch you idle? Are you then your own master, be ashamed to catch yourself idle, as Poor Dick says. When there is so much to be done for yourself your family, your country, and your gracious king, Be up by peep of day: Let not the Sun look down and say, Inglorious here he lies. Handle your tools without mittens; remember that the cat in gloves catches no mice, as Poor

Richard says, "Its true there is much to be done, and perhaps you are weak handed, but stick to it steadily, and you will see great effects, for constant dropping wears away stones, and by diligence and patience the mouse ate in two the cable; and little strokes fell great oaks, as Poor Richard says in his Almanack, the Year I cannot just now remember."

"Methinks I hear some of you say, must a man afford himself no leisure? I will tell thee, my Friend, what Poor Richard says, Employ thy time well if thou meanest to gain leisure; and, since thou art not sure of a minute, throw not away an hour. Leisure is time for doing something useful; this leisure the deligent man will obtain, but the lazy man never; so that, as Poor Richard says, A life of leisure and a life of laziness are two things. Do you imagine that sloth will afford you more comfort than labour? No, for, as Poor Richard says, Trouble springs from idleness, and grievous toil from needless ease. Many without labour would live by their wits only, but they break for want of stock, whereas industry gives comfort, and plenty, and respect: Fly pleasures, and they'll follow you...

But with our Industry, we must likewise be steady, settled and careful, and oversee our own affairs with our own eyes, and no trust too much to others; for, as Poor Richard says...

He that by the Plough would thrive,
Himself must either hold or drive.

And again, the eye of a Master will do more work than both his hands; and again, want of care does us more damage than want of knowledge; and again, Not to oversee workmen, is to leave them your purse open... And further, If you would have a faithful servant, and one that you like, serve yourself...

So much for Industry, my friends, and attention to one's own Business, but to these we must add frugality, if we would make our industry more certainly successful. A man may, if he knows not how to save as he gets, keep a groat at last. A fat kitchen makes a lean Will...and , if you would be wealthy, says he, in another Almanack, think of saving as well as of getting: the Indies have not made Spain rich, because her outgoes are greater than her incomes. Away then with your expensive follies, and you will not have so much cause to complain of hard times, heavy taxes, and chargeable families; for, as Poor Dick says,

Women and Wine, Game and Deceit,
Make the Wealth small, and the wants great.

And further, what maintains one Vice, would bring up two children. You may think perhaps, that a little tea, or a little punch now and then, diet a little more costly, clothes a little finer, and a little entertainment now and then, can be no great matter; but remember what Poor Richard says...**Beware of little expenses; a small leak will sink a great ship;** and again, who Dainties Love shall beggars prove...

Here you are all got together at this vendue of fineries and kincknacks. you call them goods, but if you do not expect they will be sold cheap, and perhaps they may for less than they cost; but if you have no occasion for them, they must be dear to you, remember what Poor Richard says, Buy what thou hast no need of and ere long thou shalt sell they necessaries. And again, at a great Pennyworth pause a while: He means, that perhaps the cheapness is apparent only, and not real; or the bargain, by straitening thee in thy business, may do thee more harm than good...many a one for the sake of finery on the back, have gone with a hungry belly, and half starved their families; silks and satins, scarlet and velvets, as Poor Richard says, Put out the kitchen fire, these are not the necessaries of life, they can scarcely be called the conveniences, and yet only because they look pretty. How many want to have them. The artificial wants of mankind thus become more numerous than the natural; add, as Poor Dick says, for one poor person, there are a hundred indigent. By these, and other extravagencies, the genteel are reduced to poverty, and forced to borrow of those whom they formerly despised, but who through industry and frugality have maintained their standing; in which case it appears plainly, **That a ploughman on his legs is higher than a gentleman on his knees,** as Poor Richard says, Perhaps they have had a small estate left them, which they knew not the getting of ; they think it's day, and will be night; that a little to be spent out of so much, is not worth minding (a child and a fool, as Poor Richard says, imagine twenty shillings and twenty years can never be spent) but, always taking out of the Meal-tub, and never putting in, soon comes to the bottom; then, as Poor Dick says, When the well's dry, they know the worth of water. But this they might have known before, if they had taken his advice; if you would know the value of money, go and try to borrow some; for, he goes a borrowing goes a sorrowing...

Fond pride of dress, is sure a vary curse;
E'er fancy you consult, consult your purse.

...when you have bought one fine thing you must buy ten more, that your appearance may be all of a piece; but Poor Dick says, It is easier to suppress the first desire, than to satisfy all that follow it...

But what madness must it be to run in debt for these superfluities we are offered, by the terms of this vendue, six months credit; and that perhaps has induced some of us to attend it, because we cannot spare the ready money, and hope now to be fine without it. But, Ah, think what you do when you run in debt. You give to another power over your liberty. If you cannot pay at the time, you will be ashamed to see your creditor; you will be in fear when you speak to him; you will make Poor Pitiful Sneaking Excuses, and by degrees some to lose you veracity, and sink into base downright lying; for as Poor Richard says, The second vice is lying, the first is running in debt. And again, to the same purpose, lying rides upon debt's back...

"And now to conclude, experience keeps a dear school but fools will learn in no other, and scarce in that; for it is true, we may give advice, but we can not give conduct, as Poor Richard says: However, remember this, they that won't be counselled, can't be helped as Poor Richard says...

Thus the old gentleman ended his Harangue. The people heard it, and approved the Doctrine, and immediately practised the contrary, just as if it has been a common sermon; for the vendue opened, and they began to buy extravagantly, notwithstanding all his cautions, and their own fear of taxes."

In England, despite his struggle to press on Britain the importance of self-governance to colonies, he was gradually forced to realize that there could be no reconciliation and that his dream of a British empire with self-governing nations would not come true. In 1751, he celebrated the rapid increase of colonial population as a great "accession of power to the British empire" – a big and happy family where in the prosperity of the parent and the growth of the children were normally beneficial. He, therefore, published about 125 papers on current problems and controversies. He left England in 1775 to America anticipating war and was a delegate to second continental congress and served on committees, specially for the drafting of the declaration of independence and on a commission to vainly bring Canada into the war as an ally.

In September, 1776 Congress agreed to send a commission of three to France to seek economic and military assistance. Franklin was one of them and soon he became a hero in France by his diplomatic skill. The treaty with France was signed and about 12,000 soldiers and 32,000 sailors had left France to support General George Washington in America. Before these forces could reach, the British General and 6000 men surrendered at Saratoga. Viewing America's place in the world as his mission to France drew to a close, Franklin combined realism to idealism. "Our firm connection with France" He noted "Gives us weight with England and respect throughout Europe." Franklin thought "A New Year of Peace will improve, will restore and increase our strength; but our future safety will depend on our Nation and our virtue." Many time he said **"No such thing as a good war or a bad peace."**

The British, in their vexation and frustration with the Americans, refused to treat captives—especially men captured at sea from American warships and privateers – as prisoners of war, instead, they crowded them into wretched prisons, threatened them with transportation to British colonies in Asia and Africa, and then cynically offered them the opportunity of volunteering to fight aboard British ships. Franklin protested this treatment in a blazing letter to the British Ambassador Lord Stormont. Stormont returned the letter with a note: "The King's ambassador receives no letters from rebels but when they come to implore His Majesty's mercy."

Paris, April 2, 1777

> "We did ourselves the honour of writing sometime since to your Lordship on the subject of exchanging prisoners. You did not condescend to give us any answer, and therefore, we expect none to this. We however take the liberty of sending you copies of certain depositions which we shall transmit to Congress whereby, it will be known to your court that the United States are not unacquainted with the barbarous treatment their people receive when they have the misfortune of being your prisoners here in Europe. And that if your conduct towards us is not altered it is not unlikely that severe reprisals may be thought justifiable from the necessity of putting some check to such abominable practices. For the sake of humanity it is to be wish'd that men would endeavour to alleviate as much as possible the unavoidable miseries attending a State of War. It has been said that among the civilized Nations of Europe the ancient horrors of that state are much diminished. But by compelling men by chains, stripes and famine to fight against their friends and relations, is a new mode of barbarity which your nation alone has the honour of inventing. And the sending American prisoners of war to Africa and Asia remote from all probability of exchange and where they can scarce hope ever to hear from their families even if the unwholesome-ness of the climate does not put a speedy end to their lives, is a manner of treating captives that

you can justify by no prece-dent or custom except that of the black savages of Guinea."

At first Franklin had not the slightest thought about America's separation from Britain. He had grown up with allegiance to Britain and had a deep appreciation of the culture of the country of William Shakespeare, John Milton, Joseph Addison and Alexander Pope.

Franklin was the premier American representative in Europe for 7 years, conducting normal diplomacy and acting as purchasing agent, admirality of the court and intelligence chief, loan negotiator etc., and retained French good will.

Franklin was an ideal ambassador to France. In his letter to Josiah Quincy, his old Boston friend, he told how much he enjoyed the French people. He then developed a theme that was to dominate many of his letter: Americans should do more for themselves.

Passy, April 22, 1779

"It is with great sincerity I join you in acknowledging and admiring the dispensations of providence of our favour. America has only to be thankful, and to persevere. God will finish his work, and establish their freedom; and the lovers of liberty will flock from all parts of Europe with their fortunes to participate with us of that freedom, as soon as peace is restored.

I am exceedingly pleased with your account of the French politeness and civility, as it appeared among the officers and people of their fleet. They have certainly advanced in those respects many degrees beyond the English. I find them here a most amiable nation to live with. The Spaniards are by common opinion supposed to be cruel, the English proud, the Scotch insolent, the Dutch Avaricious etc., but I think the French have no national vice ascribed to them. They have some frivolities, but they are harmless. To dress their hair so that a hat cannot be put on them, and then wear their hats under their arms, and to fill their noses with tobacco, may be called follies, perhaps, but they are not vices. They are only the effects of the tyranny of custom. In short, there is nothing wanting in the character of a Frenchman, that belongs to that of an agreeable and worthy man. There are only some trifles surplus, or which might be spared.

Will you permit me, while I do them this Justice, to hint a little censure on our own country people, which I do in Goodwill, wishing the cause removed, you know the necessity we are under of supplies from Europe, and the difficulty we have at present in making returns. The interest Bills would do a good deal towards purchasing arms, ammunition, clothing, sailcloth, and other necessaries for defence. Upon enquiry of those who present these bills to me for acceptance, what the money is to be iaid out in, I find that most of it is for superfluities, and more than half of it for tea. How unhappily in this Instance the folly of our People, and the avidity of our merchants, concur to weaken and impoverish our country. I formerly computed that we consum'd before the war, in that single article, the value of £500,000 sterling annually. Much of this was sav'd by stopping the use of it. I honoured the virtuous resolution of our women in foregoing that little gratification, and I lament that such virtue should be of so short duration. Five hundred thousand pounds sterling, annually laid out in defending ourselves, or annoying our enemies, would have great effects. With what face can we ask aids and subsidies from our friends, while we are wasting our own wealth in such prodingality?

Franklin left France in 1785 and landed in Philadelphia to the cheers of his country men. Honoured as a living sage, he accepted election for 3 years as President of the Supreme Executive Council of Pennsylvania, became President of the Pennsylvania society for promoting the abolition of slavery and resumed his activity in drafting the constitution of U.S.

Drafting of the Constitution for America

Benjamin Franklin played a Central role in the great crisis

(disobedience of stamp act) that led to the declaration of independence in 1776. But his most notable service, however, was his attendance at the early sessions of the constitutional convention during the summer of 1787. Too infirm to speak much in debate and less creative in political philosophy than some of his younger colleagues, he bolstered the confidence of the convention and through good humour and suggestions for compromise, helped prevent its disruption in animosity. He gave decisive support to the 'Great Compromise' over representation and dozens of times calmed volatile tempers and frayed nerves. At the convention's close, he asked each member, who like himself might not entirely approve of the constitution to "doubt a little of his own infallibility" and **sign the document to give it a chance as the best frame of government human ingenuity could at that time produce.** His last public service was to urge ratification of the constitution and to approve the inauguration of the new government under his longtime friend **George Washington.**

Last Days

A few days later Benjamin suffered an attack of pleurisy. He had agonizing pain for several days. And on April 17, 1790 at the age of 84, he explained to his daughter Sally that he simply wanted the bed made, so that he might "die in a decent manner." Sally replied she was praying that he would get well and live many more years. "I hope not", Franklin replied. A few hours later, an abscess in his lung burst. He died at eleven O'clock at night on the same day.

Philadelphia gave him the most impressive funeral that city had ever seen, and in France, where Louis XVI was imprisoned in the Tuileries, eulogy after eulogy poured-forth to the man who to the French was the symbol of enlightenment and Freedom. All Europeans remembered the epigram of Turgot, the French Economist;

> *"He snatched the lightning from*
> *the skies and the sceptre from tyrants."*

Franklin's life and his quest for excellence should inspire our youth of today.

Reading List

1. Abbot, J.S.C. : The Life of Napolean Bonaparte, London, 1897.
2. Bijli, S.M. : A Tribute to Sir Syed Ahmad Khan, A.M.U., News & Views, Aligarh Oct., 1995.
3. Carlyle, Thomas : On Hero's, Hero worship and the Heroic in History, Oxford, 1946.
4. Carter : Pioneers of the Modern World, Arnold & Sons Ltd., London.
5. Egan, Eilien : Mother Teresa, such a vision of the great, Sidgwick & Jackson, London.
6. Franklin, Benjamin : Biography in his own words Edt. by Thomas Freening. Harper & Raw Pub. in Corp.
7. Franklin, Benjamin : Memoirs edited Max Furrad, University of Calif, Press 1949.
8. Gardner, John N.V. : Excellence Harper & Raw Pub., N. York.
9. Jafferson, Thomas : Life & Works, Modern Library, Random House, 1944.
10. Jafferson, Thomas : Letters to George Washington Q/F Henry A Washington (etd). The writings of Thomas Jafferson, 1853–54, Vol. III.
11. Jacques, Bergun : The house of intellect, Harper Br. 1959.
12. Macaulay, Thomas B. : On the Athenian orators (Aug. 1924) Macaulay's complete works. Vol. XI Speeches & Poems & Misc. Writings, Longman Green & Co. 1898.
13. Porte, John : Emerson & Thoreau Transcendentalists in conflict, Weslayan, University Press, 1965.
14. Rashdal, Hastings : The theory of good & evil, Vol. II, Oxford, 1907.
15. Russel, G.W.E. : Collections and recollections, Herper Bros., 1903.
16. Schillip, Paul Arther : The philosophy of Alfred North Whitehead, N.Y. Tudor, Pub. Co. 1957, Library of Living Philosophers.
17. Thomas Henry & Thomas Dena Lee : Living Biographies of great philosophers, 1964.
18. Turner I.E. : Philosophic basis of moral obligation, a story in ethics, McMillan & Co. Ltd., St. Martin street, London, 1924.
19. Timur : Theory of Morals, Elek Books London.
20. Winthrop, Robert C. : Oration at the inauguration of the statue of Benjamin Franklin 'self-made man.' Boston, 1836, Rutgars University Press, 1954.

2

Emperor Marcus Aurelius

Philosopher King

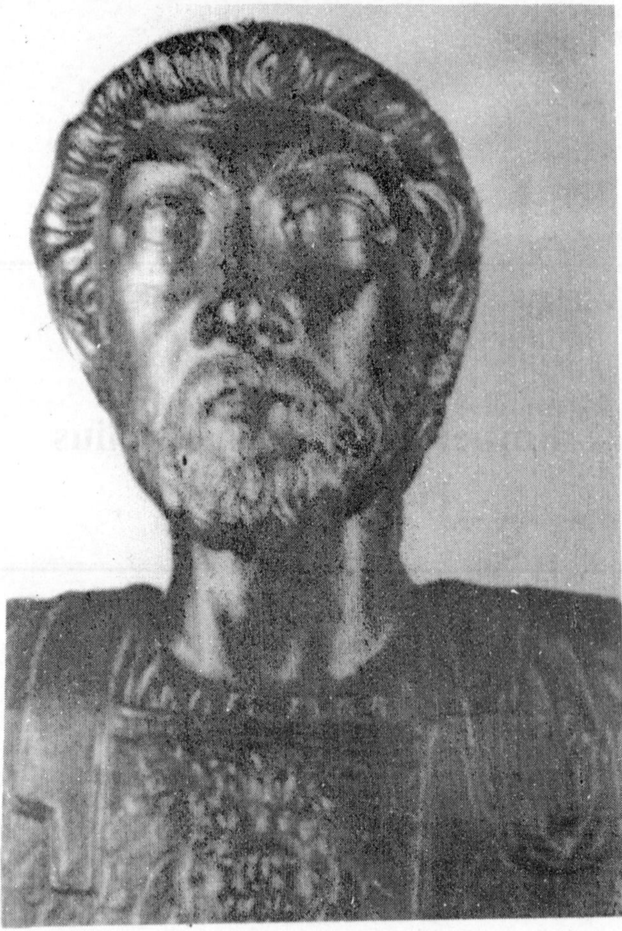

'Spend no more time in stating the qualifications of a man of virtue, but endeavour to get them.'

—Marcus Aurelius

'Mildness and temper are not only more humane, but more masculine too'.

—Marcus Aurelius

Introduction

Plato said, philosophy begins in **wonder.** In modern times, it usually begins in **doubt.** Now, doubt has become a serious and disturbing human ailment. There never was a time when so many people were so uncertain about so many things as at present. Many are uncertain about the best form of government, best economic and social system, what things are right and what are wrong, about the existence of God, and about the soul and its destiny. We are uncertain whether people are better behaved today than they were in the times of our fathers or whether they were better then, than now.

Again, philosophy has been defined as the 'attempt by use of scientific methods to understand the world in which we live.' Among the Greeks, it means the cosmos or as we should say the universe. The philosophers of all ages set themselves to their courageous task of setting a theory of the universe, its extent and duration (space and time) its Creator (God), its purpose, its primary stuff or material, its relation to man and his soul and destiny. To this end, laboured Democrites and Plato, Aristotle and St. Augustine, Bruno and Descartes, Spinoza and Kant, Hegal and Spencer and others of the great philosophers, and these immense world problems still haunt us and must be studied.

In our modern individualistic way of thinking and living, we turn more to immediate interests, and the 'World' means something else to us. With our climate, our living, our big cities, crowded population and social life, the world we live is not an astronomical world, it is rather a social, political, literary, moral and religious world.

The Greeks in ancient times were much troubled by the problem of permanence and change, for, by change they meant physical change, the motion of material atoms and particles, the phenomenon of growth and decay. These questions still remain unanswered, but our interests now are with another kind of changing world,–changing social customs, changing political relations, changing morals, changing religions, and changing literary status. But this kind of work is quite as much in need of interpretation as the other, and so philosophy remains with us – only now, it becomes the interpretation of life, its value and meaning, the ways of the mind, problems of conduct and society, have come in to foreground. But it is true as ever, that philosophy is an attempt to understand the world we live.

The spirit of fresh enquiry is everywhere, but the trouble is that owing to our intensely social life, time is lacking for careful and persistent study of the life problems. In the study of philosophy, we simply take time to think some of our problems through.

Be it as it may, Plato in his 'Republic' had visualized an ideal state. He says power and authority must be given to those who have the knowledge and the character to use them rightly. If this is not done, we shall not even be able to secure that the few men and women who are capable of achieving and exercising such knowledge and power are given the opportunity and the work to acknowledge their potentialities. By providing the necessary training for the few, we shall secure the appropriate moral and political guidance for the many. The wisdom of an individual man's mind is the whole man's wisdom; the wisdom of the philosopher kings, is the wisdom of the whole community. 'My body must be governed by my mind; the desires and impulses that are the lower orders of the city, that is my soul must be informed and directed by my understanding.' Therefore, the ideal state should be ruled by a philosopher. Marcus Aurelius who became Emperor of Rome was a philosopher. Being a philosopher he could not reconcile with the wars, pomp, ambition, his victories, his triumphs etc. which to him was all vanity. 'Yet, glory is nothing but a vapour, and after fame is oblivion'. Aurelius believed in contentment and peace. He believed in the Fatherhood of God and Brotherhood of Man. He believed not in wars and killing but in peace, not in vengeance but in forgiveness. He said all human beings are created equal. He hated the horror of hurting the feelings of others. That was the philosopher king Marcus Aurelius, and to my mind Plato's dream that philosophers will govern well proved not very successful. Aurelius was great as a man.

In this monograph, I have started by explaining first the meaning of philosophy in a simple language so that the young reader may easily grasp the philosophical thoughts of both ancient and modern philosophers, ranging from Protogoras, Socrates, Plato, Aristotle, Epicurus, Schupenhour, Spinoza, Emerson, and the philosophy of life as viewed recently by no less a scholar and humanist than Professor B. Shiek Ali. The youth may find it interesting reading and may be eager to assimilate the thoughts, put in a simple understandable language, which may help to shape their character and way of life.

Understanding Philosophy

Philosophy is a difficult concept, whose simplest meaning is, love of wisdom, which calls for clear thinking on the doctrine of ideas, causality, natural laws, behavioural pattern, regularities, direction of development and a host of other concepts. **"Philosophy is the mother of all knowledge, the science of sciences, the knowledge of the Ultimate, the adviser to man, and the search for the meaning of life."*** In the words of Professor B. Sheik Ali, **"Religion is the foundation of philosophy and philosophy is the mansion of religion. Philosophy without religion has no heart, and religion without philosophy has no mind. They are the true inseparables in the realm of wisdom and understanding."** The problem of philosophy is to make people adopt virtue without the stimulus of super-natural hopes and fears.

* Ali, B. Sheikh.

It is an attempt to answer questions which have so long evaded satisfactory answers. It deals with such abstract concepts as Human Soul, Ultimate Reality, Truth, Beauty, Honour, Virtue and Morality.

Life is a gift of God, and good life is the gift of wisdom. A healthy society needs to know what constitutes good life, what values are ingrained in the rich experience of man, and what factors promote peace, prosperity, happiness and creative vision. The goal of mankind is not pleasure but knowledge, and that knowledge which results in wisdom and understanding. The society that aims at enhancing wisdom and understanding would surely produce superior minds who form the real wealth of a nation, unlike that society which is lost in creature comforts, apparently having all the glittering glow of prosperity; but in reality like artificial roses emitting no fragrance.'

'Man is the measure of all things' says **Protogoras,** and 'know Thyself' (a saying from the Delphic oracle echoed by **Heraclitus and Socrates** among others). Both reflect the specific orientation of philosophical anthropology, as humanism which takes man as its starting point, and treats man and the study of man as the centre, or origin on which all the disciplines ultimately depend.

❖ ❖ ❖

To Plato and Socrates, the meaning of the mission of philosophy is the establishment of justice among men. "Justice is the only happiness" said Socrates. The unjust alone are unhappy. 'No one has ever condemned injustice or praised justice (apparently he was unaware of the teachings of Hebrew Prophets). No one has ever investigated, how it happens that injustice is the greatest of all evils that the soul has with in it, and justice the greatest good.' And so, it is in order to ascertain the meaning of justice that Plato composed his immortal Dialogues. To him, the sum of human happiness depends on justice, beauty and love. The goodman, the happy man–for to be good is to be happy–is the just man, the harmonious man, the man whose perfectly attuned character always plays the right note in the symphony of social cooperation.

The ideal man of **'Plato's Ideal Republic'** is consecrated to the creation of beauty, either in living off-springs or in works of art or in noble deeds. For, beauty is the password to immortality. By creating a thing of beauty, we conquer death. Such was the philosophic dream of Plato. The ideal state must always be governed by the best says Plato. And in his *'Republic'* the philosophers are both by training and by natural ability the choicest of the best men and women that the state has been able to produce.

Man is born for only one purpose–to be happy says Plato. But what is happiness? It is the pleasant state of mind which is brought about by the habitual doing of good deeds. No man can be called unhappy if he acts in accordance with virtue. For, such a man will never do anything harmful or mean. And happiness consists in doing of good deeds. 'But the only man who is fully happy is he who is active in accordance with complete virtue, is sufficiently equipped with wealth, health, friendship (not for some chance period) but throughout a complete life.'

❖ ❖ ❖

But if happiness is the result of virtue, what then is virtue? To the ancients, the word did not mean as it does to us, moral excellence alone. It means any kind of excellence. A virtuous person in **Aristotle's Philosophy is a person who possessed physical prowess, technical competence and mental virtuosity. To these three qualities, Aristotle adds a fourth requisite for happiness – Moral Nobility.** The all round excellence, therefore, was needed for Aristotle's 'happy warrior in the battlefield of life.' But the world always is phenomenal, and virtue subordinates it to the mind. With the above thoughts, Aristotle drew a picture of an ideal or magnanimous man, some two thousand years ago.

'The ideal or magnanimous man is one who does not expose himself to danger, but is willing in great crisis to give his life if necessary. He takes joy in doing favour to other men, but feels shame in having favour done to him by other men. For, it is a mark of superiority to confer a kindness, but inferiority to receive it. His unselfishness is, however, but a higher form of selfishness, of 'enlightened selfishness.' 'The doing of a kind deed is not an act of selfsacrifice, but of self-preservation.' For, man is not an individual self, but a social self. Moreover, every good deed is a profitable investment. It is bound sooner or later to be returned with interest.

The ideal man behaves with moderation under both good fortune and bad. He will know how to be exalted and how to be abased. He will neither be delighted with success, nor, grieved by failure. He is reticent and somewhat slow in speech, but speaks his mind openly and boldly when occasion calls for it. He is apt to admire, for nothing is greater to him. **He overlooks injuries and does not speak evil of others,** even of his enemies, unless, it be to themselves. He never feels malice, and always forget injustices. He is not given to talk about himself or about others, for, he does not care that he himself should be praised or that other people should be blamed. He does not cry out about trifles and craves help from none. He is the healthy, the wise, the fundamental, the manly man. Furthermore, the work of this man will be inspiring, affirmative, and ethical. He must be moralist for whom nature is a discipline in moral truth. In short, he is a good friend to others, because he is himself his best friend.

The brave man is magnanimous as well as gentle. He does not take even an enemy at a disadvantage, nor strike a man when he is down, and unable to defend himself. Even in the midst of deadly strife, such instances of generosity have not been uncommon.

The honest man is antagonistic to fraud, the truthful man to lying, the justice loving man to oppression, the pure minded man to vice and iniquity. Such men have in all ages represented the moral of the world. Inspired by benevolence, and sustained by courage, they have been the main stays of all social renovation and progress. But for their continuous antagonism to evil conditions, the world were for the most part given over to the domination of selfishness and vice. Intellectual interpredity is one of the vital conditions of independence and self-reliance of character. **A man must have the courage to be himself, and not the shadow of the**

echo of another. He must exercise his own powers, think his own thoughts, and speak his own sentiments. He must elaborate his own opinions and form his own convictions. He who dare not form a opinion, must be a coward; he who will not, must be an idler; he who can not must be a fool.

Philosophical Theories

Ever since men became capable of free speculations, their actions in innumerable important respects, have depended upon their theories as to the world and human life, as to what is good and what is evil. This is as true in the present days as at any former times. **To understand, therefore, an age or a nation, we must understand its philosophy, and to understand its philosophy, we must ourselves be to a certain extent philosophers. The circumstances of men's lives do much to determine their philosophy, but conversely, their philosophy does much to determine the circumstances.**

It is a matter of common experience that men's characters are powerfully affected by misfortune, bereavement, poverty and disgrace. Adversity is, not of course, uniformly and necessarily productive of moral improvement. But no one will deny that under certain circumstances, and with men of certain temperaments, great moral changes are often produced indirectly through the awakening of religious emotions. In either case, of course, all that the misfortune does is to create conditions unfavourable to their action. When men have been struck a great bodily blow in their material fortunes, they turn to the affairs of the mind. It is only through periodic illness, that the world reflects, and it is only through reflection, that the world is worthy of survival. For philosophy, as some one has rightly said, thrives in the sick chamber of civilization.

Philosophy like theology consists of speculation on matters as to which definite knowledge has so far been ascertainable, but like science, it appeals to human reason rather than authority, whether that of tradition or that of revelation.

Some of the questions which often come to our mind are:

Is the world divided into mind and matter, and if so, what is mind and matter?

Is mind subject to matter or it possessed of independent power?

Has the universe any unity or purpose?

Is it evolving towards some goal? Are there really laws of Nature? Is there any way of living that is noble and what does it consist, and how shall we achieve it? Must the good be eternal, in order to deserve to be valued, or is it worth seeking ever if the universe is inexorably moving towards death? Is there such a thing as wisdom, or is it what seems such merely the ultimate requirements of folly?

To these questions, the contribution of great philosophers represent an adventure in thinking. And when we study them, we find, that the process of man's thoughts can be exciting a spectacle as the pageants of man's deeds. It is just enchanting to plunge into new ideas as it is to penetrate into new lands. Our horizon of activity expands, imagination richer, desire to learn and to know increases, our life becomes more coloured and most joyful as a result of companionship with the travellers of spirit and Pioneers of thought. We gain an insight into the minds of various philosophers which contribute to an interesting and important discovery.

Philosophy, therefore, is man's search for aspects of his existence hitherto unknown to him, regarding which his curiosity is naturally aroused, and his answers to this search holding true universally. A philosopher with his thought and intuition changes the course of mankind, and takes human consciousness one step forward. Rationalist philosophers from Aristotle to Bertand Russel have given philosophy, methods of conducting syllogistic inferences and logical analysis, and down the ages, the techniques have become so synonymous that philosophy and the practice of the philosophic explorations so rare, that today, the practice of logical analysis has erraneously been taken to mean the principle of philosophy of the self and the species. And, of course, the ultimate functions, of man's thoughts is to lead him to God – perfection – and to help himself realize God. The purpose of man's thoughts, his philosophy is to help him attain fulfilment in his worldly existence and lead him to perfec-tion. The philosopher is one who is curious to know certain aspects of human existence. He possesses some original ideas which compells him to become curious to research and to reveal his self.

❖ ❖ ❖

Aristotle (384BC–322BC) says: **God is not the Creator of the universe, but the cause of its motion. For, a creator is a dreamer, and a dreamer is a dissatisfied personality, a soul that yearns for something that is not, an unhappy being who seeks happiness – in short, an imperfect creature who aims at perfection. But God is Perfect, and since He is Perfect, He cannot be dissatisfied or unhappy. He is therefore, not the maker, but the MOVER of the universe.** As Nizami said:

'Say it is in the mind of every knowledgeable Person, that
Every moving object has a mover behind it.'

—Nizami

But what sort of Mover? To this question, Aristotle replies that God is the **Unmoved Mover** of the universe. Every other source of motion in the world, whether it be a person or thing or a thought, is (according to Aristotle) a **moved mover.** Thus, the plough moves the earth, the hand moves the plough, the brain moves the earth, the desire for food moves the brain, the instinct for life moves the desire for food, and so on. In other words, the cause of every motion is the result of some other motion. The master of every slave is the slave of some other master. Even the tyrant is the slave of ambition. But God can be the result of no action. **'He is the source of all actions, the Master of masters, the Investigator of all thoughts, the Unmoved Mover of the world as a beloved object moves the lover. Without being itself, it produces motion within all of us by being loved.'**

Plato (427BC–347BC) says: **"Love is the Hunger of the Human Soul for Divine Beauty."** The lover is eager not only to find beauty but to perpetuate it, to plant the seed of immortality in the mortal body. That is why the sexes love each other – to reproduce themselves and thus prolong time into eternity. And that is why parents love their children. For, the soul of the loving parents create not merely children, but seekers and partners of co-workers, and successors in the eternal quest of beauty. "What is this, beauty that we are all seeking to perpetrate through love? It is wisdom and virtue, honour and courage , justice and faith. In a word, beauty is truth and truth is the way that leads directly to God."

To Plato, religion must be purified in all its savages, myths and miracles and superstitions. 'We must have only the religion which is compatable to reason.' Our lives and laws are not judged by divine superiority, but simply by human perfection. **'It is man' says Aristotle 'who is the measure.'** Similar sentiments were echoed by **Allama Iqbal** in his six Lectures on the reconstruction of Islamic Thought, when he said, "Religion is not a departmental affair, it is neither mere thought, nor mere feeling, nor mere action; it is the expression of the whole man." **The essence of religion according to Iqbal, is faith, and faith is more than mere feeling.** "Islam finds the foundation of world unity in the principles of 'Towhid' (belief in the oneness of God)." It **demands loyalty to God and not to the Throne.**

❖ ❖ ❖

Epicurus (342BC–270BC) founded a religion based upon the pleasures of the mind. Epicurus says, "if men try to become more divine, they will succeed in becoming more humane. By worshipping the gods we become more God like, more refined, more indifferent to the buffetting of fate and the vicissitudes of life. True religion, therefore, does not consist of sacrifice or superstition or fear." It consists rather in a pious imitation of the Gods–**that is in "the contemplation of the nature of the world with a mind at rest."**

Epicurus conceived a negative rather than a positive theory of pleasure. **The greatest pleasure, he said is the complete absence of pain.** He says, death is the end of our existence. The soul like the body is mortal. It was born with the birth of the body and it dies with its death. Outside the body, there is no thought, no feeling, no sensation, no memory, no life. Dust thou art, to dust returnst is equally true of the human body and the human soul. He gives us a sad cold, bleak science – an intricate machine without a mechanic, a super human spectacle with out a divine plan. And then proceeds to give us an equally sad, cold, bleak philosophy – a system of pleasure without joy, the negative tranquillity of death as an escape from the positive perplexities of life. "The earth we live in, he reminds us, is rented to us for a little while, and when the time comes for us to move on we are dispossessed without a moment's notice." "But if we can not conquer death, let us at least overcome the fear of death". "Let us not grieve over the brevity of human life. Instead let us accept it with a placid heart." "For there is no consciousness after death, no pain and no punishment in hell for any mistakes that we may have made, during our stay on earth." "The white hand of Death soothes us into a sweet and dreamless sleep. For Death is the friendly warden who signs the papers of our release from the mad house of the world. He is the gentle physician who cures the most dreadful of all diseases–life."

There was however one positive aspect to Epicurus negative philosophy of pleasure. And this was his insistence upon the gospel of friendship. Epicurus had a genius for friendship. **Though he lived on bread and water, he always tried to break his bread in the company of a friend. "It is more important to know with whom we are to eat" "than what we are to eat." His philosophy, to be sure, was self centred. The only way to be happy, he said, is to invite others to partake of your happiness – not because it is expedient.** "It is not possible to live pleasantly without living wisely and justly and generously." "Treat others as you want them to treat you. Inflict no injury in order that you may suffer no injury. Live and let live". For this life of ours is meant to be a festival of friends. **"Cultivate the genius of friendship. Make a religion of it. Worship it."** For friendship is a sweet and beautiful and holy thing. The sympathy of true friendship is the only certain gift we possess in this world of doubtful worth. "If the sufferings of life can reconcile us to death, then the holiness of friendship can reconcile us to life."

The sympathy of his friends reconciled Epicurus to his own sufferings. Poverty, bereavement, and disease made his life indeed a thing of doubtful value. No philosopher has ever been more revered and no philosopher has ever been less understood.

Like **Epicurus, Schopenhour** (1788–1860AD) too was a pessimistic philosopher. He said, "Man is essentially a creature of pain. Suffering, therefore, is a condition of genius." It is the will that is fundamental in man; and it is the will that rules. His will is constantly driving him on to desire one object after another in life. But the moment he obtains his desire what follows? A terrible boredom, an empty void. Existence becomes again an unbearable burden. So he arrives anew. What is life but a pendulam swinging between pain and emptiness, desire, and boredom. For all satisfaction in this life is a negative quality. The only positive state is pain.

He said: 'does anyone believe he can enjoy his pleasure while his neighbour suffers pain?' On the contrary, "he who seeks for himself a happy life in a world of tempestuous sea of evil, is like a beggar dreaming he is king." This is the law of eternal justice. **"There is no gulf between mine and thine, my happiness and your happiness, my will and the general will of mankind." Let the wisemen proclaim this transcendent truth–that each and everyone of us must bear all the sufferings of the world as his own.** "And we, who have sipped from the fountain of eternal wisdom, we who have dedicated ourselves as humanitarians and saviours of men, let us pray out our hearts to all those who suffer, that in so doing we may relieve our own sufferings."

Man according to **Nietzsche** (1844–1900AD) suffers because he wills to be free. He is struck down because he dares to practice his rights against the interest of Gods who would keep him enslaved. Such was the fate of Prometheus who was chained to a rock and tormented by the elements. "And, such too was the fate of Adam and Eve who were driven from the garden of Eden." **"The Lord" observes Nietzsche "can not tolerate a rebel, yet the greatest rebels have been the supreme liberators of mankind."**

Only by suffering the tragic consequences of such an ascension, can man grow in the strength and worthiness of his freedom. **For, tragedy forges the will in to a mighty instrument of power. Nietzsche says, "Man must use his will not to die but to live. It is cowardly to will death as a release from suffering. On the other hand, it is noble to will life, inspite of suffering. Such a positive assertion of the will raise us above ourselve. Indeed it transforms man into God."**

Baruch Spinoza (1632–1677AD) believed in the doctrine of Pantheism. He says, God is the universe. The stars, the planets, the trees, the flowers, the oceans and mountains, the clouds – these are the body of God. The spirit that gives them shape and colour and motion and beauty is the mind of God. Every human body is part of God's mind. This philosophical doctrine is called Pantheism, for, the Greek word Pan (the white, or everything) and theos(God). This doctrine of Pantheism is more than a mere theory. It has a tremendous practical and ethical implications. For, if all humanity is one body and one soul, it follows that no individual can hurt others without hurting himself. "To do an injury to your neighbour is to cut off your own finger or to pluck out your own eye." The happiness of each of us depends upon the well-being of the whole body of mankind. For the human race, like every human being, is a united living organism. We are more than brothers of a single human family under the Fatherhood of God. We are members of a single human entity which in turn is an integral part of the divine essence of God.

Spinoza believes in happiness – the presence of pleasure and the absence of pain. It is our business to seek pleasure and to avoid pain. Our chief interest in life is to love ourselves. Each man, writes Spinoza, "must love himself and seek what is useful to him." This sound like the height of egoism. But Spinoza goes on to prove that it is the height of altruism. For, as Spinoza points out, "in order to love yourself you must love others. Love, pleasure, happiness – these are treasures of the soul, best enjoyed when most generally shared. We have already met this doctrine of enlightened selfishness in the philosophy of Aristotle. Spinoza amplifies the idea and applies it to modern life. The wise man, declares Spinoza, knows that he can help himself only by helping others. He realizes that individual happiness is mutual happiness. He avoids envy because envy produces not happiness but pain. He avoids hatred because hatred begets hatred. He avoids hurting others because he knows that injury is repaid with injury, that he who takes up the sword is destined to perish by the sword. He avoids conquest because he realizes that every military victory sows the seeds for a future war of revenge. **"Our greatest victories** writes Spinoza, **"are won not by arms but by greatness of our soul"**

The truly good man, therefore, the truly happy man will be the truly wiseman. He will be generous to others because he knows that in this way he will be most generous to himself. And so our ultimate object in life is to seek happiness through knowledge, through the acquisition of wisdom, through the enlightened understanding of the vital interrelationship that exist between man and man. He who understands this, will hate nothing despise nothing, injure nothing, and fear nothing. He will live a life not of individual ambition but of mutual cooperation. He will adhere to the teachings of the ancient prophets and to the principle of the Golden Rule. He will desire nothing for himself which he will not also desire for the rest of mankind. For, all men are equally important parts of God. And, so, asserts Spinoza, in order to be happy you must love yourself, **But to love yourself is to love mankind, and to love mankind is to love God. And this is the reason for which we have come in to the world."**

"Let us remember our united destiny, learn to be satisfied with little, to return love for hatred and to accept with a smiling courage whatever our individual fate may have to offer." This is the sum and substance of the happy life, the whole method, as Spinoza would say, of the superior man's wisdom. Above all he urges, "learn to take joy in your intimate relationship with the rest of the world. Bear constantly in mind the fact that your own and your neighbour's existence, however insignificant they may appear to you, are necessary threads in the weaving of the tapestry of universal life." "The greatest good is the knowledge of the union which the mind has with the whole of nature." "If the world has not been made for you, be happy in the thoughts that you have been made for the world. You are an important page in the book of life. Without you the book would have been incomplete."

Spinoza had not only one of the most universal minds of modern times, but one of the most sympathetic hearts. In 1882 when his statue was unveiled at The Hague (Holland), Earnest Renan concluded the dedicatory exercise with these words:

"Here came perhaps the truest vision ever had of God. He might have added the words, 'because here came perhaps the noblest affection ever entertained for man."

❖ ❖ ❖

According to **Emerson,** the life of a man is a quest for friendship, a striving for the class re-union of the human soul. But true friendship is not merely a passion but it is also an action of the soul. It is a divine game of give and take. **"The only way to have a friend is to be one." 'We must learn to grasp heroic hands in heroic hands'.** The active and heroic conception of friendship is to Emerson, the only solid thing in a world of shadows. It is a substance of such reality and duration that compared to it, the Alps and the Andes come and go as rainbows."

Emerson says "cultivate the art of friendship and you come close to the heart of reality." "You stop looking at the rainbow and you begin to see the true source of light." If man could be inspired with a tender kindness to the souls of men and should come to feel that every man was another self, this feeling would cause the most striking changes of external things. He, therefore, said "Every man I meet, I consider him more superior to me."

❖ ❖ ❖

Professor B. Sheik Ali's view on the philosophy of life is appealing. He says, "Returning good for evil is justice and not generosity, for a tree does not deny shade even to its wood-cutter. If that is the behaviour of an inanimate object, ours should be higher. It is Scorpion's nature to sting, but our nature should be to save its life, even if it stings. To do good and be good is the essence of all ethics. To see good, to seek good, to know good and to love good, are all the limbs of morality. **Wisdom and Knowledge do not descend from Heavens.** We have to earn them by our efforts, our love, our labour, our devotion and our skill. Given the parameters, life leaps like a geyser. It will prompt us to find the best within us, and also in others. The best certainly exists all around us, if only we have the eyes to see, and will to acquire. When we give the best, the best will come back to us, even if it doesn't, we get the peace of mind which is most precious. With peace of mind, we need nothing else; without it, it does not matter what else we have. If we are not satisfied with anything but the best, the chances are, we will get the best."

"When the mind is **tuned** to this kind of wave-length, the renaissance of wonder starts, and we begin to know the meaning and purpose of life. One should know that one's life must be like a candle, which burns itself, but throws light to others; like a tree which stands in the scorching sun, but gives shade to others; and like wood which destroys itself, but cooks food for others. One should never be desperate in misery, for, we have to laugh when we are sad, and sober when we are elated. Those who weep would be made to rejoice one day, for, destiny is a wheel that churns bad into good. In affliction we have to remember that it is fire that purifies the gold and human life everywhere is a state in which much is to be endured, and little is to be enjoyed. Our sweetest songs are those that tell us of the saddest thoughts."

❖ ❖ ❖

From the above brief sketch of the philosophical thoughts of some of the philosophers, we find that all philosophies exhibit an intrensic unanimity of thought. It is specially true in the field of ethics. Different schools of philosophy–be it ancient or modern, stoic or epicurian, mystic or Christian, Pagan or idealistic, are in practical agreement with different systems of religion. The philosophers and the philosophy alike are united in the belief as to the fundamental purpose of life. And the purpose is to ensure the happiness of man through the cooperation of mankind. The search for metaphysical certainly has been the source of much that is profound and significance in the history of thought. What can a human mind know with certainty? How does opinion differ from knowledge? What is real? What can be known? These are the problems with which metaphysics deals.

We all human beings share a common destiny in a universe whose mystery still remains unfathomed. Men have a social conscience and sometimes, it is very sensitive. We are both equal but are made unequal by the way we are brought up. Reverence for personality is the central principle of all ethics. Unfortunately, in our practice we have overlooked them.

The optimists feel that, life is essentially worth living. It may have its moments of pain and sorrow, but it is valuable because of these things, and the reward which even a glimpse of self-knowledge brings. It is not right to think that only those who are unhappy can understand the sufferings of others. When we help others out of deep sympathy, our desire to help is rooted in the joy we feel in life. Unhappy people sometimes become embittered and want others to suffer also. **Human beings are born to love and be loved. (Mother Teresa's example). Happy people are those who are most thankful to life's opportunities and responsibilities than to its rewards and prizes. The indispensable conditions for happiness is to be without some of the things we badly need. Tagore** believes in man's capacity for joy, and of his power to live in harmony with the natural and universal forces that surround him.

Character is one of the greatest motive force in the world. It is moral order seen through the medium of individual nature. Men of character are the conscience of the society to which they belong. In its noblest embodiment, it exemplarifies human nature in its highest forms, for, it exhibits man at his best. Men of genius always command admiration and men of character most secures respect. The former stand to society in the relation of its intellect, and the latter of its conscience; and while the former are admired, the latter are followed.

The youth will certainly take lessons from the experiences of the great men whose quest for excellence are unparalleled.

With the above brief background of philosophy as expounded by some of the great philosophers, and men of wisdom, I would now turn to my favourite thinker and philosopher **Marcus Aurelius** – the philosopher king of Rome and his philosophical thoughts.

Brief Background

"Until philosophers are kings, and the princess of this world have the spirit and power of philosophy, and political greatness and wisdom meet in one, cities will never cease from ill–no, nor the human race, as I believe–and then only, will our state have a possibility of life, and see the light of the day. The truth is, that the state in which the rulers are most reluctant to govern is best and most quietly governed, and the state in which they are most willing is the worst."

Thus writes Plato in his Republic, laying down the conditions, which even to him appear impossible, under which a state may be wisely governed. "The rule must be a philosopher as well as a king; and he must govern unwillingly, because he loves philosophy better than dominion." Once in the history of the world these conditions were fulfilled: **in Marcus Aurelius we find the philosopher king, the ruler who preferred the solitude of the student to the splendour of the palace, the soldier who loved the arts of peace better than the glory of war.** It is with no small interest that we turn to the records of history to see that was the outward life led by this king; but even more willingly do we open the precious record of his own thoughts, which reveal to us the inner life of the philosopher.

Marcus Aurelius Antoninus was the adopted son of the Emperor Antoninus Pius, who died in 161 A.D. He had been brought up with the utmost care by his adoptive father, and received the best instruction in poetry and rhetoric, at that time the staples of a liberal education. But his favourite study was philosophy, and when only eleven years old he assumed the philosophers' simple dress, adopted their mode of life; and finding that his inclination was chiefly towards Stoicism, he attached himself to this – the strictest of the philosophic schools. A discipline of monastic severity, that bade its followers disregard all bodily comfort, all that is commonly called pleasure, and care for nought but virtue, was indeed a strange training for one destined for the imperial purple, and it hardly appeared to be a fitting preparation for the cares of what was then the one great Empire of the world. True, the Stoics loved to call themselves citizens of the world, and to inculcate that cosmopolitanism that is broader and nobler than mere patriotism; but while they maintained in theory that the wise man should take part in politics, in practice there was always something in the existing state of things which made his doing so unadvisable. But Marcus Aurelius could not choose his own lot. Destined for the throne already by the Emperor Hadrian, associated in the empire even in his adoptive father's lifetime, he could but accept his lot, and in striving to practise the noble principles he had learnt, pay to his Stoic teachers the truest tribute.

His was a troubled reign. The Roman Empire, which in the vigorous days of the Republic had been gradually but surely extending its boundaries, had been consolidated, and newly administered by Julius Caesar and Augustus. On the death of the latter, it extended from the Atlantic on the west to the Armenian mountains and Arabian deserts on the east. On the south, the African deserts had alone stopped the conquering arms, while on the north, a line of natural boundaries was traced by the English Channel, Rhine, Danube, Black Sea, and Mount Caucasus. Warned by the ill-success that attended the later campaigns of his generals on the Lower Rhine, Augustus had cautioned his successors to aim at preserving rather than increasing their dominions. Thus it came about, that between the years 114 and 161 A.D. when Marcus Aurelius succeeded to the throne, only two fresh conquests had been made; Britain, a source of more trouble than profit to the empire, and Dacia, conquered by Trajan in 106 A.D.

Natural boundaries and Roman legions kept peace and security for many years within the circle of Roman dominion. But there were two weak points on these borders. On the north, the hardy German tribes on the Danube and Upper Rhine, themselves hard pressed by Slavonian intruders from Russia, threatened to invade the Roman dominion; on the east the "insolent Parthians," long the terror of the Roman arms, was a constant source of trouble and danger. The peace-loving Marcus Aurelius was obliged to cope with both these enemies. The arms or rather the army, of the insolent and profligate Lucius Verus for a time subdued the Parthians, but no lasting peace was destined Marcus Aurelius. He himself conducted the campaigns on the Danube, and again and again beat back the northern enemy in wars, of which the chief interest to us now consists in the scant notes in the Meditations–"This among the Quadi," "this at Carmuntum," showing how these precious records of a pure and serene soul were composed amid the storms of battle and the elation of victory. Nor were his troubles confined to foreign wars. The plague, imported from the East, ravaged Italy, though it did the state good service in carrying off Lucius Verus, Marcus's adoptive brother, whom, in obedience to the wishes of Antoninus, he had associated with himself in the empire. There were famines too in the land, with which the Emperor tried to cope by schemes of carefully-organised charity. And, lastly, Avidius Cassius, one of his most trusted and alert generals, revolted in Syria, and tried to obtain for himself the empire, deeming it an easy matter to overcome a Master who was so full of generosity and compassion that he could only inspire contempt in the mind of the unphilosophic soldier. The revolt was soon put down, but the leader was killed by one of his own officers. The Emperor expressed only his regret that he should have been thus deprived of the luxury of forgiveness, and he carefully destroyed all documents that could implicate any others in the revolt. Thus in all the trials of his life, his philosophy inspired noble action, and he might worthily be added to the short list of those whom the Stoics acknowledged as really good and great.

Emperor Marcus Aurelius
121–180 A.D.

Cherished the ambition 'never to give pain to another.'

When Marcus Aurelius commenced his reign (in 161 A.D.) the Roman Empire had passed the vigour of its youth. It was rapidly approaching the decline of old age. Under the Caesars the Empire delighted in its conquests; now, under the Antonines, it was ripe for philosophy. For philosophy thrives in the sick chamber of civilization. In the case of Greek philosophy a great disaster, the destruction of the Athenian Empire, had set the stage for Plato, Aristotle, the Epicureans and the Stoics. These teachers as we have observed earlier, tried to discover a path of moral conduct along which the individual might safely travel whilst the pillars of his national civilization lay in ruins.

Plato had dreamed of a new ideal state to rise above the ruins of the old. The ideal state was to be ruled by a philosopher-king. If ever a man was destined to remake the world and to raise its citizens to the stature of demigods, it would be such a ruler. With great material resources at his disposal and with great resources of the mind as well, with the armies of men to follow him and with the wisdom of God to lead him on, such a philosopher-king might bring the Utopian dream of Plato to a practical reality. But he must have good material to build with. There must be a great empire for the great emperor, a healthy body for the healthy mind.

Such was the dream of Plato. And it seemed as if the Rome of Marcus Aurelius might fulfil that dream. The Roman Empire, stretching from the northern tip of England to equatorial Africa and from the Atlantic Ocean to the Euphrates, had at long last, in Marcus Aurelius, received its philosopher-king. But Plato's dream was as far from fulfilment as ever. For Rome under the rule of Marcus Aurelius presented the spectacle of an unhealthy body with a healthy mind. Rome was powerful, but it was not sound. In its long and aggressive fight for victory this overambitious empire had bled itself dry.

❖ ❖ ❖

Caesar Marcus Aurelius Antoninus Augustus was born on 26th April 121 A.D. at Rome died on March 17, 180 A.D. at Vindobona (Vienna) or Sirmium, Pannonia. Marcus Aurelius has symbolized for many generations in the West the Golden Age of the Roman Empire. Best known for his "Meditations" on Stoic philosophy, his thoughts pursued during the troubling involvement of his reign. His day to day political thoughts can be understood by reading the "Meditations". The 'Meditations' (the thoughts of a philosopher-king) have been condemned by many generations, are of the great books of all times. Though they were Marcus's own thoughts, they were perhaps not original. They were basically the moral tenets of Stoicism learnt from Epictatus. "The cosmos is a unit governed by an intelligence, and the human soul is a part of their divine intelligence and can therefore stand, if needed and alone atleast pure and undefiled amidst chaos and futility. One or two of Marcus's ideas, perhaps more, though lack of rigorous understanding, than anything else, diverged from the stoic philosophy and approved that Platonism that was itself then turned into the Neoplatonism into which all Pagan philosophies except Epicuranism, were destined to merge. But he did not deviate so far as to accept the comfort of any kind of survival after death.

At the age of eleven, Marcus Aurelius decided he would be a philosopher. He adopted the shabby cloak of the Cynics, ate simple food and slept on a hard cot. His imagination was fired by the personalities of the gnarld old patriarchs from Athens who brought to Rome their schools of philosophy and their vermin. They walked with bowed heads and with hands folded behind the backs, and **lectured on the greatness of the universe and the littleness of man.** And they practised what they preached, these Cynics who derived pleasure, and these stoics who ignored pain. They retired from the world of men and became voluntary prisoners behind the bars of their principles. But these men were no emperors. In renouncing the world they had nothing to lose but their sorrow. It was something new for a prince to be converted – a prince in the mightiest empire of the ancient world.

When Marcus Aurelius was eighteen, his uncle the Emperor Pius Antoninus, had adopted him as his son and successor to the vast realm. But meanwhile the precocious lad had discovered an even vaster realm—the realm of the spirit. He was annoyed that he couldn't devote the rest of his life to philosophy, but he resigned himself to his fate. Already he showed within him the makings of a Stoic.

His uncle spared no effort in educating Marcus to the throne. He gave him the foremost teachers in rhetoric and in history. He hardened him to the saddle of the war horse. He started him on a career of statesmanship. He bestowed upon him the title of Caesar. In the palace, the young prince received the flattery of the courtiers; in the barracks he was drilled in army manoeuvres; in the quiet of his study he speculated on the "wherefore of empire, the whence of ambition and the wither of life." The conservative and practical-minded nobility would have been gravely shocked had they realized what was going on in the mind of their future emperor. The Romans were a nation who acted first and speculated afterwards. And irony of ironies, here was a royal philosopher in their midst!

He ascended the throne at the death of his foster father–the throne of the Caeser-founded in treachery, dedicated to oppression, sustained with bloodshed. As he **donned the purple** he made a mental reservation to himself: "Take care not to become Caesarified." Other idealists had been compelled to renounce poverty for riches. It was hard for a philosopher to content himself with a crown. It was distasteful for a scholar to plunge into a career of politics and battles. He had inherited an empire of snarling beasts. He must devote his life to the solution of quarrels not of his own making; he was tied to the crimes and follies of his ancestors. The barbarian hordes throughout the Empire, smarting under the lash of five centuries of Roman aggression, were ready to revolt. And when the philosopher **Marcus Aurelius** ascended the throne the storm broke. The barbarians had no respect for the meditations of an emperor; they respected only his armies.

He sent an army to put down the uprising of the Parthians, east of the Tigris. The war was terminated successfully by Lucius Verus, an adopted brother of his, whom Aurelius had made co-ruler of the Empire at his accession. He had hoped that Lucius would attend to the practical business of the state whilst he himself attended to his philosophy. But Lucious Verus died, and Marcus Aurelius was left alone with his kingdom–a dangerous toy for which he had no taste. His head was full of philosophy but his hands were full of trouble. At the same time that Marcus was securing his trans-Danubian frontiers, Egypt, Spain, and Britain were troubled by rebellions or invasions. By 175 A.D. the General Avidius Casius who earlier had served under Verus, had virtually become a perfect of all of the eastern provinces including control of important Province of Egypt. In that year Avidius Cassius took the occasion of a rumour of Marcus' death to proclaim himself Emperor. The barbarians had flamed into a new revolt. The Quadi and the Marcomani had swept into the provinces of the Danube. The races north of the Alps were feasting their eyes on Italy and their hearts on a desire for plunder. The mighty Roman structure was sagging. Marcus Aurelius rose to the occasion. He collected money for defence by selling the Royal silver-ware and the palace jewellery at a public auction. He conscripted the gladiators from the Coliseum, the slaves from the markets, the thieves and the murderers from every corner of the Empire; and at the head of this non-descript army, he placed himself and his books. He marched to the East, pitched his tent and sat down to wait the onrush of the Quadi. **At**

night, by the flicker of an oil lamp, as the wind whistled against the canvas flap, and the wolves howled in the distance, he set down his thoughts on the sadness of fate and the savagery of war. Most of the remaining years of his life, he spent in the warrior's tent at the battle front to safeguard the Empire that had been wished upon him but to his pen. Another warrior before him had divided his time between the sword and the pen. But Julius Caesar had exploited his literary talent to further the glory of his vanity. Marcus Aurelius undertook a more modest and more noble task—to demonstrate the vanity of his glory.

❖ ❖ ❖

The Roman Legions defeated the Quadi. Some of the soldiers believed it was the triumph of the doctrine of brotherhood that had turned the trick. For there were strange description among the emperor's legion's-men who professed to follow the teachings of a certain Nazarene. And they called up to their leader in heaven to stop the barbarians. The Quadi, with their greater numbers, had surrounded the Romans. They had cut them off from their water supply. Suddenly the great clouds in heaven burst open and the rain came down. The hard-pressed warriors of the Emperor held out their helmets and drank to their hearts content. And then another miracle happened. Lightning stuck down with swift vengeance from the sky. The Quadi were engulfed in a hundred fires. But—so went the story—not a Roman was touched. It was a mighty victory for Marcus Aurelius. But the little band of Christians spread the news of this miracle through out the world and hailed the battle as a victory for Christianity.

Though a pagan in training, the emperor—philosopher Marcus Aurelius was tender and kind at heart. He rejected the miracle of the conquest. For he didn't believe in the God of battle. **He did, however, believe in the God of love. He believed in the fatherhood of God and in the brotherhood of Man.** He sympathised with his fellow men, his co-partners in the universal brotherhood of sorrow. "I can not be angry with my brothers" he wrote, "or sever myself from them, for, we are made by nature to help one another, like the feet, the hands, the eyelids, the upper and the lower rows of teeth."

Yet the Christian brothers of Marcus Aurelius were outlaws in the Roman state. The slaves, the burdened toilers, the discouraged peasants were robbed of their freeholdings, and herded by a class of wealthy exploiters into farm Gangs on the soil. Society had failed the common man, and the common man, having lost his faith in this world was passionately in search of a hope for the next world. Marcus Aurelius's kindness and feelings for his people cheered them up and gave new hopes.

Though Marcus disliked the Christians, there was no systematic persecution of them during his reign. Their legal status remained as it had been under Trojan and Hadrian. Christians were *ipsofacto* punishable but not to be sought out. It appears though the Christian blood flowed more profusely in the reign of Marcus Aurelius the philosopher than it had before. He was not an initiator of persecution.

The thinkers of the Roman world had also lost their faith. For they saw about them an aggressive monster, the victorious Roman Empire – **a power that knew how to divide and rule but not how to unite and govern.** They saw a political and social and military system which implanted in the hearts of the people, no allegiance but only hatred and cynicism and fear. Yet, they were unwilling to subscribe to a cult of emotional propaganda that placed revelation above reason. Instead they flocked to the schools of philosophy to find a way out. They remained indifferently loyal to the apparently indifferent old gods. Their chief concern was with the certain sorrows of this world, rather than with the uncertain joys of the next. They didn't expect to control their own thoughts. They sneered at the Christian reformers who sought to remould the fellowship of the earth into something more akin to their dream of heaven. The Roman philosophers were not communists who believed in social equality; they were anarchists who had no social beliefs whatsoever. They divided themselves into two main groups: the Epicureans and the Stoics. The one group advocated, "Enjoy life while you can, for tomorrow you may be dead." The other,

"Endure life while you can, for tomorrow you may still be alive to suffer."

Yet the **Gentle Carpenter** had gone a step beyond the Stoics. "Do not accept suffering "he had said: "choose it. Help one another to bear life's common cause that in so doing you may lighten one another's burden."

Marcus Aurelius was half believer and half Stoic. And he had good need for both the patience and his Stoic indifference. For troubles were heaping themselves upon his head. Rumours had reached him that one of his most trusted generals, Avidius Cassius, was raising the standard of revolt in Syria. "Avidius," jested the punters, "is avid to be emperor," This ambitious soldier had gained a name for himself through his vigorous suppression of rebellions in Arabia and in Egypt. He dreamed, it was whispered, that he was another Brutus whose mission it was to free Rome from the emperor dictator. He was a restless soldier who chafed at his comparative inactivity under the military leadership of a philosopher. Born under the hot oriental sun, he was a dark-skinned man with a dark mind that could easily harbour disloyal thoughts. But Marcus Aurelius shrugged his shoulders at the rumours of disloyalty. "He is a good general, strict and brave; the state cannot do without him." Besides, no one had stepped forward with a direct accusation. There was no concrete evidence for the whispered charges. Confidently the emperor turned his mind to other matters. He must reject the human urge to indulge in petty recriminations against his friends. Life was too serious for that sort of thing. The philosophic soul must jump to no hasty decisions. "Do every deed, speak every word, think every thought in the knowledge that you may end your days at any moment," he confided to his books.

Meanwhile the treachery of Avidius, so the rumour went, had taken a more dangerous turn. The ambitious general, it was whispered, was now casting his eyes not only upon the emperor's kingdom but upon the emperor's wife. This new titbit of gossip took on like wildfire. People began to hint that the marriage between the emperor and his cousin, Faustina, had never been sanctioned with the blessings of love. And yet there were many instances to convince the intimate friends of the royal family that Marcus Aurelius was a tender husband. Hadn't he written numerous letters to his old tutor, Fronto, expressing his affection for Faustina? Hadn't she borne him over a dozen children? Was she not always, when her royal husband was at home, as solicitous about his comfort as he was about hers? And now that he had pitched his tent on the field of battle, she was as faithful as **Penelope, insisted** their friends-weaving in the palace and waiting for his return.

But Avidius was not willing to wait. He suddenly spread a report that the emperor was dead. He rallied his legions to back him as the new emperor. The people of Antioch followed him to a man, the governor of Egypt joined him.

When the news of the rebellion reached Marcus, he called his troops together. Addressing them he said: "Fellow soldiers, my very best friend has plotted to overthrow me and has forced me against my will to take the field. I enter upon this campaign with the conviction that I have neither committed any act of injustice against Avidius nor left undone anything that I ought to have done for him." "He had no indignation to express, no complaint to voice" he told his legions. "There is only one thing I am afraid of, fellow soldiers – for I shall speak the whole truth to you – and that is that Avidius Cassius may kill himself to avoid the shame of coming into my presence or that someone else, knowing that I am on the way to take the field against him, may do the deed. **Then I shall be robbed of the greatest prize of the victor such as no man ever had. And what was this prize? To forgive the man who has done me the wrong, to remain a friend to him who has broken his friendship with me."**

The revolt lasted only a hundred days. As Marcus Aurelius had predicted, one of Avidius own followers assassinated him. "I shall spare his wife and his children." announced the philosopher-warrior. He sent the senate a message in which he enjoined them from putting to death any of the soldiers who had taken part in the rebellion. "Let the banished come home, let the proscribed take back their property. I wish I could recall from the dead the poor victims who have already suffered the penalty."

The hardened politicians of the Empire shuddered at the mercy of their emperor. They wondered whether he was fair to his own family in thus sparing the family of the arch-traitor. But Marcus Aurelius quieted their fears with a shrug of the shoulders. For he was a Stoic and a fatalist. "If my family deserves to be loved more than the family of Avidius, the gods will enable us and not them, to sit upon the throne."

Having thus disposed of the conspirator's family, he set out, together with Faustina and with his son Commodus, to visit the cities that had joined the conspiracy. But he came with a message of forgiveness and not of revenge. When he reached the village of Halala, at the foot of Mount Taurus, Faustina fell ill and died. In spite of the scandalous stories he had heard about her behaviour, inspite of his own suspicions. he had never ceased to love his queen. Her death was a terrible blow. He built a golden image of Faustina to accompany him on his campaign. He founded a home for destitute girls in her memory. He offered prayers and tears to her statue. And yet, though he sorrowed over death, he did not fear it. Nor did he fear life. He must live his life, as he would meet his death, bravely. He returned to the old front, for the barbarians had not yet ceased to make trouble. Existence was "a warfare and a journey in a strange land." He went back to his battles and his books, "victorious over pain and pleasure, independent of what others may do or may fail to do...For the life of the body is but a river, and the life of the soul a misty dream."

Finally, in 179 A.D., he defeated the last of the rebellious tribes. The Empire was secure–for a time. But the emperor had contracted a disease from his exposure in camp, and he lay deathly ill. Sickly all through his life probably plagued with a chronic ulcer he took daily dozes of drugs.

The Stoic Philosophy of Marcus Aurelius, was a product of the East. The founder of Stoicism, the Semitic Zeno, was a spiritual brother of the old Hebrew prophets. His people were Phoenicians. He had come to Greece from the island of Cyprus and had set up a school of philosophy at Athens. A swarthy Isaiah, careless of the opinions and the conventions of society, a sunburnt rebel with a passion for justice, a hardened cynic with gentle eyes; a citizen of the universe, looking upon the mortals of the earth and the immortal stars in the heavens as his fellow citizens. Like his brother dreamers in Judea, he was inspired with the conviction that god is One. "God is ether. God is air. God is the spirit of ethereal fire. God goeth to and fro throughout all that is. God is mind, God is nature." The Hebrews called Him Jehovah. The adopted son of Athens identified him with Zeus. **One God, one human family, one law "Ye shall all have one law and one custom–like a flock, herded under one crook, that feedeth together."** This was echoed by Sri Narayana Guru in the early 20th century–'one God, one law and one human family.'

This Stoic philosophy of Zeno, like the other schools of Athenian thought, had emigrated to the Imperial City when Greece came under the conquering orbit of Rome. The Romans appropriated these alien schools of philosophy, as they appropriated their alien captives, and pressed them into the service of their practical life. They rejected the metaphysics of the various philosophies and accepted their ethics. For, they cared little about the mysteries of the heavens. They were concerned mainly with the realities of the earth.

The realistic philosophers of Rome found Stoicism especially to their liking. For, the Stoics taught that if man couldn't banish the sorrows and the evils of the world he could at least discipline his own will to endure them courageously. And furthermore, by a process of intellectual acrobatics, the Stoic could even become optimistic about the imperfections of the world. For actually – he maintained – there was nothing evil in experience. Only popular credence made it so. **The world was good, for it was governed in accordance with the laws of nature. "All events are merely natural progresses and have no intrinsic moral values, whether good or bad."** If we feel that providence has struck us too keen a blow, we must remember that we are in no position to judge the workings of the entire universe from our own mortal–and moral–vantage spot. **There is nothing good and nothing bad, but thinking makes it so. We suffer from our opinions, from our**

limited vision. It is possible for us to make ourselves misfortune-proof by adopting a simple formula. If unfulfilled desires are the bane of our existence, let us limit our desires to the scope of our ability to fulfill them. Since the material goods of life are so fleet and rare, let us be content with our spiritual goods–a good mind and a good character. Call these the positive virtues. Fix them as the ultimate meaning of life. And consider that every thing else is indifferent. Health, illness, pleasure, pain, riches, poverty–all these have no meaning. Even death, though, it destroys the mind as well as the body, the good character, as well as the good fortune, must be regarded as a negative event. For death may destroy the philosopher but not his philosophy. It kills the mind of the individual, but it does not disturb the majesty of the world. The majestic order of nature is bound to outlast all the little minds of those who seek to define it. Learn, therefore, to be indifferent to your fate. For all of us are subject to the same fate in the end. All of us alike, from the highest to the lowest, are the equally helpless puppets of an inevitable and impartial destiny.

This creed denied all the artificial criteria whereby men were divided into classes of master and slave, king and commoner, rich and poor. It struck the very keynote of democracy. All events are to be faced with equanimity; all men are equal. Interestingly enough, it was the slave, Epictetus, who converted the emperor, Marcus Aurelius, to the democratic gospel of Stoic philosophy. Men are born to different stations in life, wrote Epictetus, but at the moment of death the destitute are amply compensated. **For death serves to take away more from those who have more, or less from those who have less. And if the rich, sobered by this levelling of human fortune, had their lives to live all over again, they wouldn't take a penny less nor the poor a penny more. For, the nature has too great a sense of humour to let man profit by his experience.** Nothing changes, no human nature ever grows better or worse, more human or less human. Indeed, there is no yardstick for human progress. Man is forever stepping gingerly on a treadmill that churns the vast infinite waters of the past and the future. He has nothing to lose but his footing, nothing to gain but a few more moments in a struggle to keep his balance before he topples over. Why should he try to moralize and classify things into the beautiful and the ugly, the good and the bad, when all he can observe around him is the stretch of the earth and the heavens? They are neither beautiful nor ugly, neither good nor evil, but vast, overwhelming, eternal. They are nature. And nature is the only true reality. Let us adapt ourselves to this reality. Let us live in accordance with the laws of nature.

It is the irony of man's foolishness—observes Marcus Aurelius, that in the midst of his impotence he should be spurred on by an ambition for glory! "Camillus, Caesar, Volesus, Leonnatus, after them Scipio and Cato, Augustus, Hadrian and Antoninus all are forgotten. All things hasten to an end, shall speedily seem old fables, to be mouthed for an instant and then to be buried in oblivion". Rome too! The grandeur and the glory of an empire is but the report of gossipy narrators, a handful of pebbles and dust to be dug up by archaeologists groping among the ruins.

Is there, then, no hope for mankind? Yes, replies Marcus Aurelius, there is the ultimate hope of renouncing all hope. In thus renouncing hope, man can free himself from his greatest enemy-disappointment. Indeed, he can become **mirthless apotheosis** of jubilation, decked out in sackcloth and ashes. All he must do is to drink deep with his mind into the intoxication of complete apathy. Let us be, like the gods, indifferent to the buffetings of fate. "Take me up and cast me where you will. I shall have serene within me my own divinity." Here is the achievement of supreme triumph through supreme abnegation. Yet even the Stoic reaches the limit of self-denial. **There is margin beyond which humility pays no dividends.** When all is said and done, there is an active as well as a passive side to the philosophy of Marcus Aurelius. He is indifferent to his fortune, but he is not indifferent to his duty. And this duty is – to govern his own soul and his Roman subjects firmly but fairly. Live in accordance with nature–that is, in accordance with the laws of reason. For there is a **ruling** reason in the universe whose **ultimate** purpose is co-ordination, interdependence, reciprocity, in a word, justice.

Justice to his fellows and indifference to his fate–this was the highest virtue in the philosophy of Marcus Aurelius. This, and fearlessness in the face of death. "Banish the fear of death by regarding it not with superstition or awe but merely as one of the natural functions in the cycle of life, such as eating and drinking, sleep and sex."

Like Epicurus, Marcus Aurelius argues that death is nothing more than the dissolution of the elements of which every human being is compounded. Does not the conservation of energy preserve every atom in the universe? "And if in their successive interchanges no harm befalls the elements, why should one suspect any harm in the change and the dissolution of the whole? **Death is natural, and nothing natural can be evil."**

This is the very summit of self-conquest. For, where there is no evil there need be no fear. "If in death all sense be extinguished, there can be no sense of loss. But if a different sort of sense be acquired, you became a different creature and do not cease to live."

❖ ❖ ❖

It was the winter of 180 A.D. Marcus Aurelius lay dying in his tent. He was only fifty-nine years old. A stranger, paradoxical, discontented failure of a man, **this emperor soldier – philosopher who had preached contentment all his life the Dr. Jekyll and Mr. Hyde of the ancient world. At night, in the quest of his study,** he had been the ardent scholar and sensitive poet who was searching his own heart and weaving the substance of his thought into the plan of a better world for happier men. But in the daytime, amidst the clash of arms, he had become the perfect commander who swept to victory by the Roman formula of no surrender and no mercy. His convictions had been greater than his courage. "My city and country, so far as I am Marcus Aurelius, "he had written in his Meditations, "is Rome; but so far as I am a man, it is the world." Yet in actual life he had forgotten that he was a man; he had merely remembered that he was Roman. **He had taught magnanimity to**

his fellow men. "If you cannot maintain a true magnanimous character, go courageously into some corner where you can maintain it; or if ever there you fail, depart at once from life." Yet, in his treatment of the Christians he had been the direct opposite of magnanimity. Regarding their gentleness as a menace to the imperialistic dreams of the Roman Empire, he had ordered their leaders to be crucified. He was a good man in bad company. Living in Rome, he had been compelled to do as the Romans.

And now as he lay dying in his tent he thought of his miscast role in the fitful drama of life. His mind had been fashioned "for nobler times and calmer hearts." He had aimed at contentment and he had won glory instead. Yet "glory is nothing but a vapour, and after fame is oblivion."

Vanity of vanities. The life of Marcus Aurelius, his pomp, his ambitions, his wars, his victories, his triumphs, all vanity!

The Romans were glad to see him go. They wanted a leader who was less of a philosopher and more of a warrior. His son Commodus and his other heirs were anxious, foolish little men, to come into their worldly inheritance. The dying emperior clasped his mantle tightly about him. "I am leaving a life from which my very partners, for whom I toiled and prayed and planned, are wishing me to depart. Why, then, strive for a longer life?"

❖ ❖ ❖

There is a story that when Marcus Aurelius died, the Olympian gods held a banquet in his honour. At his right sat the emperors Augustus, Tiberius and Vespasian. At his left sat the other great Roman emperors—Nerva, Trajan, Hadrian and his own foster father, Antoninus Pius. Nero and Calagula, however, had been refused admittance at the door. Jupiter announced a contest to decide as to which of the emperors had been the greatest Roman. Each one stood up in turn and made a short address in his own behalf. Most of them boasted of their conquests, the injuries they had inflicted, the wealth they had looted, the territories they had annexed etc. and when the time came for Marcus Aurelius to speak, he merely said: **"I, a humble philosopher, have cherished the ambition never to give pain to another."**

Marcus Aurelius, concludes the story, was thereupon crowned the greatest of Romans. But not the greatest of men, for Marcus Aurelius the philosopher was thwarted in his ambition by Marcus Aurelius the king.

In Sum

Mind is a divine genius that dwells in every man, and Marcus Aurelius was a super man. Indeed loves Marcus Aurelius, as one man may love another whose mind is in harmony with his own.

With him reigned philosophy; through him the world was for one short moment guided by the last and greatest man of the day.

In the family of the Antonines, among whom Marcus Aurelius was brought up, Wisdom and beneficence were heirlooms. His mind did not reconcile with the magnificently cruel and vicious Caesars.

With the intuition of the Philosopher, Marcus had apprehended the vanity of all joys, and full of a gentle but deep seated disenchantment with regard to life, he had ceased to expect any satisfaction from power.

❖ ❖ ❖

"The Meditations" the thoughts of the philosopher king have been considered by many generations one of the great books of all times. Though they were Marcus's own thoughts, they were not original. They were basically the moral tenets of Stoicism, learnt from Epictetus: the cosmos is a unity governed by an intelligence, and the human soul is a part of that divine intelligence and can therefore stand, if naked alone tallest pure and undefiled, amidst chaos and futility. One or two of Marcus' ideas, perhaps more through lack of rigorous understanding than anything else, diverged from the stoic philosophy and approached that Platonism that was itself their turning in to Neo-Platonism into which all Pagan philosophies, except Epicurianism were destined to merge. But he did not deviate so far as to accept the comfort of any kind of survival after death.

A more intimate contact with thoughts pursued by Marcus Aurelius during the toubling involvements of his reign, his day-to-day political thoughts, can be understood by reading the meditations.

Meditations of Marcus Aurelius

The imperial philosopher Marcus Aurelius gave to the world in his 'Meditations', "the gospel of those who do not believe in the Supernatural."

These Meditations, were not written as a whole–probably they were never intended for publication; they are simply the Emperor's commonplace book, where he entered his reflections, often quite unconnected on the things of time and eternity. By this means he seems to have adopted his own counsel of withdrawing into his own mind, there to seek calm and quiet. It is noteworthy that in Marcus Aurelius the claims of natural affection are never disregarded. Book I is entirely devoted to recording his obligation to his parents, friends, and teachers for the benefit of good training or example. For all those helps and advantages which can be traced to none of these, he simply thanks "the gods," without further discussion or inquiry into their nature. The same loving disposition gives life to the Stoic doctrine of the citizenship of the world. Marcus Aurelius truly finds himself akin to all mankind. "Mankind are under one common law; and if so, they must be fellow-citizens, and belong to the same body politic from whence it will follow that the whole world is but one commonwealth" (Med. iv. 4). "Now a social temper is that which man was principally designed for" (vii. 55). This brotherhood of man will lead us to strive for the common good, and reckon nothing else our own advantage. "That which is not for the interest of the whole swarm is not for the interest of a single bee" (vi. 54). It will lead us also to pity and forgive our enemies. "And since it has fallen to my share to understand the natural beauty of a good action and the deformity of an ill one; since I am satisfied the person disobliging is of kin to me, and though we are not just of the same flesh and blood, yet our minds are nearly related, being both extracted from the Diety, I am convinced that no man can do a real injury, because no man can force me to misbehave myself; nor can I find it in my heart to hate or be angry with one of my own nature and family. For we are all made for mutual assistance, as the feet, the hands, and the eyelids; as the rows of the upper and under teeth" (ii. 1) Marcus Aurelius loves to dwell on the instability and insignificance of all things. "The vast continents of Europe and Asia are but corners of the creation; the ocean is but a drop, and Mount Athos but a grain in respect of the universe, and the present instant of time but a point to the extent of eternity. These things have all of them little, changeable, and transitory beings" (vi. 36). We should accustom ourselves to watch the eternal course of destruction, and realise that the universe itself sustains no harm. The death of one thing is the birth of another. "The universal nature works the universal matter like wax. Now, for the purpose, it is a horse; soon after you will have it melted down and run it into the figure of a tree; then a man, then something else. And it is but a little while that it is fixed in one species. Now a trunk feels no more pain by being knocked in pieces than when it was first put together" (vii. 23). "Death and generation are both mysteries of nature, and somewhat resemble each other; for the first does but dissolve those elements that later had combined"(v. 5). Amid all this change the only true good is philosophy, which teaches us to keep our guiding principles pure and untainted by bodily impressions. "Toss me into what climate or state you please. For all that, I will keep my divine part content if it but exist and act in accordance with its nature" (viii. 45). Nothing external can influence us, unless we pronounce it good or evil. This is in accordance with the Stoic doctrine, that all sensations make a material impression on the soul; but it is left to the reasoning or guiding principle to decide whether they are true or false, good or evil. "Hold in honour your opinionative faculty, for this alone is able to prevent any opinion from originating in your guiding principle that is contrary to nature or the proper constitution of a rational creature" (iii. 9.) "Do not suppose you are hurt, and your complaint ceases; cease your complaint, and you are not hurt" (iv. 7), writes the Emperor, using, as he so often does, an obscure dogma to point a practical moral.

Such practical teaching abounds in Marcus Aurelius; but he rises to higher flights. **How gladly he quotes Antisthenes's comment on the kingly prerogative. "It is a royal thing to be ill-spoken of for good deeds" (vii. 36). How well he satirises the craving for gratitude, so aptly defined by a French writer as the 'usury' we extract for our good deeds. "Some men, when they do you a kindness, at once demand the payment of gratitude from you; others are more modest than this.** However, they remember the favour, and look upon you as their debtor in a manner. A third sort shall scarce know what they have done. These are mush like a vine, which is satisfied by being fruitful in its kind, and bears a bunch of grapes without expecting any thanks for it. A fleet horse or greyhound do not make a noise when they have done well, nor a bee neither when she has made a little honey. **And thus a man that has done a kindness never proclaims it, but does another as soon as he can, just like a vine that bears again the next season.** Now we should imitate those who are so obliging as hardly to reflect on their beneficence" (v. 6). And how scathing is this criticism of the affectation of virtue! "How fulsome and hollow does that man look that cries – 'I am resolved to deal straighforwardly with you.' Hark you, friend, what need of all this flourish? **Let your actions speak; your face ought to vouch for your speech. I would have virtue look out of the eye, no less apparently than love does in the sight of the beloved.** I would have honesty and sincerity so incorporated with the constitution that it should be discoverable by the senses" (xi. 15).

Here is another gem that sparkles with especial brightness – **"The best way of revenge is not to imitate the injury"** (vi. 6).

Very noble is this conception of the true function of prayer – "This man ... invokes the gods to set him free from some trouble; let it be your petition that your mind may never put you upon such a wish. A third is very devout to prevent the loss of his son. But I would have you pray rather against the fear of losing him. Let his be the rule for your devotions" (ix. 40).

To quote from the Meditations is a tempting task, but they lie before the reader, and he can make his own choice. We must however briefly inquire how Marcus Aurelius treats those great questions to which each system must find some answer, or else abandon its claims to be a guide through life. The origin of evil is a difficulty that every system has had to meet. It is the first and most obvious argument against the existence of an All-wise Providence. The Stoics boldly faced the difficulty, and denied the facts. The world is perfect, they said; all that seems evil is required for the general good. **On this point Marcus Aurelius is perfectly orthodox, but he condemns too curious inquiry. "Does your cucumber taste bitter? – let it alone. Are there brambles in your way? – avoid them then. Thus far you are well.** But, then, do not ask, 'What does the world with such things as this?' For a natural philosopher would laugh at you. This expostulation is just as wise as it would be to find fault with a carpenter for having sawdust, or a tailor shreds, in his shop." **Epictetus had said: "As a mark is not set up for the purpose of missing it, so neither does the nature of evil exist in the universe;" that is, there is no absolute evil, it is all subordinate to good.** So too Marcus Aurelius: "Wickedness generally does no harm to the universe: so too in particular subjects it does no harm to anyone" (viii. 55). At times he points not to the universal law, which he regards as the providence of the universe, but to the existence of gods, who must direct all things for the best. But he never asserts this with any certainty. The alternative is between gods and atoms, between providence and chance; and though Marcus Aurelius pronounces for the former, he desires to show that even under the latter a man may be content. As to the future life, he never speaks with any certainty. The guiding principle of the soul can never perish, since it is a part of the Deity; but whether there is a future self-consciousness existence is a question he scarcely touches on. This life is all that concerns us. "Though you were destined to live three thousand, or, if your please, thirty thousand years, yet remember that no man can lose any other life than that which he lives now, neither is he possessed of any other than that which he loses" (ii.14).

The Stoic Emperor cannot say with our modern poet –

"What is our failure here but a triumph's evidence
For the fullness of the days? Have we withered or agonised?
Why else was the pause prolonged but that singing might issue thence?
Why rushed the discords in, but that harmony might be prized?"–

but he draws a noble moral from the transitoriness of our being. Not "let us eat and drink, for to-morrow we die," is the teachings of the Meditations, but rather, "let us use this life well, since we have no other." The consolation for death must be sought in the consciousness of duty done. If we have lived well, we should be content to die, no matter whether our years be many or few. Epicurus bade his followers depart from life as a guest from a banquet satisfied with his entertainment; the Stoics, in sterner language, bid us leave the stage as an actor who has performed his part. "Hark ye, friend; you have been a burgler of this great city. What matter whether you have lived in it but five years or three? If you have observed the laws of the corporation, the length or shortness of the time makes no difference. Where is the hardship, then, if Nature, that planted you here, orders your removal? You cannot say you are sent off by a tyrant or an unjust judge. No, you quit the stage as fairly as a player does that has his discharge from the master of the revels. But I have only gone through three acts, and not held out till the end of the fifth, you say. Well, but in life three acts make the play entire. He that ordered the first scene now gives the sign for shutting up the last. You are neither accountable for one, nor the other. Therefore, retire well-satisfied, for he by whom you are dismissed is satisfied also" (xii. 36).

Perhaps there never was an age that more needed, such teaching than our own. On the one hand, sectarian hatred and dogmatism almost obscure the great truths common to all mankind;

on the other, merciless and destructive criticism, in undermining much that used to be generally accepted, seems at times to threaten even the foundations of truth. Marcus Aurelius was Great. His Quest for Excellence is unparalleled. The present day youth may take lessons from his meditations.

A few more reflections on Aurelius' Meditations

The true worth of a man is to be measured by the objects he pursues.

❖ ❖ ❖

Be always doing something serviceable to mankind and let this constant generosity be your only pleasure, not forgetting in the mean time a due regard to the Diety.

❖ ❖ ❖

Your manners will depend very much upon the quality of what you frequently think on; the soul is as it were tinged with the colour and complexion of thought.

❖ ❖ ❖

Reason and the reasoning faculty need no foreign assistance, but are sufficient for their own purposes. They move within themselves, and make directly for the point in view. Wherefore, acts in accordance with them are called right acts, for they lead along the right road.

❖ ❖ ❖

Now think a little, and tell me what is there more delightful than greatness of mind, and generosity, simplicity, equanimity and piety. And what can be more delightful than prudence, than to be furnished with the faculty of knowledge and understanding which keeps a man from making a false step, and help him to good fortune in all his business.

❖ ❖ ❖

Further, consider the temper of those you converse with, and you will find the best hardly do; not to mention that a man has work enough to make himself tolerable to himself.

❖ ❖ ❖

What honesty prompts you to say or do anything never held it beneath you? Never be misled by the apprehension of censure or reproach. Other people have their own guiding principles and impulses, mind them not. Go on in the straight road, pursue your work and the common interest. For, to speak strictly, these two are approached by one and the same road.

❖ ❖ ❖

Wit and smartness are not your talent. What then? There are a great many other good qualities in which you can not pretend nature has failed you; improve them as far as you can and let us have that which is perfectly in your power. You may, if you please, behave yourself like a man of gravity and good faith, endure hardship, and despise pleasure; want but a few things, and complain of nothing, you may be gentle and magnanimous if you please, and have nothing of luxury or trifling in your disposition.

❖ ❖ ❖

Look thoroughly into matters and let not the peculiar quality or intrinsic value of anything escape you.

❖ ❖ ❖

Happiness lies all in the functions of reason, inwarantable desires and virtuous practice.

❖ ❖ ❖

Mildness and temper are not only more humane, but more masculine too.

❖ ❖ ❖

Spend no more time in stating the qualifications of a man of virtue but endeavour to get them.

❖ ❖ ❖

Nothing is more scandalous than false friendship, and therefore, of all things avoid it.

❖ ❖ ❖

You should resolve to live no longer than you can live honestly; for, in earnest reason would rather you were nothing than a knave.

❖ ❖ ❖

When anybody's misbehaviour disturb you, immediately turn to yourself and be think you whether you have not been guilty of the same fault; for instance whether you have not over valued money, or pleasure, or fame or the like. Such reflections will quickly make you forget your anger, especially if you consider that the offender was not altogether his own man, but under some untoward compulsion.

❖ ❖ ❖

You will do well of remember that the world is just as it was formerly, and will go on at the rate. If you either dip into history or recollect your own experience, you will perceive the scenes of life strangely uniform, and nothing but the old plays revived. Take a view of the courts of Hadrien, Antoninus, Pius, of Philip, of Alexander or Croesus, and you will find entertainment the same, only the actors are different.

❖ ❖ ❖

It is a great folly not to part with your own faults which is possible, but to try instead to escape from other people's faults, which is impossible.

❖ ❖ ❖

Do not run riot. Keep your intentions honest and your convictions sure.

❖ ❖ ❖

Make an experiment upon yourself and examine your proficiency in a life of virtue. Try how you can acquiese in your fate, and whether your own honesty and good nature will content you.

❖ ❖ ❖

Do but return to the principles of wisdom, and those who take you now for a monkey or a wild beast, will make a god of you in a week's time.

❖ ❖ ❖

Do not act as if you had ten thousand years to throwaway. Death stands at your elbow. Be good for something, while you live and it is in your power.

❖ ❖ ❖

There are three things which belong to a man – body, soul, and mind. Sensation belong to the body, impulse to the soul, and the reason to the mind.

❖ ❖ ❖

Such practical teaching abounds in Marcus Aurelius; but he rises to higher flights.

Reading List

1. Arm Strong, A.H. : Plotinus, George Allen and Unwin Ltd., Ruskin House, Museum St. 1953, London.

2. Butler. Cuthbent : Western Mysticims, Harper Torch Books, The Cathedral Library, Harper and Row Publishers, 49, East 33rd St. N.
York, 1966.

3. Costelloc, B.F.C. & Muirhead, I.H. : Aristotle and the earlier Peripatetics (Being a translation from Zellers Philosophy of the Greeks). Longman Green & Co., 39, Paternoster Road. London, 1897.

4. Duff, Robert A. : Spinoza's Political and Ethical Philosophy. James Mcle House and Sons, Glasgow, 1903.

5. Edel, Abraham : Aristotle and His Philosophy Crown Helm Ltd., London, 1982 (University of North Carolina Press).

6. Emerson, R.W. : On the conduct of life, N. York.

7. Emerson R. W. : Essays, Coulten House, N.York, 1962.

8. Henies, C.A. : Marcus Aurelius (A revised text and translation into English) The meditations of Marcus Aurelius translated by Jermy Collier. Revised with introduction and notes by Alice Zimmerman. London Walterscott Peternoster square.

9. Henieman. Williams : Communication with himself of Marcus Aurelius Antonines, together with his speeches and sayings, Harvard University Press, London, 1966.

10. Iqbal, Sir Mohammed : Six lectures on the reconstruction of Islamic Thought, Lahore, 1932.

11. Manning, Frederik : Epicurus's Morals, Peter Davis Pub., Convent Garden, London, 1926.

12. Mead. G.R.S. : Select works of Plotinus, London Bell and Sons Ltd., 1914.

13. O'Dea, Thomas F. : The sociology of religion. Foundations of Modern Sociological series. Prentice Ha!l India (Pvt. , Ltd.) New Delhi, 1963.

14. Plato : 'The Republic' translated by A.D. Lindsay Dent London, Everyman's Library, 1984.

15. Patric, George and Thomas white Patrick : Introduction to philosophy, Surjeet Publication 1978, Delhi.

16. Pollock, Sir Fredereic : Spinoza – His Life and Philosophy, London, Duke University, McMillan, 1899, N. York.

17. Ralph, William : Philosophy of Plotinus, Vol. I & II, Longman Green and Co., London, 1923.

18. Rajagopalchari, C. : Marcus Aurelius, 1960.

19. Rendall, Gerald H. : Marcus Aurelius, Antonines to himself (rendered in English), London, McMillan & Co. 1905.

20. Russel, Bertrand : History of Western Philosophy. Unwin Paper Backs. Museum Street, London, 1970.

21. Shariff, M.M. : Nietzche's Ethical Doctrine. Muslim University Journal, Series Vol. 1., March 1943, Aligarh.

22. Thomas, Morris, V. : The Concept of God, Oxford University, Press 1987.

3

Emperor Napoleon Bonaparte

A Versatile Genius—'a man of destiny'

God gave to me a mind that has not been mortgaged to the opinion of any man or any set of men: a mind that I was to use, and not to surrender.

—Napoleon.

A great man does not bear malice, his anger and his ill-humour do not last beyond the moment. He no longer sees persons, he sees only events, their significance, and their consequences.

—Napoleon.

Introduction

This is the third of the series on Excellence. The first two were on Benjamin Franklin and Marcus Aurelius respectively.

In choosing Napoleon Bonaparte for the third series I have two reasons. Firstly, he was my hero since childhood. Secondly, both as a soldier and a Statesman he rose superior to all his contemporaries. Of the greatness of his genius, there can be no question, and Europe owes him an unspeakable debt of gratitude. His self-confidence was colossal. He did not make an extravagant statement when he said "**Centuries may pass before circumstances combine to produce another such as I was.**" At St. Helena where he was a captive, Napoleon said with true prophetic instinct:

"I will tell you what will happen when I am personally out of question in thirty years, the Government will be obliged to yield public opinion, and raise a monument to me for the glory of the nation." His prophecy came true.

One writer has truly said that "There is no age, no personality in history of great interest either to France or to the world, than the Napoleonic era and Napoleon." His military genius is universally accepted. His rapidity of movements, his power of inspiring his armies to perform extraordinary feats, his knowledge of detail combined with his gigantic grasp, his prodigious triumphs, makes cool judgement difficult. In short, the military genius of Napoleon in its results is unsurpassed. He was a great administrator as well.

He controlled every wheel and spring, large or small of his vast machinery of Government, it was, as it were a plaything. He was his own war office, his own foreign office, his own administrator, his own ministry of every kind. **His financial management by which he sustained a vast empire with power and splendour but with rigid economy, and with out a debt, is a marvel and a mystery.** In all offices of state, he knew everything, guided everything, inspired everything. He himself aptly enough compared his mind to a cub-board of pigeon holes, to deal with any subject, he opens the pigeon hole relating to it, and closed the others. When he wished to sleep, he closed them all. Moreover, his in exhaustible memory made him familiar with all men, and all the details, as well as with all machinery of Government.

There, he-was a great legislator as well. The positive and permanent part of his work is, of course, the Code (Code Napoleon) which remains, and profoundly affects the character of the nation, as well as other races to which it has been extended. The enactment have, for example, had more potent effect in moulding the social and political life of a community, and the provisions of this code for the compulsory division of property. It checks population, it enforces equality, it constitutes the most powerful and conservative of landed interest. That was something very great Napoleon did. Again, he wanted to unite all countries of Europe in to one powerful bloc, and used the very phrase "United State of Europe" as expressed in his ideal. "The same law" he said "must run through Europe". "I shall fuse all nations into one." Napoleon wanted a common legal code, a common court of appeal, common coinage, and weights and measures throughout Europe. If he had achieved his aims then, Europe would have become one nation, and anyone who travelled in it would always have been in a common Fatherland. However, the vision of Napoleon came true in 1952 when, after the World War II, France and the then West Germany signed the agreement constituting the European Coal and Steel Community (popularly called the Schuman plan) pooling the iron and coal resources of both the countries to achieve the economies of scale. The success of the ECSE laid the foundations for a European

Common Market in 1958 when six countries (viz.) Belgium Luxumbourg, the Netherlands, West Germany, France and Italy signed the treaty constituting the European Common Market. Subsequently, other countries joined the Common Market. Today, Napoleon's dream takes a practical shape after nearly two centuries, when all European countries agreed for a uniform currency and coinage to complete the integration of Europe with the common currency—the EURO. How farsighted Napoleon was! Hats off to that statesman who had a vision and a mission regarding the future of Europe.

As a student, Napoleon consecrated his days and nights with untiring assiduity to study. In all mathematical studies, he became highly distinguished. All books upon History, upon Government, upon the practical sciences, he devoured with utmost activity. The poetry of Homer and of Ossien he read, and re-read with great delight. His mind combined the political and the practical in most harmonious blending. In a letter to his mother during this time he says, **"with my sword by my side, and Homer in my pocket, I hope to carve my way through the world." The "lives of Plutarch" he studied as thoroughly and with such profound admiration, that his whole soul became imbued with the spirit of the illustrious men.** All the thrilling scenes of Grecian and Roman stories, the rise and fall of empires, and deeds of heroic daring, absorbed his contemplation. **So great was his ardour for intellectual improvement that he considered every day as lost in which he had not made perceptible progress in knowledge.** By this rigid mental discipline, he acquired that wonderful power of concentration by which he was ever enabled to simplify subjects the most difficult and complicated.

His extra-ordinary faculty of intense and continuous exertion, both of mind and body was his distinguishing characteristic through life. **"Napoleon did not blunder in to renown. His triumphs were not causalities, his achievements were not accidents; his grand conceptions were not the brilliant flashes of unthinking and unpremeditated genius.** Never did man prepare the way for greatness by more untiring devotion to the acquisition of all useful knowledge, and to the attainment of the highest possible degree of mental discipline. That he possessed native powers of mind of extra-ordinary vigour is true, but these powers were expended and energized by herculian study." On one occasion when he was a student, a mathematical problem of great difficulty having been propounded to the class, Napoleon, in order to solve it, secluded himself to his room for seventy-two hours and solved the problem. His mighty genius impelled him to the sacrifice of every indulgence and to sleepless toil.

His mind was characterized by great logical accuracy, united with the most brilliant powers of masculine imagination. His conversations—laconic, graphical, oracular—arrested every kind. Had the vicissitudes of life so ordained his lot, he would undoubtedly have been as distinguished in the walks of literature, and in the halls of science as he became in the field and in the cabinet. His visionary zeal has been tremendous.

At St. Helena, Napoleon had in his possession a memoir on the subject of opening the ancient canal from Suez to Cairo. "He thought practicable, and it was his intention to have done it. He had ascertained that the Nile at Cairo was nearly on a level with the Red Sea. He proposed effecting this by means of the waters of the Nile, the embankment of which are 4 ft. higher than the Red Sea."

Napoleon, as is well-known, had very elaborate plans for establishing the French power in Egypt, and for using Egypt as a stepping stone to India. In addition to the Canal from Suez to Cairo, he had in his mind one from the Red Sea to the Mediterranean. The Red Sea has been carefully surveyed, the proposed canal was declared practicable, the expenses was calculated to amount to about 18,000,000 Francs and two years labour would, he thought suffice for its construction.

That he was one of the profoundest thinkers all admit; and his eloquent proclamations re-sounded through Europe, rousing the army to almost a frenzy of enthusiasm, and electrifying alike the peasant and the prince. Napoleon had that comprehensive genius which would have been pre-eminent in any pursuit to which he has devoted the energies of his mind. Great as were his military victories, they were no means the greatest of his achievements.

One is tempted in following this astonishing career, to attribute, as he did, part of its success to general chance. "It is chance that makes great men" he once said. Yet, chance could too have been so consistent. All powerful leaders of men have certain traits in common which seems essential ingredients of their prestige. To begin with, they attach little value to the things that ordinary beings covet. Never did a leader had so much wealth at his disposal as Napoleon, and kept as less for himself. Then there is the fact that men of genius see things as they are not as they wished them to be. Napoleon, throughout the peak period of his career was a realist and had no time to systems. Later, he went into decline, because he had ceased to manoeuvre. But at bottom, he remained a great man. As he did not expect men to be perfect, he was fairly quick to pardon their faults. A quick and expansive mind, an incredible capacity for work, intellectual honesty, no illusions about his fellow men, a way of charming them without flattering them, these are the qualities that could have kept fortune on his side.

His vision and foresight, his liberalism and humanism are qualities rare with any military general or statesmen in power. There, is grandeur about the name Napoleon. We speak of the 'Napoleonic era', and the 'Napoleonic legend', and the 'Napoleonic wars'. We say that a man is a 'Napoleon of Industry' when we meant that he is a powerful and controlling personality. **Napoleon knew that he was destined for great things, and this belief has led men to speak of him as the man of destiny. It would be difficult to think of any other man in the history of the world whose name suggests so much.**

There are some who can speak contemptuously of Napoleon Bonaparte. They are to be pitied, rather than blamed. Some persons cannot discern differences of colours, others cannot perceive discord or harmony; and these are those who are incapable of appreciating grandeur of character. They are to be judged harshly. It is their misfortune.

Whatever, one may think of the drama of his life, no one

can deny the grandeur of his death. Like Prometheus bound to his only rock, Napoleon suffered pain and humiliation, with the dignity of a martyr. In his defeat, he was also victorious.

The study of Napoleon's life is therefore, very valuable, and I thought it worth to include in this series under the caption **"In Quest of Excellence"** to enlighten the young men and women, about his greatness which may inspire them to follow his ideals, more so in this confused world of ours where people have lost all respect, for moral and ethical values.

"From noble men we learn nobility,
Base friends destroy our natural quality."

(cf. Memorabillia)

'A good government may indeed redress the grievances of an injured people: but a strong people can alone build up a great nation. To be strong, a people must be self-reliant, self-ruled, and self-sustained. The dependence of one people upon another, even for the benefits of legislation, is the deepest source of national weakness.'

— *Napoleon.*

Synopsis

I. The background—admiration for Napoleon—as a man of industry—his courage—his rise from a corporal to Emperor—his belief in the equality of man—All appointments based on merit and talents— discarded the old belief of hereditary privileges—selected Artisans as Marshalls and Dukes—Displeasure of the bourgeois of Vienna and London etc.—England forming a coalition of states to fight against Napoleon—Napoleon's first abdication to Elba—Reasons for his escape from Elba—Entering Paris to re-ascend the throne as Emperor without shedding a drop of blood—Fury and anger of the combined coalition to crush Napoleon and to Place Barabons on the throne—Napoleon surrenders, and abdicates to England—ends his political career—goes as guest of England in the British ship 'Bellorophon' seeking asylum—Arrest of Napoleon at Southhamton port—Not allowed to disembark—Taken prisoner to St. Helena—Protest of Napoleon to British Govt.—Mental and physical tortures at St. Helena by Sir Hudson Low, Governor of St. Helena—6 years of Captivity — Napoleon seriously ill—dies at St. Helena—buried at St. Helena—world opinion in favour of Napoleon—France demands the ashes of Napoleon after 19 years—Britain agrees and restores the ashes to France—

"To be worthy of your destiny, pass only laws that are wise and moderate. Carry them out with force and energy. Encourage the spread of intelligence and respect religion.

Napoleon.

Emperor Napoleon Bonaparte

(August 15, 1769—May 5, 1821)

'The destinies of great men are unpredictable.'

—Napoleon.

Napoleon is my hero. I am his admirer. A adore him for his excellence. He abhored war, and did everything in his power to avert that dire calamity, because he merited the sovereignty to which the suffrage of a grateful nation elevated him; because he consecrated the most extra-ordinary energies ever conferred upon a mortal to promote the prosperity of his country; because he was regardless of luxury and cheerfully endured all toil and all hardships that he might elevate and bless the masses of mankind; because he had a high sense of honour, revered religions, respected the right of conscience and nobly advocated equality of privileges and the universal brotherhood of man. Such was the character of Napoleon Bonaparte.

Hostile historians have stigmatized him as a usurer, while admitting that the suffrages of the nation placed him on the throne. They have denounced him as a tyrant inexorable as Nero, while admitting that he was the adoring love of his subject; he is called a blood-thirsty monster delighting in war, yet is confessed that he was, in almost every conflict struggling in self-defence and imploring peace. It is said that his insatiable ambition led him to trample remorselessly upon the rights of other nations, while it is confessed that Europe was astonished by his moderation and generosity in every treaty which he made with his vanquished foes; he is described as a human butcher reckless of suffering, who regarded his soldiers merely as food for power, and yet at the same pages, we are told that he wept over the carnage of the battlefield, tenderly pressed the hand of the dying, and won from those soldiers who laid down their lives in his service, a fervour of love which earth had never seen parallelled. It is recorded that France atleast became weary of him and drove him from the throne, and in the next paragraph we are informed that as soon as the bayonets of the Allies had disappeared from France, the whole nation rose to call him back from his exile (Elba)* with unanimity so unprecedented that without shedding a drop of blood he traversed the whole of France, entered Paris and re-ascended the throne. It is affirmed that a second time France weary of his despotism, expelled him, and yet it is at the same time recorded, that the same France demanded of his executioners, his mortal remains from St. Helena, received them with national enthusiasm, consigned them to a tomb in the very bosom of Paris, and has reared over them such a mausoleum as honours the grave of no other mortal in Europe. Such is Napoleon as described by his enemies.

The reason is obvious. Why the character of Napoleon should have been maligned. He was regarded justly as the foe of aristocratic privileges. The English oligarchy was determined to crush him. (Napoleon did not gird at the rich, but claimed that at the other end of the social scale shall be free holders, artisans and small tradesmen, able to live out their lives in comfort. He made no war on the rich, but was resolved to level up the poor to the standard which ensured atleast a medium of enjoyment). After deluging Europe in blood and woe, during nearly a quarter of a century, for the accomplishment of the efforts to crush Napoleon, it becomes necessary for Britain to prove to the world, and specially to the British people who were tottering beneath the burden of taxes which these were engendered, that Napoleon was a tyrant, threatening the liberties of the world, and that he deserve to be crushed.

No doubt Napoleon incurred the displeasure of the nobility of London and Vienna regarding the reforms he introduced in agriculture. **If ever a nation was authorized to engage a war of**

---

* See Annexure-1. Escape from Elba.

self-defence, Napoleon was right in this endeavour to resist those unrelenting foes whom no plea for peace could disarm. Napoleon declared at St. Helena where he was captive that his object was to destroy the whole of the feudal system organized by Charlamagne. And with this view, he created a nobility from among the people, in order to swallow up the remains of the feudal nobility. **The foundations of his ideas of fitness were, abilities and personal worth, and therefore, he selected the son of a farmer or an artisan to make a Duke or a Marshall of France.** He sought for true merit among all ranks of the great mass of French people, and was anxious to organize a true and general system of equality. He was desirous that every Frenchman should be admissible to all the employment and dignities of the state, provided , he was possessed of talents and character, equal to the performance of the duties whatever might be the family. In a word, he was eager to abolish to the last trace, the privileges of the ancient nobility, and to establish a government which at the same time, that it held the reigns of government with a firm hand, should still be a popular government. The oligarchs of every country of Europe soon perceived his design, and it was, for this reason that war to the death was carried on against him by England. "The noble families of London and Vienna thought themselves prescriptively entitled to the occupation of all the important offices in the state, and the management and handling of public money. Their birth was regarded as a substitute for talents and capacities; and it is enough for a man to be son of his father, to be fit to fulfil the duties of the most important employment and highest dignities of the state. "They are somewhat like kings by divine right. The people in their eyes are merely milk cows, about whose interests they felt no concern, provided the treasury is full always, and the Crown resplendent with jewels." In short, in abolishing the hereditary nobility, Napoleon had three objectives in view.

(i) to reconcile France with the rest of Europe;

(ii) to reconcile old with new France;

(iii) to put an end to all feudal institutions in Europe, by re-connecting, the idea of nobility with that of public services, and detaching it from all prescriptive or feudal notions.

The whole of Europe as governea by nobles who were strongly opposed to progress of the French Revolution, and who exercised an influence which proved serious obstacles to the development of French principles. It was necessary to destroy this influence and with that view to clothe the principal personages of the empire with titles equal to theirs.

Secondly, Napoleon was very sore with the Pope as well, who had been preaching rebellion. He declared that "the Pontiff cannot surely believe that God considers the rights of the throne as less sacred than those of the Papal Tiara, for, kings, existed long before Popes." "Priests are not made to govern." "Jesus declared that His kingdom is not of this world. Why will not the Pope render Caesar what is due to Caesar. Is he greatest on earth than Jesus was?" and so on. "Religion is clear." "Jesus and His apostles preached it on the house tops so that it might be known to all." "If you are dominated by the pride and ostentation of the world, we shall consider you a demon as spoiled by pride and worldly interest, and as the enemy of religion, our throne and our people." "Your influence is powerful, your empire is great when you remain within the limits traced by Jesus; but your power becomes ridiculous and despicable, when you wish to march with the potentates of the earth surrounded by pride, menaces and force." "You have enough to do when confining yourself to spiritual affairs and the care of souls." "Do not meddle with matters that do not concern you. I recognize you for my spiritual chief, but I am your Emperor" said Napoleon.

But when the differences between them became irreconcilable, Napoleon gave a practical application to his homily on unworldliness by dethroning the Pope and detaining him at Savona. Early in 1811, Napoleon wrote a furious letter to prince Borghese, Governor of the Transalpine Province ordering him to press severely on the Pontiff.

"....As I desire to protect my subjects from the rage and fury of this ignorant and peevish old man, I hereby order you to notify him, that he is forbidden to communicate with any church of mine, or any of my subjects, on pain of the punishment consequent on his disobedience, and theirs. You will remove all suspicious persons from the Pope's household. You will leave only the number of persons necessary to wait on him, and you will not permit any one of any kind to visit him. You will take steps to increase the garrison of Savona. You will take care to have all the Pope's papers, books, and documents taken from his, and you will have them sent to Paris. If the Pope should indulge in any extravagant behaviour, you will have him shut up the citadel of Savona, which you will have taken care of provision, and furnish with all necessaries before hand..... The examination of the Pope's papers must be skilfully done. You will leave him no paper, nor pen, nor ink, nor any means of writing. You will give him a few French servants, and you will remove the unsatisfactory ones. Besides this the people of his household can be forbidden to go out."

Thereafter, the Pope was removed to Fountainbleau and treated with rigour.

From the above it is clear how sore the Emperor Napoleon was both with the Kings and the Pope. In campaigns of hatred against the Priests and Kings the important fact was bound to be overlooked until too late, that no man is free so long as another man possess the power to inflict starvation upon him. It was inevitable, therefore, that Napoleon should be opposed by kings and church concerned about the magic of blood privileges, by financial liberals with their magic of freedom without food, by that Jacobins with their class magic and by the promise-lenders. The kings called him usurper; the liberals called him tyrant; the Jacobins (always partial to blood privileges) bourgeois. And all these parties seeking eagerly to over-throw him, turned to the financiers for help. **Armies began to march against France;** the sons and daughters of financial liberalism spent their wits in holding up to ridicule the 'dynasty of Ajaccio'; Jacobins raised to public offices abused secretly the 'Emperor of the Praetorians.' And in Paris, Ouverand acting for international finance, prepared a pitfall in which he believed, the Corsican and all his schemes, most inevitably fall.

In the meanwhile, two of Napoleons generals Tallyrand and Fausche betrayed him secretly conspiring with the Allies, resulting in the defeat at the battle of Waterloo, and the surrender of this Great Emperor. Napoleon wanted to go to USA to seek asylum, but could not do so because the British fleet were all around, and he had the fear, his ship might be intercepted and he taken prisoner. Hence, he decided to surrender to Britain by "ending his political career" and wrote to the Regent of England that he comes to England like Themistocles to seat himself at the hearth of the British people under the protection of the laws of England, and demanded this grace from His Royal Highness the Regent of England, as the most powerful, most steadfast and the most generous of his enemies. However, surrendering unconditionally to his worst enemies was a gesture worthy of Plutarch: Napoleon felt that his letter to Prince Regent would make a fine page in history.

Before embarking the British ship *'Bellerphon'*, his faithful generals told him that there is great risk in going to Britain, for which the Emperor said to Gen-Bertrand.

"There is always a danger in putting one's trust in one's enemies, but it is better to trust in their honour than to fall in their hands as a prisoner."

When the ship reached Postsmouth (England), it was surrounded by a thousand boats of all description. The armed guard boats continually rowering around to keep the large crowd under control that had gathered in admiration of his greatness, and with acclamation and enthusiasm, and with instinctive sense that he had ever been the friend of the people. The Emperor was never been so cordially greeted even upon the banks of the Seine River at Paris. Notwithstanding libels of the ministers, the returned British soldiers from the war front in France during the Napoleonic wars had narrated in every cottage, stories of his magnanimity, his kindness, his sympathy with the poor and the oppressed. He was the man of the people instinctively surrendered to him their love of homage. From all parts of England, multitudes were crowding towards Plymouth. **The enthusiasm was so intense, and universal, that the British Government became actually apprehensive that Nepoleon might be rescued even on board a British liner of Battle ships in a British harbour.** Two frigates were, therefore ordered to lie as guards on the *'Bellerophon'* and sentinals were doubled and trebled both by day and night' says Sir Walter Scott. The emperor was firm, thoughtful and silent. His friends were overwhelmed with Consternation. Admiral Lord Keith who was in command at Plymouth but a few miles from Torbay, wrote to Captain Maitland, "Tell the emperor that I shall be happy in being made acquainted with anything which may be agreeable to him, and that I will do everything in my power to comply with his wishes. Thank him in my name for the generous attention shown to my nephew who was brought a prisoner to him after being wounded at Waterloo." In Britain, Lord Liverpool wrote to Castlereagh "You know enough of the feelings of people in the country not to doubt that he would become an object of curiosity immediately, and possibly of compassion in the course of a few months. "The innumerable visitors who flocked to see him at Plymouth confirmed the Pre-science of our Premier." There was indeed an extra-ordinary glamour about the fallen monarch of which he himself was quite aware. Similarly, when Napoleon left *'the undaunted'* which conveyed him to Elba during his first abdication, the Boatswain on behalf of the ships company had wished him "long life and prosperity in the island of Elba and a better luck another time." After two short meetings, both Hotham, the Admiral, and Senhouse, the flag captain of *'the undaunted'* felt all prejudices evaporate. "The admiral and myself" writes Senhouse have both discovered that an inveteracy has oozed out like the carnage of Acres in the Rivals." There was a more sublime peril yet. "Damn the fellow" said Lord Keith, after seeing Napoleon "if he had obtained an interview with the Prince Regent, in half-an-hour's time they would have been the best friends of England." These were the opinions of British generals.

On the evening of 30th July, 1815, Sir Henry Banbury, Under-Secretary of State came on board the *'Bellerophon* with Admiral Keith, and from a scrap of paper without signature, read to the emperor, the following illegal and infamous decision...

"As it may perhaps be convenient for General Bonaparte to learn, without further delay, the intentions of the British

Government, your lordship will communicate the following information....

"It would be inconsistent with our duty towards our country and the Allies of His Majesty, if General Bonaparte possessed the means of again disturbing the repose of Europe. It is on this account, that it becomes absolutely necessary that he should be restrained in his personal liberty, so far, as this may be required by the foregoing important object. The island of St. Helena has been chosen as his future residence. Its climate is healthy and its local position will allow of his being treated with more indulgence than could be admitted in any other spot, owing to the indispensable precaution which it would be necessary to employ for the security of his person." It was then stated that General Bonaparte might select a surgeon and any three officers, excepting Sarkaj and Lallemond to accompany him, and also twelve domestics, that those persons would be regarded and treated as prisoners of war, and that Sir George Cock Burn would sail in a few days to convey the captives to their prison." Sir George received very vigorous instructions to recognize Napoleon not as an Emperor, but simply as a General. The members of the household of the Emperor, in the various capacities of household service were also informed that if they wished to accompany the Emperor, they may be subjected to all the restrictions which might be necessary for securing the person of the distinguished captive. This was regarded—says Busy "as an effort to deter his friends from accomponying the exile to his destination, by informing them with an idea of punishment for vague and undefined offences, and of having before them a life of disquietude from espionage and arbitrary control." If such were really the intention, however, it signalled failure: its sole effect being to concentrate the affections of those whom it sought to testify.

Thus, trampling upon the British constitution, and indefiance of all justice and law, was an illustrious foreigner condemned to imprisonment for life, without trial and even with out accusation. The ministers were so fully conscious of the illegality of the measures, that they did not venture even to sign their names to the act. The Emperor listened to the reading of this atrocious document in silence with profound calmness, and without manifesting any emotion. He had obtained such wonderful control over his own spirit, that, it tones gentle and dignified and with great mildness of manner and countenance, he simply, yet eloquently replied...

"I am the guest of England, not her prisoner. I have come of my own accord, to place myself under the protection of the British Laws. In my case the Government has violated the laws of the country, the laws of nations, and the sacred duty of hospitality. I protest against their right to act thus, and appeal to British honour."

The Emperor was to be shifted from *'Bellerophon'* to the *'Northumberland'*, under the command of Admiral Cockburn, was to convey the Emperor to St. Helena. The ship was ready for long a voyage at Portsmouth and consequently urged to hasten the departure of the ship. Under these circumstances, on the advice of an English Lawyer, the Emperor wrote the following protest to be forwarded to the British Government.

Protest

"I hereby solemnly protest in the face of Heavens and mankind, against the violence that is done to me, and the violation of my most sacred right in disposing of my person and liberty. I voluntarily came on board *'Bellerophon'*. I am not the prisoner, I am the guest of England. I came at the suggestion of the Captain himself, who said he had orders from the Government to receive and convey me to England together with my suite, if agreeable to me. I came forward with the confidence to place myself under the protection of the Laws of England. When once on board the *'Bellerophon'*, I was entitled to the hospitality of the British people. **If the Government in giving the Captain of the *'Belleraphon'* orders to receive me only wished to lay a snare, it had forfeited the honour, and disgraced its flag. If this act be consummated, it will be in vain for the English henceforth to talk of their sincerity, their laws, and liberties.** British faith will have been lost in the hospitality of the *'Bellerophon'*.

I appeal to history, I will say that an enemy who made way for twenty years against the English people, came spontaneously, in the hour of misfortune, to seek asylum under their laws. What more striking proof could he give of his esteem and confidence? But how did England reply to such an act of magnanimity? It pretended to hold out a hospitable hand to the enemy, and on giving himself up with confidence, he was immolated."

Napoleon.

Bellerophon at Sea, Aug. 4, 1815

Mackintosh in his history of England (Vol. III, 133) writes: The English Government felt so embarrassed by conscious guilt, that, a year after, they passed a law to sanctify the crime. Drawing a parallel between Napoleon and Marry, Queen of Scotts, says: "Neither of them was born a British subject or had committed any offence within the jurisdiction of England; consequently, neither of them were amenable to English law. The imprisonment of neither was comfortable to the laws of England or the laws of Nations."

Some of the admires (British) of Napoleon were keen that he should be brought to London on some pretext. It being understood that a writ of *habeas corpus* of Subpoena has been taken out to remove him to London to appear as evidence at some trial in consequence of which it was determined that their ex-emperor should be removed at Sea. This affair of the Subpoena seems to have arisen out of an article in the leading opposition paper, 'the Morning Chronicle', in which one Mr. Capeld Lofft stated that Bonaparte having appealed to the laws of Great Britain, might demand from the Lord Chancellor, a writ of *habeas corpus;* some one suggested the bringing of a libel suit against a naval officer in which Napóleon was to be called as a witness. A lawyer than started to Plymouth and chased Admiral Lord Keith, who however successfully dodged him, by moving from one place to another, from one boat to another seeing that the lawyer was following him to deliver the Subpoena. The ships departure was, therefore, hastened with the imperial prisoner.

The emperor was, in the meanwhile shifted from *'Bellerophon'* to *Northumberland;* and was ready for voyage from Postsmouth to St. Helena. The Emperor Napoleon fascinated Capt.

Maitland who took the Emperor Napoleon to England in the *Bellerophon,* as he fascinated Usshar, who had conducted him to Elba in *'The Undaunted.'* Maitland* caused enquiries to be made, after Napoleon had left the *'Bellerophon'* as to the feelings of the crew, and received the result "well they may abuse that man as much as they please: but if the people of England knew him as well as we do, they would not touch a hair of his head."

The admiral and his crew of *'Northemberland'* was in a state of scarcely suppressed mutiny. They refused to get up anchor at Plymouth until a large military force was brought on board to compel them. On the voyage, their language and conduct were beyond description, they thought nothing of striking the mid shipmen. A guard was placed outside the Emperor's cabin to prevent communication between the captive and the crew. Napoleon, then said to have told Cockburn, that he did not doubt that he could get many to join him. When Napoleon left *'The Northumberland'* the crew opined. "He is a fine fellow who does not deserve his fate." After nearly two and a half months of sailing** at last the ship *'Northumberland'* reached the rocky island of St. Helena situated between the tropics in latitude 15° 55' and longitude 5°—43' W. Yellow fever and liver diseases are common and the water dirty and polluted. The island of St. Helena sprang due to a volcanic eruption and is rocky. "Nothing can possibly be less pre-possessing, nay, more horribly forbidding, than the first appearance of this isolated, and apparently burnt up barren rock which promises neither refreshment, nor pleasure."

The mighty conqueror has run his course. His 'star' has led him far from insignificant Ajaccio, and was now leading him still further. Unknown lad, cadet, lieutenant, General, Emperor, Statesman Constructor, he had been all and more. **Destiny had now set him a far more difficult task, namely, to reign over himself.**

---

* See Annexure V.

** See the diaries of Admiral, Sir Thomas Usshar (on Board the 'undaunted') and John R. Glover, Secretary to Rear Admiral Cockburn (on board 'the 'Northumberland', London, T. Fisher Unwin, Adelphin Terace MCMVI 1906.

Sir George Cockburn disembarked and went to meet the Governor of St. Helena, Col. Wike, and after a long private conference, they both went up together when the later was introduced to this wonderful man. Longwood was fixed for his residence. A house in town was prepared for him, until the necessary preparation for his reception, he should be made to Longwood. Napoleon landed at Jamestown St. Helena on October 17, 1815 at dusk*. Bonaparte was provided with a horse, and in his rides at St. Helena in the first year of captivity, he was fond of talking to the slaves, occasionally gave them gold and has in fact already got in to all their good graces. He deplored the condition of slavery, and encouraged those who had any pretence to claim their freedom consequently, examination to that effect were daily taking place at the police office.

After nearly eight months, Sir Hudson Lowe arrived on April 15, 1816 to take over as Governor of St. Helena. Sir Hudson, it seems 'looked like a hangman and whose behaviour was clumsy'! Every one who befriended the emperor at St. Helena in the first year of his captivity were persecuted by Sir Hudson Lowe. The English who had never recognized the victorious. Emperor, dealt harshly with the imperial prisoner. The wooden huts at Longwood were he was lodged had been built for the cattle. In that hot suffocating climate, the emperor was deprived of basic needs, food, clothing, diet and medicine and even bath. Isolated from the human habitation, spied on by soldiers of the British Army which had done so much to bring about his down fall, but surrounded by a little band of faithful, loyal and devoted men and women who refused to desert him in his last days of trial and despair, he spent the remainder of his life, which has been lived to the full. Sometimes, his old enthusiasm would revive as he reviewed the history of a campaign with his biographers; at others, he would show his distrust to his executioner Sir Hudson Lowe, the Governor of the island whose behaviour was mean, ridiculous and incredible.

To one of the British doctors who attended on him, he dictated the following:

* T.H. Brook's letter dated Oct. 18, 1815.

"I had come to seek the hospitality of the British people. I asked for a generous protection. To the subversion of every right held sacred upon earth, chains was the reply I received. I should have experienced a different reception from Alexander. The Emperor Francis would have treated me with more respect and kindness. Even the king of Prussia would have been more generous. It was reserved for England to deceive and excite the sovereigns of Europe, and to give the world the unheard of spectacle of four great powers cruelly leaned against one man. Your ministers have chosen this horrible rock, upon which the lives of Europeans are exhausted in less than three years, in order to end my existence by assassination. And how have I been treated since my arrival here! There is no species of indignity or insult that has not been eagerly heaped upon me. The simplest family communications which have never been interdicted to anyone, have been refused to me. No news, no papers from home, have been allowed to reach me. My wife and son no longer existed for me. I have been kept six years in the tortures of close confinement. The most uninhabitable spot on this inhospitable island—that where the murderous effect of a tropical climate are most severely felt—has been assigned to me for a residence; and I who used to ride on horse back all over Europe have been obliged to shut myself within four walls, in an unwholesome atmosphere. I have been destroyed piece-meal by a pre-meditated and pro-tracted assassination. The infamous Hudson Lowe has been the executionar of these atrocities of your ministers. **You will end like the proud republic of Venice, and, I dying upon this dreamy rock, far from those whom I hold dear, and deprived of everything, bequeath the approbrium and horror of my death to the reigning family of England. "Europe will one day Stigmatize with horror, that pertidious and wicked man Hudson Lowe. All true Englishmen will disown him as a Britain."**

In a letter from the Cape to Lady cleaving by one of the suits (anonymous) that their prospect was so much darkened and that the situation so much changed for the worse since the departure of Admiral Cockburn, that Napoleon had observed that "being at St. Helena was not the worst torment which had been put in execution against him; adding that there was nothing English in the manner in which he was treated that it resembled more the police of Sicily."

"All feeling and reasonable people agree that the precautions lately put in practice, are unjust and ridiculons, even oppressive to the military who execute, and that, by carefully guarding the outlets of the ravines leading towards the Sea sides, following Napoleon by signals whenever he went into the interior of the island, and guarding the sea coast in the manner now practices, by boats and brigs, every point in regard to safe custody would be attained with greater possible simplicity and successes, which is all that human prudence and wisdom can acquire under such circumstances."

"I could tell much more upon this subject which would both surprise and grieve you. **The spectacle of persecution and injustice has been always revolting to me. You may judge them, what I felt, when I beheld the victor of sixty great battles, once the arbiter of many nations, and their rulers, thus basely tormented, I said with in myself:**

"I respect thee with the crown of thorns, that force has now placed on thy brow, even more than when numerous diadems encircled it."*

Misgivings of the future, self-reproach from the past, the monotony of a suppressed life, these were the daily torments that corroded his soul. For six years, he supped the bitterness of slow, remorseful desolate death.

Moreover, with his restless energy thrown back on himself, he was devoured by his inverted activities. He could not exist except in a stress of work. Work, he said, was his element; he was born and made for work. He had known, he would say, the limits of his powers of walking or of seeing, but had never been able to ascertain the limits of his power of work. His mind and body, says Chaptal, were incapable of fatigue. How was employment to be found at Longwood for this formidable machine? The powers of brain and nerve and body which had grappled with the world now turned on him and rent him.

---

* Napoleon in his own defence. Letter from Cape to Lady cleaving by anonymous pp. 158-159.

To read books for which he was always crazy, to learn English enough to read in the newspapers what was going on in Europe which he had controlled, to dictate memoirs, to gossip about his custodians, to preserve order and harmony among all those who followed him to St. Helena (his trusted friends) these were the crumbles of existence which he was left to mumble. There is no parallel to his position. The world has usually made short work of its Caesars when it has done with them. Napoleon had sought death in battle, and considered suicide as cowardice. The constant efforts to assassination by the Allied Government had failed. The hope of Britain that the French Government would shoot or hang him has been disappointed. **So Europe buckled itself to the unprecedented task of gagging and paralysing an intelligence and "a force which were too gigantic of the welfare and security of the world."** That is the strange, unique hideous problem which makes the records of St. Helena so profoundly painful.

But the bad treatment to which Napoleon was subjected, served the emperor's final purpose. With his genius for stage craft, he found St. Helena all the ingredient for his fifth act. He said:

"Misfortunes also have their heroism and their glory." "My career lacked adversity. If I had died on the throne, in the clouds of my omnipotence, I would have remained incomplete for many people. To day, thanks to misfortune, I can be judged for what I really am."

At St. Helena Napoleon knew that surrounded by biographers, each of whom will publish his memoirs, and not unnaturally he present himself in a light that is most likely to flatter him, in the eyes of posterity. He seeks to please, and does, in fact, do so by undergoing an unexpected mental and emotional resurgence by recovering something of his lost youth. He started his life as a man of letters: he ends it as he promised the soldiers of Fountainbleau while bidding farewell on his abdication to Elba on April 20, 1814 "dictating the history of great battles."

"Soldiers, I bid you farewell. For twenty years that we have been together your conduct has left me nothing to desire. I have always found you on the road to glory. All the powers of Europe have combined in arms against me."

"A few of my generals have proved untrue to their duty and to France. France herself has desired other destinies; with you and the brave men who still are faithful, I might have carried on a civil war; but France would be unhappy. Be faithful, then, to your new king, be obedient to your new commanders, and desert not our beloved country."

"Do not lament my lot; I will be happy when I know that you are so. I might have died; if I consent to live, it is still to promote your glory. **I will write the great things that we have achieved.**

I can not embrace you all, but I embrace your General. Come, General Petit, that I may press you to my heart! Bring me the eagle, that I may embrace it also! Ah! dear eagle, may this kiss which I give thee find an echo to the latest posterity! Adieu, my children: the best wishes of my heart shall be always with you: do not forget me."

It is perhaps a more dramatic ending to so marvellous a story than if you had fallen in battle. Many men have met their death in that way, but there has been one imperial prisoner at St. Helena, the exiled monarch who on the night of 4th May, 1821 was on his death bed unconscious. A tornado of frightful violence which swept the black rocks of the island uprooting the trees which Napoleon cherished, now laid prostrate in the rain and mud, the dying Emperor unconscious of everything which was passing around him tossed restless upon his pillow. On the 5th of May he was lying upon his back—"A pleasant and peaceful expression was spread over his face." **Just as the sun was sinking behind the clouds of that sombre and tempestuous day, the spirit of Napoleon passed the earthly veil and entered the vast unknown.**

"The glories of our blood and state
Are shadows, not substantial things;
There is no armour against fate;
Death lays his icy hands on kings;
Sceptre and Crown, must tumble down,
And in the dust be equal made with the poor crooked
scythe and spade."

Misfortunes also have their heroism and their glory.

—*Napoleon at St. Helena.*

Application was immediately made to Sir Hudson Lowe for permission to remove the remains to Europe. In reply he informed the friends of Napoleon that the orders of his Government were imperative that the body was to remain at St. Helena. The aristocrats of Europe feared Napoleon even in his grave!

Napoleon had earnestly expressed the wish in his will that his remains might repose on the banks of the Seine in the midst of the French people whom he had loved so well: but if that privilege were denied, he prayed that his body be taken to his native island and deposited in the tomb of his father's at Ajaccio; but if the English Government declined also granting that request, he entreated his friends to bury him in a secluded spot which he had selected at St. Helena, beneath the weeping willow which overshadowed the limpid spring from which he had received so many draughts of cold water. With his growing affection he loved the spring as if it had been a personal friend.

On the afternoon of 8th May 1821 the funeral took place with such simple pomp as the island could afford. The coffin on which lay the sword and the Mantle of Marengo was borne by British soldiers to a car drawn by four of the Emperor's horses, and thence again by relay of British soldiers to a spot which Napoleon had himself chosen, should burial in France was refused. It was at the bottom of a deep ravine under the shade of two weeping willows which overshadowed the limpid spring from which the Emperor received so many draughts of cold water, had the grave been dug. (See Anexure VI).

The inmates of Longwood followed the chief mourners Count Monotholin, Bertrand, Lascasses etc. Then came Sir Hudson Lowe, Montochem, and the officials, Civil, Naval and Military of the island. After the burial service was conducted by the Abbe Vignali, the heavy triple coffin of tin, lead and Mahogany was interred in the heavy Chamber of massive masonry deep in the earth, and successive volleys from a battery of fifteen guns discharged over the grave, reverberated along the cliffs and crags of St. Helena in salute. (See Annexure VIII. Letter from T.H. Brooke).

Immediately after his death, Chatearbriand in a poetical and overstrained language wrote the following which created a deep impression on the whole civilized world.

"The solitude of Napoleon in his exile and his tomb has thrown another kind of spell over a brilliant memory. **Alexander did not die in sight of Greece; he disappeared amid the pomp of distant Babylon. Bonaparte did not close his eyes in the presence of France; he passed away in the gorgeous horizon of the torrid zone. The man who exhibited such powerful reality vanished like a dream:** his life, which belonged to history, co-operated in the poetry of his death. **He now sleeps for ever, like a hermit or a pariah, beneath a willow, in a narrow valley, surrounded by steep rocks, at the extremity of a lonely path. The depth of the silence which weighs upon him can be compared only to the vastness of that tumult which once surrounded him. Nations are absent; their throngs have retired, the bird of the tropics, harnessed to the car of the sun, as Buffon magnificently expresses it, speeding his flight downwards from the planet of light, *rests alone, for a moment over ashes, the weight of which shook the equilibrium of the world.*"**

"Bonaparte crossed the ocean to repair to his final place of exile, regardless of the beautiful sky which delighted Columbus, Vasco da Gama, and Camoens. Stretched upon the ship's stern, he did not perceive that unknown constellations glittered over his head. His powerful glance for the first time encountered their rays. What to him were stars which he had never seen from his bivouacs and which had never shone over his empire? And yet each one of them fulfilled its destiny; one half of the firmament shed its light over his cradle, and the other half illuminated his tomb."

On the 27th of May, the devoted household of Napoleon sadly embarked for Europe. The day before their departure they went in a body to the tomb of the Emperor, and covered with flowers and "with tears which could not be expressed." **They had endured five and a half years of exile and woe, and where they also won the homage of the world by their devotion to greatness and goodness in adversity. One of the members, Sergeant Hubert refused to abandon the grave of the emperor. For Nineteen**

years he guarded the solitary tomb of his master. Hats off to that faithful sergent.

The history of most men terminate with the grave. It is not so with Napoleon. The long agony of St. Helena engrossed the attention of the world during this period. 'As prophesised by Napoleon at St. Helena, that in July 1880, the entire French nation rose as one man and expelled the Barabons for the third time, and the crown was placed on Louis Phillips the Duke of Orleans. Two months later, the Chamber of deputies requested that the mortal remains of the French Emperor Napoleon might be claimed of the British Government and restored to France. On the 5th of May, the anniversary of Napoleon's death application was made to the Government of Great Britain to this regard through its Ambassador and Minister Plenipotentiary. The response from Britain was 'speedy and cordial.' On 9th of May 1840 Lord Palmerston transmitted the following reply to the French Government:

"The Government of Her Britanic Majesty hopes that the promptness of its answer may be considered in France as a proof of its desire to blot out the last trace of those national animosities which during the life of the Emperor, armed England and France against each other. Her Majesty's Government hopes that if such sentiments survive elsewhere, they may be buried in the tomb about to receive the remains of Napoleon."

On the 12th of May 1840 His Royal Highness Prince Joun'villa proceeded to St. Helena with frigates. After two and half months of sailing and after 9 hours of digging with huge cranes, the casket containing the mortal remains of Napoleon were raised, and lo! when they opened the casket, they found him fresh as if Napoleon died a few minutes ago. After the guard of honour and Salute, the Casket was loaded in the ship with full military honours, and set sail to his motherland France. After two and half months of sailing, on 18th October 1840 (after twenty-five years and 3 days from the time Napoleon landed upon the Island of St. Helena as captive, to pass through the long agony of death) the convoy entered the mouth of River Seine on December. 9, 1840 amidst the jubilation of the French people for a magnificent funeral.

The Mayor of Roven, in preparation for the reception of the remains of the Emperor, thus addressed the inhabitants of the city:

"Beloved fellow citizens! After twenty-five years of exile in a foreign land, Napoleon is, atlast restored to us. A French Prince—the worthy son of our citizen king, brings back to France what remains of the great Emperor. In a few days these glorious ashes will rest in place under the national safeguard of his glory, and the remains of his invincible Phalanxes. A few moments only are allowed to salute the Coffin of the hero who caused the French name to be respected throughout the world. Let us employ them in solemnly manifesting the sympathies which are in the hearts of a population, over whom the Emperor once extended his powerful and protecting hand. Let us, unite, with a religious feeling, in the triumphant funeral reserved to him by the city, where his glory and genius are stamped with immortal grandeur."

With full military honours, his ashes repose in the bosom of beautiful Paris amid the imperishable monuments of wisdom, his goodness and his glory. The faithful soldier Sergent Hubert who accompanied the Coffin from St. Helena was present at the *'Invalides'* amidst embraces by the French Generals and officers. France raised the most noble tomb that the genius of modern times has conceived. It is a sacred place for pilgrimage to every son and daughter of France, and men and women of other nations pass a continual stream before the massive Sarcophagus. None who enters the solemn and sacred place fails to bow the head before the ashes of the Great Emperor. France established in grateful commemoration of the virtues of her illustrious Emperor, an annual religious celebration of the return of his ashes, to be observed through all coming times on 15th December at his tomb, beneath the dome of the *'Invalides'*.

In Sum

The history of Napoleon's fall is a microcosm of the fall of European civilization. First the religious basis of his monarchy was destroyed; the monarchy was changed by a ceaseless opposition in to party leadership. Secondly, the Emperor and people were separated so that the conscription becomes a symbol of abominable tyranny and the defence of the fatherland. The truth is, and the circumstances themselves alters it, that this great soldier fought because he had to fight. The choice was not between war and peace, but between the betrayal of his few generals and the refusal of the Allies for Peace.

If we analyse the short, at the same time, a very extraordinary career of Napoleon, we can observe that it fell in to three periods: **in the first the meteor shot in to the sky: in the second, it lit the whole of Europe with its blaze; in the third, it fell to earth.**

It was in Italy, that the meteor first appeared in the sky. There were two reasons for Napoleon's early success in Italy, where he fought the Austrian masters of Lombardy. One was the spirit of the army; for, it was a peoples army, fighting for France, and for the ideas of the Revolution. Later on, his army was composed only partly of Frenchmen and many of his troops served unwillingly and without ideals. The Italian campaign showed Napoleon at its best.

The other reason for his success was of course, his own character. He knew he was destined for great things. His addresses to his soldiers, his proclamations struck the right note. They were full of spirit, urging his men to sacrifice themselves for France, praising them for their courage and assuring them of further victories. He always praised his armies and rewarded gallantry with many decorations. In this, he was a great contrast to Wellington, who was inclined to belittle his troops.

The French Republic had lost Italy three years after Napoleon's victory at Lodi. But before re-conquering Italy, Napoleon suddenly overturned the French Government *(The Directory)* and made himself First Consul in 1799. He then showed that he had statesmanship as well as military genius. Peace, order and efficiency reigned once more in France. His system of law *(the Code Napoleon)* survives to a great extent today, and was due very largely to the energy and imagination of Napoleon himself. He let the peasants keep the land, they had seized during the Revolution; he made friends with the Church, and built roads and schools and universities. In 1804 he seized the Imperial Crown from the Pope, and Crowned himself and his wife Josephine in Paris at the Notre Dame Cathedral.

Thereafter, over eight years (1804–12) Napoleon's greatest glory. He was forty-three, Emperor of France and King of Italy. Married an emperor's daughter (Marie Louise) and had an heir. His empire covered nearly all Europe, and he reigned an absolute monarch over a hundred million people. In 1805 at Ulm and Austerlitz, he crushed Austria; in 1806 at Jena he crushed Prussia; in 1807 at Friedland, he crushed Russia. From Ulm to Austerlitz, from Jena to Friedland, his military genius in those battles was triumphant over Europe. His victory at Friedland was followed by the Treaty of Tilsit, concluded on a barge on the River Niemen. By this treaty, Napoleon—who had just abolished the ancient Holy Roman Empire—combined with the Czar Alexander, to dominate Europe.

The last period (1812-15) his life was one of failures. His overwhelming ambition led him into blunders as great as victories. The Egyptian expedition had been a blunder, and so were the blockade against England, the Spanish war, and the invasion of Russia. By forbidding other countries to trade with England, he caused great sufferings to his Allies, and roused England to even greater efforts against Napoleon. In 1812 when he wanted to teach a lesson to Russia with a huge army, he saw the Russians burning the standing crops of wheat rather than submit.

In 1813, therefore, there was uprising of the nations of Europe in the name of liberty to destroy Napoleon. Napoleon was defeated by the Allied forces at Leipzig. Then followed the exile at Elba, his defeat at Waterloo after his return from Elba and ascending the throne of France. Napoleon was deceived by his two generals Talleyrand and Fouche. Exiled to St. Helena—a series of tragedies and failures.

The life which began in obscurity ended in failure, long magnetized Europe. His name still dwarfs all others of his century. His was the most splendid genius that has happened on earth. His personality, his sense of destiny, his energy, his soaring ambitions made even failure seem like success.

Outliving his mighty empire, girt around by a thousand miles of imprisoning ocean, guarded by his most steadfast enemies, humiliation by Sir Hudson Lowe, the Jailor at St. Helena, his son a captive at the court of Hapsburgs, and his empress Marie Louisie openly faithless, bereft of his mother, brother, sister, friends and his people, Napoleon sinks from sight like a battered derelict. He was brave and courageous to bear the mental and physical torture. He once said to Bertrand at St. Helena, 'it requires courage to stay here in this horrible island bereft of his near and dear ones'.

Despite his prodigious failures, he was superlatively great in all that pertains to Government, the quickening of human energies, and the art of war. His greatness lies not only in the abiding importance of his best undertakings, but still more in the Titanic force that he threw in to the inception and accomplishment of all of them—a force which invests the storm-blasted monoliths strewn along the latter portion of his career with a majesty unapproachable by a tanner race of toilers. **After all, the verdict of mankind awards the highest distinction, not to prudent mediocrity that shuns the chance of failure, and leaves no lasting mark behind, but to the eager soul that grandly dares, mightily achieves, and holds the hearts of millions even amidst his run and theirs. His work on the orderly reconstruction during the consulate was the outcome of Statesman like qualities of the highest order.**

Such a wonder-worker was Emperor Napoleon. The man who briddled the Revolution and re-moulded the life of France who laid broad and deep the foundations of a new life in Italy, Switzerland, Germany, the Netherlands, Belgium etc. and **who rolled the West in on the East in the greatest moment known, and finally drew the Yearning thoughts of myraids to that solitary rock in South Atlantic, must ever stand in the very forefront of the immortals of human story.**

Providence uses such men, while they serve its mysterious designs for the uplifting of the race. It casts them aside when their renovating work is accomplished.

That perhaps is the mystery of creation.

"You may die young, but not if you have lived without glory, useless to the fatherland, and leaving no trace of your existence; for, that is not to have lived at all."

–Napoleon

(Advice to his younger brother Jerome Bonaparte).

The Personality of Napoleon

Early Life

Born at Corsica of a noble family but very poor, losing his father at an early age, with nothing but himself to depend upon, he had raised himself to the rank of General in the French army by no other arts than those of industry and steadfastness, high character and devotion to duty, supported, no doubt, by talents almost without example. In these first twenty-three years of his life there is not a single example of meanness or of dishonesty, or of any derogation from the high standard of conduct which he had set before himself. At Brienne, disgusted with the abandoned morals of those surrounding him, he was forced to hold himself aloof; but he made, it seems many friends, and was far from being the gloomy misanthrope which some biographers have declared him to have been. "At Paris he was the life of a chosen circle, and he showed the same firmness in the selection of his friends, and the same courage in asserting his principles, which distinguished the whole of his youth." Whatever may have been his desire for personal advancement, his care for himself was at least equalled by his love of his family and of his native land. Thrown by accident into an epoch of Revolution, he trod the difficult path of safety with marvellous wisdom and self-command. If the idea of the regeneration and independence of Corsica (his birth place) ever occurred to him, he soon became convinced that the prosperity of his island was indissolubly bound up with its connection with France. Disapproving of the execution of the king and of the persecution of the Girondists, and sympathizing very little with the excesses of the mountain, he saw that a patriotic Frenchman must follow the main course of French political feeling, and that any other action would lead to civil war. Arriving in France a fugitive and an exile, burdened with the heavy charge of an exiled family, he raised himself in a few months to a position which any officer might envy. Surely, in his case also, the youth is father of the man; and twenty-three years spent under the most difficult circumstances which could try the qualities of a character, crowned by high success legitimately gained, are not likely to have been followed by twenty-three other years stained by universal ambition.

Ambition

Ambition seemed to expel from his mind every other passion. The craving to obtain renown by the performance of great and glorious deeds; the desire to immortalize his name, as one of the distinguished men, an illustrious benefactor of the human race, had infused itself so intensely throughout his whole nature, that animal passion even was repressed, and all the ordinary pursuits of worldly pleasure became, in his view frivolous and contemptible.

Back in the last benches of his class, Napoleon was dreaming of, and admiring Alexander and Julius Caesar to excel them in his future ventures, and he succeeded. He felt that he was destined for great things, and this belief led men to speak of him as a 'man of destiny'. His temperament was serious, thoughtful and pensive. The grand and the mysterious engrossed and overawed him. His ambitions were not exulting and exhilarating, but sombre, majestic and sublime. He thought of herculean toil, of sleepless labour, and of heroic deeds. For ease and luxury, and self-indulgence, he had no desire, but he wished to be the greatest man accomplishing more than any other mortal had ever accomplished. Even in youth, life had but few charms for him, and he took melancholic view of man's earthly pilgrimage, often asserting that existence was not a blessing.

When at St. Helena drawing near to the close of life, he exclaimed that he had known but few happy moments upon earth, and that for those few, he was indebted to the love of Josephine.

'Good taste is the highest attainment of civilization.'

—Napoleon.

In the army, he turned with disgust from the licentiousness and dissipation which ever disgrace the presence of an army, and with a sternness of morality which would have done honour to any of the sages of antiquity, secured that respect which virtue ever commands.

"My extreme youth" said Napoleon "when I took command of the army in Italy rendered it necessary that I should evince a great reserve of manners and the utmost severity of morals. This was indispensable to enable me to sustain authority over men so greatly my superiors in age and experience. "I pursued a line of conduct in the highest degree irreproachable and exemplary. In spotless morality, I was a Cato, and must have appeared such to all. My supremacy could be retained only by proving myself a better man than, any other man in the army. Had I yielded to human weaknesses, I should have lost my power."

He was temperate in the extreme, seldom allowing himself to take even a glass of wine, and never did he countenance by his presence any scene of baochanalism rivalry. For gamering in all its branches, he manifested them, and through the whole of his life, the strongest disapproval. **He ever refused to repose confidence in anyone who was addicted to that vice.** It seems, one day at St. Helena, he was conversing with Les Cases, when some remark which was made led Napoleon inquire, "were you a gamester?"

"Alas Sire"! Les Cases replied: " I must confess that I was, but occasionally."

"I am very glad" replied Napoleon "that I knew nothing of it at that time, you would have been ruined in my esteem. A gamester was sure to forfeit my confidence. The moment I heard that a man was addicted to that vice, I placed no more confidence in him."

Influence of Napoleon's Mother

From where did this young soldier imbibe these elevated principles? Licentiousness, irreligion, gambling had been the trinity of revolutionary France, and Napoleon was reared in the midst of those demoralizing influences. And yet, how sullied does his character appear when compared with that of his companions in the camp, and on the throne! Napoleon informs that to his mother he was indebted for every pure and noble sentiment which inspired his bosom. His mother Letizia was a woman of extraordinary endowment. She had herself hardly passed the period of childhood, being but 19 years of age, when she heard first wailing cry of Napoleon, her second son. She was a young mother to train and educate such a child for his unknown but exalted destiny. She instilled in to the bosom of her son those elevated principles of honour, and self-respect which, when surrounded by every temptation **earth** could present, preserved him from the degraded doom of the inebriate, of the voluptuary, and of the gamester, **and which made the court of Napoleon, "the most brilliant court this world has ever known, also the most illustrious for the purity of its morals and the decorum of its observances."** It was a mother's influence which inspired a dutiful son to a magic change which transformed France from a Pagan to a religious land. It was the calm gentle persuasive voice of Letizia which was embodied in the Consular decree.

Napoleon ever regarded his mother with the most profound respect and affection. He repeatedly declared, that the family were entirely indebted to her for that physical, intellectual and moral training which prepared them to ascend the lofty summits of power to which they finally attained. He was so deeply impressed with the sense of these obligations that he often said:

"My opinion is that the future good or bad conduct of a child depends entirely upon the mother." One of the first acts, on attaining power, was to surround his mother with every luxury which wealth could furnish. And when placed at the head of the government of France, he immediately and energetically established schools for female education, remarking that **"France needed nothing so much to promote its re-generation as good mothers." By the same token Emerson said, "Men are what their mothers made them."**

The dignified character of this exalted lady is illustrated by the following anecdote.

Soon after Napoleon's assumption of the Imperial Purple, he happened to meet his mother in the gardens of St. Cloud. The Emperor, surrounded by his courtiers, and half playfully extended his hand for her to kiss.

"Not so my son" she gravely replied at the same time presenting her hand in return, "it is your duty to kiss the hand of her who gave you life."

"She watched over us with a solicitude unexampled. Every low sentiment, every ungenerous affection, was discouraged and discarded. "She suffered nothing but that which was grand and elevated to take root in our youthful understandings. 'She abhorred falsehood, and would not tolerate the slightest act of disobedience. **"None of our faults were over looked.** Hard in her affections, she punished and rewarded without distinction, good or bad. She made all feel it. She was too parsimonious, even ridiculously so. This was due to excessive foresight on her part. She had known want, and her terrible sufferings were never out of mind." "Losses, privation, fatigue, had no effect upon her. "She endured all, braved all. She has the energy of a man combined with the gentleness and delicacy of a women. In other words, her's was a man's head on a women's shoulders."

At St. Helena Napoleon said, he loved to hear from his mother's lips the story of her hardships and sufferings, as with her husband and the vanquished Corsicans (the birth place of Napoleon). She fled from village to village, and from fastness to fastness before their conquering enemies. "My mother was probably but little aware of the war like spirit she was thus nurturing in the bosom of her son, but with her own high mental endowments, she could not be sensible to the extra-ordinary capacities which had been conferred upon the silent, thoughtful pensive listener." "There was no mirthful tendencies in the character of Napoleon, no tendencies in childhood, youth or manhood to frivolous amusements or fashionable dissipation."

Seal of Napoleon Bonaparte

Liberty and property are both ruined by over-solicitude.

—Napoleon.

"My mother" said Napoleon at St. Helena "loves me. She is capable of selling everything for me, even to her last article or clothing." "Left without guide, and without support" says Napoleon "my mother was obliged to take the directions of affairs upon herself. But the task was not above her strength. She managed everything, provided her everything with a prudence which could neither have been expected from her sex, nor, from her age. Ah! What a woman! Where shall we look for her equal?" Exclaimed Napoleon. "This woman whom it would have been so difficult to extract even five francs, would have given up everything to secure my return from Elba, and after Waterloo she offered me all she possessed to restore my affairs."

The distinguished lady died at Marsaillies in the year 1822 about a year after the death of her illustrious son upon the island of St. Helena. Seven of her children living at that time, to each of whom she bequeathed nearly two million dollars; while to her brother cardinal Fasch, she left a superb palace, embellished with the most magnificent decoration of furniture, paintings and sculpture which Europe could furnish.

Honor to Letizia the mother of Napoleon.

Napoleon's Views on Sentiments

The man had from the very first the faculties of reason and of sentiment, that he desired society and love, and that primeval man was capable of feeling pity, friendship, love, and also gratitude and respect. Unless reason and sentiment were inherent qualities of man, virtue would neither be a duty nor a pleasure.

He defines happiness as the enjoyment of a life which is most suited to our organization. But our organization is two fold—animal and intellectual—one as strong as the other. "Our intellectual appetites are as imperious as our animal appetites, and happiness cannot be possible without their complete development." Sentiment and reason are qualities peculiar to man, they are his titles to the supremacy which he has acquired, and which he preserved. "It is sentiment that is the source of our activity, which makes us friends of the noble and the just, and enemies of the oppressor and the villain. In sentiment lies conscience, the source of our actions, and should be their invariable rule. Reason saves men from the precipice of passion, and tempers in him the desire to press his rights. Society has its origin in sentiment, and its support in reason. A man to be happy must eat, sleep, beget children, but he must also have sentiment and reason.

Sentiment is the bond of life, of society, of love, and of friendship. It unites the son to the mother, the citizen to his country. It is blunted by sensuality, but revived by misfortune. "Climb one of the peaks of Mount Blanc, see the Sun, gradually rising, bring consolation and hope to the cottage to the labourer, let its first ray be received into your heart, remember the sensation which it gives you. See the sun set on the sea, melancholy will overcome you, you will abandon yourself to it, the melancholy of nature cannot be resisted. Stand beneath some Roman monument, your imagination will move in distant ages with Aemilius, Scipion and Fabius, you will see the plain where a hundred thousand Cimbri lie buried. The Rhone flows in the far distance, swifter than an arrow, there is a road on the left, the little town of Tarascon is not far off, flocks pasture in the meadows, you dream, doubtless—it is the dream of sentiment. Sleep in the hut of a shepherd, lying on skins, a fire at your feet, midnight sounds, the herds are led forth to pasture: What a moment to enter yourself and to meditate on the origin of nature in tasting the most delicious pleasure! Thus also the silence of the starlit night after the fierce heat of a summer's day, the calm reflection of a solitary evening after your family have retired to rest, a night spent alone in some great cathedral, a tent life on the island of Monte Cristo, under the wall of a ruined monastery, lulled by the roaring of the waves breaking on the rocks. All these situations will fill you with sentiment."

The stress which Napoleon lays on the importance of sentiment to the character, of its universality, and its intimate connection with the rest of a man's nature is surely very remarkable and come from his deepest heart. But listen to this: "You return to your country after four years of absence, you visit the sites where you played in your earliest age, where you first experienced the knowledge of men and the awakening of the passions. In a moment you live the life of your childhood, you enjoy its pleasures, you are fired with the love of your country, you have a father and a tender mother, sisters still innocent, brothers who are like friends; too happy man, run, fly, do not lose a moment. If death stop you on your way you will never have known the delights of life, of sweet gratitude of tender respect of sincere friendship. These are the real pleasures of life, and they are greater if you have a wife and children. If your soul was as burning as the furnace of Etna; if you have a father, a wife and children, you never need be afraid of the weariness of life. Thus, by sentiment we enjoy ourselves, nature, our country, and the men who surround us."

A Man of Energy and Imagination

As far as his capacity to work was concerned, he was a formidable machine. A disciplined soldier and a staunch believer in justice and fairplay he was concerned with the welfare of his soldiers and their family, and the nation. His army was very well disciplined as he was. He never pardoned any one who does not work or shirk his responsibilities. Once Napoleon said:

"If people come to know that their king is a kind man, his administration is a utter failure."

A soldier of his consular guard on one occasion committed suicide from a disappointment of love. Napoleon issued the following order of the day.

"The grenadier Gobain has committed suicide from love. He was, in other respects, an excellent soldier. This is the second incident of the same nature which has occurred with in a month. The First Consul directs it to be inserted in the order-book of the guard, that a soldier ought to know how to vanquish the pangs of melancholoy of the passions; that there is as much true courage in bearing up against mental sufferings with constancy as in remaining firm on the wall of a battery. To yield ourselves to grief without resistance, or to kill ourselves to escape affliction, is to abandon the field of battle before the victory is gained."

His organisation of France during the consulate shows his extra-ordinary breadth of view and his mastery of detail, a powerful imagination, a largeness of perception, the possession of an infinite patience—such were some of the qualities which he possessed in a marked degree. Often when he refused to listen to suggestion, it was found that he had more knowledge of the facts than those who tended the advice. "His Majesty's Character" writes Gourgard, "is a combination of contrasts".

Before, however, Napoleon could show his remarkable genius for organisation, by not only making the constitution workable, but by using it as a means for establishing himself as the despotic ruler of France, it was necessary first to establish order at home and then to deal with the external foes of France.

Roederer, a competent and independent judge, who, at the beginning of the consular government, sees Bonaparte daily at the meeting of the Council of State, and who notes down every evening the impressions of the day, is carried with admiration. "Punctual at every sitting, prolonging the session five or six hours, discussing before, and afterwards the subjects brought forward, always returning to two questions, 'It that just?' 'Is that useful?' Examining each question in itself, under both relations, after having subjected it to a most exact and elaborate analysis; next, consulting the best authorities, the times, experience, and obtaining information about bygone jurisprudence, the laws of Louis XIV. and of Frederick the Great... Never did the council adjourn without its members knowing more than the day before; if not through knowledge derived from him, at least through the researches he obliged them to make. Never did the members of the Senate and the *Corps Legislatif*, or of the tribunals, pay their respects to him without being rewarded for their homage by valuable instructions. He cannot be surrounded by public men without being the statesmen, all forming for him a council of state." "What characterizes him above them all," is not alone the penetration and universality of his comprehension, but likewise, and especially "the force, flexibility, and constancy of his attention. He can work eighteen hours at a stretch, on one or on several subjects. "I never saw him tired, I never found his mind lacking in inspiration, even when weary in body, nor, when violently exercised, nor, when angry, I never saw him diverted from one matter by another, turning from that under discussion to one he had just finished or was about to take up. The news, good or bad, he received from Egypt, did not divert his mind from the civil code, nor the civil code from the combinations which the safety of Egypt required. Never did man more wholly devote himself to the work in hand, nor better devote his time to what he had to do. Never did mind more inflexibly set aside the occupation or thought which did not come at the right day or hour, never was one more ardent in seeking it, more alert in its pursuit, more capable of fixing it when the time came to take it up,"—He himself said later on: "Various subjects and affairs are stored away in may brain as in a chest of drawers. When I want to take up any special business I shut one drawer and open another. None of them ever get mixed, and never does this inconvenience me or fatigue me. If I feel sleepy I shut all the drawers and go to sleep." Never has brain so disciplined and under such control been seen, one so ready at all times for any task, so capable of immediate and absolute concentration. Its flexibility is wonderful, "in the instant application of every faculty and energy, and bringing them all to bear at once on any object that concerns him, on a mite as well as on an elephant, on any given individual as well as on an enemy's army... When specially occupied, other thing do not exist for him; it is a sort of chase from which nothing diverts him." And this hot pursuit, which nothing arrests save capture, this tenacious hunt, this headlong course by one to whom the goal is never other than a fresh starting point, is the spontaneous gait, the natural, even pace which his mind prefers, "I am always at work," says he to Roederer. "I meditate a great deal. If I seem always equal to the occasion, ready to face what comes, it is because I have thought the matter over a long time before undertaking it. I have anticipated whatever might happen. It is no genius which suddenly reveals to me what I ought to do or say in any unlooked for circumstance, but my own reflection, my own meditation... I work all the time, at dinner, in theatre. I wake up at night in order to resume my work. I got up last night at two o'clock. I stretched myself on my couch before the fire to examine the army reports sent to me by the Minister of War. I found twenty mistakes in them, and made notes which I have this morning sent to the minister, who is now engaged with his clerks in rectifying them." His fellow-workmen break down and sink under the burden imposed on them and which he supports without feeling the weight. When Consul "he sometimes presides at special meetings of the section of the interior from ten o'clock in the evening until five o'clock in the morning... Often, at Saint-Cloud, he keeps the counsellors of state from nine o'clock in the morning until five in the evening, with fifteen minutes' intermission, and seems no more fatigued at the close of the session than when it began." During the night sessions "many of the members succumb through lassitude, while the Minister of War falls asleep"; he gives them a shake and wakes them up, "Come, come, citizens, let us bestir ourselves, it is only two o'clock and we must earn the money the French people pay us." Consul or Emperor, he demands of each minister an account of the smallest details. It is not rare to see them leaving the council room overcome with fatigue, due to the long interrogatories to which he has subjected them; he disdains to take any notice of this, and talks about the day's work simply as a relaxation which has scarcely given his mind exercise. And what is worse "it often happens that on returning home they find a dozen of his letters requiring immediate answer, for which the whole night scarcely suffices." The quantity of facts he is able to retain and store away, the quantity of ideas he elaborates and produces, seems to surpass human capacity, and this insatiable, inexhaustible, unmovable brain thus keeps on working uninterruptedly for thirty years. Every idea entertained by him had its origin in his personal observation and it was his personal observation which controlled it. Everything else, as with his predecessors of the fifteenth century, comes to him through the original direct action of his faculties in contact with me and things, through his prompt and sure tact, his indefatigable and minute attention, his indefinitely repeated and rectified divination during long hours of solitude and silence. Practice, and speculation, is the source of his instruction, the same as with a mechanic brought up amongst machinery. "There is nothing relating to warfare that I cannot make myself. If nobody knows how to make gunpowder, I do. I can construct gun-carriages. If Cannon must be cast, I will see that it is done properly. If tactical details must be taught, I will teach them." Hence his competency at the outset—general in the artillery, major-general, diplomatist, financier and administrator, all at once and in every direction. Thanks to this fecund apprenticeship, beginning with the Consulate, he shows cabinet clerks and veteran ministers send in their reports to him what to do. "I am a better administrator than they are; when one has been obliged to rack his brains to find out how to feed, maintain, control, and animate with the same spirit and will two or three hundred thousand men, a long distance from their country, one soon gets at the secrets of administration." He takes in at a glance every part of the human machine he fashions and manipulates, each in its proper place and function, the generators of power, the organs of its transmission, the extra working gear, the composite action, the speed which ensues, the final result, the complete effect, the net product; never is he content with a superficial and summary inspection; he penetrates into obscure corners and to the lowest depths "through the technical precision of his questions," with the lucidity of a specialist, and in this way, borrowing an expression from the philosophers, his idea is found adequate to its object.

Hence, his eagerness for details, for these form the body and substance of the object; the hand that has not grasped these, or lets them go, retains only the shell, an envelop. With respect to these his curiosity is "insatiable." In each ministerial department he knows more than the ministers, and in each bureau he knows as much as the clerks. "On his table lie reports of the positions of his forces on land and on water; he had furnished the plans of these, and fresh ones are issued every month"; such is the daily reading he likes best. "I have my reports on positions always at hand, my memory for an Alexandrine is not good, but I never forget a syllable of my reports on positions. I shall find them in my room this evening, and I shall not go to bed until I have read them." He always knows "his position" on land and at sea better than is known in the War and Navy departments; better even his staff-officers; the number, size and qualities of his ships in or out of port, the present and future state of vessels under construction, the composition and strength of their crews, the formation, organization, staff of officers, material stations, and enlistment, past and to come, of each army corps and of each regiment. "The admirable condition of my armies is due to this, that I give attention to them every day for an hour or two, and, when the monthly reports come in, to the state of my troops and fleets, all forming about twenty large volumes. I leave every other occupation to read them over in detail, to see what difference there is between one month and another. I take more pleasure in reading those than any young girl does in a novel."—Cadet de Gasicourt "Voyage en Autriche". That was the hard work, and that was the secret of his success.

I have always borne the world on my shoulders and that task, afterall, does not permit me to be tired.

—Napoleon.

Napoleon on The Art of War—A Leader and Strategist

Napoleon was a great admirer of Themistocles, Xenophon, Caesar and the Spartans. It is these philosophers and generals who inspired him.

Themistocles, the Athenian Statesman and general who lived in the fourth century B.C. and who showed universal ability and application was his hero. Indeed his career proved a point made by Pericles that in Athens what counts is not membership of a particular class, but the actual ability which the man possesses. As Thucydides wrote: 'few surpassed Themistocles in practical reason'.

No doubt Themistocles showed an unmistakable natural genius, and in this respect he was quite exceptional, and beyond all others deserves our admiration. Without studying a subject in advance or deliberating over it later, but using simply the intelligence that was his by nature, he had the power to reach the right conclusion in matters that have to be settled on the spur of the moment, and do not admit of long discussion, and in estimating what was likely to happen, his forecasts of the future were always more reliable than those of others. He could perfectly well explain any subject with which he was familiar, and even outside his own department he was still capable of giving an excellent opinion. He was particularly remarkable at looking into the future, and seeing there the hidden possibilities for good or evil. **To sum him up in a few words, it may be said that through force of genius and by rapidity of action, this man was supreme at doing precisely the right thing at precisely the right moment.**

Archemedies proposed to lift the world if he could be allowed to place his lever; for myself, I would have changed it whenever I could have been allowed to exercise my energy, perseverance and budgets.

—Napoleon.

Next is Xenophon.

Xenophon was the only philosopher among them all to have adorned philosophy both in word and deed. On the one hand he writes moral virtues in his discourses, and to some extent in his historical writings also. On the other hand, he excelled in deeds and begot generals by the force of his example. **Alexander the great, atleast, would never have become 'Great' but for Xenophon.**

Xenophon who sat at the feet of Socrates, the western world's first great teacher of leadership. It was Socrates who taught, that leadership tends to be exercised by the person who knows what to do in a given situation. Consequently, he placed much emphasis upon the need to acquire the appropriate technical competence and experience if one wished to lead others. But knowledge is not the whole story. There are people who are technically competent and highly specialized in their fields. Yet they are not recognized as leaders. Something more is required. As the experience of Xenophon suggests, a good leader gives direction, sets an example, shares danger or hardship on an equal footing, and wins true support of others. He or she should win respect without counting popularity. Are there more general leadership abilities transferable from one field to another? Could they be learned?

The greatest General should be the ablest guide of the nation, when the desire for peace and order supervened. For, indeed the gifts of command and organisation are not unlike in the two spheres. A successful commander must possess the facilities of foresight as to the probable course of events, of insight in to character, and of sound sense in the adjustment of conflicting interest.

Napoleon admitted, courage and prowess were all important in the days of feudalism and chivalry: but said he, in the present age the qualities needed by a commander were foresight, power of calculation, administrative ability, ready wit eloquence such as appeals to soldiers, and above all, knowledge of men. All these are civil qualities. The General who is capable of great things is he, who possesses the finest civil qualities. He is obeyed and respected on account of his intellectual ability.

Napoleon had equally great admiration for the Spartans as well. The life of the Spartan was his ideal: for, they laid so much stress on strength and virtue. 'Virtue', he adds consists in courage and force. "Energy is the life of the soul, the main spring of reason." The excitements of Spartans were those of the strongman: and the **"strongman is good; only the weak is wicked." Courage is graceful and dignified, whilst fear in any form is mean and repulsive.** It was the enthusiasm and courage that led King Leonides (480 B.C.) of Lacedemonia along with three hundred Lacedemonian warriers defended the pass at Thermopylae by remembering glory before all things; and reputation to be acquired in the midst of dangers. A battle gained without costing the conqueror any blood is an inglorious success, while the conquered cover themselves with glory by perishing with their arms in their hands. Not one came back alive including the King. Although, it was a technical defeat, is perhaps the best example of valour. After the war, the Spartans erected a memorial on the battlefield of Thermopylae saying only.

"Stranger, tell the Lacedimonians that we lie here in obedience to their orders." Napoleon was deeply impressed by the Spartans.

Napoleon's fighting instinct throbbed in his blood during his tender years. His extra-ordinary hardiness and pugnacity, inherited from the Pietra-Santa family distinguished him from first to last, from the first charge at Montenotta to the on set of imperial Guard at Waterloo. In this combative instinct lies the secret of his power over the soldiering. Men will go anywhere, and do anything for a fighting general, provided, he cares for their interests, and touches their imagination

He used to say.

Man is governed by imagination only; without imagination, he is brute.

Napoleon was a fighter, instructor of armies, Commander-in-Chief, strategist and tactician. His genius for war was the most universal known to authentic history. **He was the real western Alexander the Great, the modern Caesar.**

Napoleon was an ideal leader as well. His exacting instinct and unquestioning obedience from the Generals, giving them abundant opportunities to enrich themselves at the expense of the liberated peoples, and finally showering them immense domains. Sometimes, he fired them with burning words.

"If your experience reverses, always remember these three things—union of your forces, activity, and a firm resolve to die with glory. These are the great principles of the military art which have made fortune favour me in all my operations. **Death is nothing, but to live Vanquished, and without glory is to die every day."** King Leonodes (480 B.C.) who perished with 300 Lacedimonians by covering themselves with glory by perishing with their arms in the hand was a source of great inspiration to Napoleon.

His Proclamations to the soldiers pulsate with national pride. From the first appeal in 1796 to march onward, and conquer or die showed a supreme art in kindling the passion for glory in the rank and file. As he said, love of glory is with Frenchmen a sixth sense. Despite great stress and strain, he used to encourage the engineers and artillerymen by standing near them, watching their toil and speaking the words that change men in to Titans, or he would go over the battlefield, feeling the pulse of the soldiers, showing genuine satisfaction when he discovered signs of life that had not been observed before. He used to love to talk with old guard asking them how long, and where they had served, the number of their wounds, and so forth.

After the victory in 1796 over the Austrians at Lodi in Italy, he wrote "I feel deeds await me, of which the present generation has no inkling. "Everything has happened as I foresaw. So will it be in the future. I shall make my way whatsoever I will." Napoleon was sure of his own future that he inspired his army to feel the same. **When Napoleon was told before the battle of Leipzig in 1814 that he was outnumbered by three to one, he replied: "I have fifty thousand men, add myself, you get one hundred and fifty thousand."** His self-confidence was colossal. The reason for his triumph and success was his determination, his will and his character. **Courage comes only when leaders have moral character.**

No man has ever better understood the value of time than

Napoleon. His remarkable saying to the pupils of a school where he once visited:

"My young friends, every hour of time is a chance of misfortune for future life" formed the rule of his own conduct. He said on another occasion.

"Victory belongs to the more persevering."

The first essential of a great leader is clearness of insight and firmness of purpose. Bonaparte early gave proof of these valuable gifts. A sign of a strong nature is the resolve to master every fact that is essential to success. Another quality needed is perfect self confidence even after a great reverse. This, Napoleon displayed in Egypt after Nelson's triumph at the battle of Nile. To keep up the spirit of the men, he instituted races, concerts, and all kinds of distractions, beside stimulating the manufacture of gun powder and the many necessaries which the army now had to supply in Egypt itself.

"Promptitude brought victory; Slackness involved disaster."

In strategy, prompt advance is a great force along the line of operation; or, in other words, the adopting of a strategic offensive in the swiftest and most effecting manner. In tactics, concentration of masses against the enemy's weak point. Strategy, that is the conduct of war in its large lines and specially, the choice of a line of operation, determine the whole course of a campaign. It is, therefore, more important than tactics, the art of arranging and handling the troops on the battlefield. "Many commanders, for instance Ney, and Blucher have fought battles well on the ordinary lines, but have lacked the imagination, the grip on the principles of war, the topographical instinct, needed by the strategist." His brain must, as it were mirror the scene of the campaign, and the position of his own and other enemy's forces, so far as he knows the latter. As Napoleon said:

"A General's mind must be in-respect of lucidity and clearness resemble the lens of a telescope, and never create any mirage. Further, the Commander needs to estimate at their true value, the obstacles in the way of either army, seeking how he may avoid them, and make them a danger to his opponent. The futility or otherwise of the country along his line of advance, and the temper of the inhabitant must also engage his attention; and last but not the least, the opportunities for forming and utilizing depots, or magazines, for the supply of his army will be his constant care. Therefore, a faulty choice of a line of operation at the outset vitiates the whole campaign.

Art of War

A proof of the unfailing vivacity of Napoleon's brain is the variety and freshness of his dicta on the art of war. Here are some of them:

* "The first quality of a soldier is fortitude in enduring fatigue and hardship; bravery is the second. Poverty, hardship and misery are the school of the good soldiers....."
* "Soldiers must in all ways be encouraged to remain with the colours: this you will attain by showing great esteem for soldiers."
* "An army is a people that obeys."

" Never attack a position in front which may be taken by turning."

"The junction of different corps should never be effected in the vicinity of the foe."

"At the commencement of a campaign, thought should be expended as to whether an advance should be made or not; but when once the offensive has been assumed it should be maintained to the last extremity."

"The strength of an army, like the amount of momentum in mechanics, is estimated by the mass multiplied by the velocity. A swift march enhances the morale of the army and increases its power for victory."

"Men must be led by an iron hand in a velvet glove."

"Courage is like love: it feeds on hope."

"In war all is mental; and the mind and opinion make up more than the half of the actual."

"The art of war is an immense study which comprises all others."

Napoleon brought all the powers of his mind to bear upon the problems of war, and was admittedly the greatest warrior of all time.

Napoleon as a Distinguished Man of Letters

All the world thinks of Napoleon as a great soldier, and a great administrator— Mr. Gladstone declared him to be the greatest man in both departments of life that the world has ever seen—but few there be who think of him as a distinguished man of letters.

Bonaparte's mind was bent entirely on literary career, opened his first campaign. Dramas, tragedies, essays fill up the leisure of the early years. At 21, he had written a history of Corsica which he dedicated to Paoli and which he sent that manuscript to the Corsican patriot Paoli for his approval. Of this, it is recorded of Paoli that "this young man is formed on the ancient model. He is one of Plutarch's men."

Napoleon clearly loved the art of writing as he loved the art of war, but in November 1793, came the earlier triumph of the young artillery officer at Toulan, and Napoleon's career as an author of books was ended for many a day. Not until he reaches St. Helena does he again subordinate everything to authorship this time, however, with Caesar and Xenophon in his mind.

The interval was filled with the brilliant achievement in war and administration with which the whole world has rung, but it has its great literary achievement in the multitude of remarkable letters, dispatches, manifestos and proclamations, which form not the least part of Napoleon's permanent achievement, although the most human note to those wonderful years is to be found in the love letters to Josephine.

There is Napoleon as the friend of literary men in his period. It is true that there was no writer of first class importance among his subjects during his too brief reign. Happily, Napoleon was destined to come in contact with one of the great men of letters—Geothe. Perhaps the high position of Napoleon in letter is best emphasised by turning to the accounts of the interviews between Goethe and the emperor. Napoleon had assembled all the European Sovereigns at the congress at Erfurt. There were besides the emperor Napoleon, and the Czar Alexander, four kings, and thirty-four Princess. Every hour, every minute of Napoleon's time was crowded with its official duties, but the moment the emperor heard that Goethe was in Erfurt, he commanded his appearance at an audience at eleven o'clock the next morning. The date was October 1, 1808. Napoleon was already the hero of fifty pitched battles, Jena and Austerlitz among the latest; Goethe was already the author of 'Werther, 'Faust', Hermann' and 'Dorothea'—atleast fifty volumes. Napoleon had read only one of these, 'Werther', but he had read seven times, and had cherished it as a companion in Egypt. Napoleon was delighted with Goethe's personal appearance.

'Voila unhomme!' He exclaimed when Goethe entered. He first enquired about Goethe's dramas, and he was reminded by Daru, who was present, that Goethe had translated Voltair's Mohamet. "That is not a good play" replied the Emperor, and then gave a detailed exposition of how improper it is that a great world conqueror should be made to give improper description of himself. After that he turned the conversation to Goethe's sorrows of Werther, and Goethe now learned for the first time that Napoleon was one of his readers*. He points out an artistic blemish in the work, namely, Werther's suicidal mania proceeded not solely from disappointed love but also frustrated ambition. Always enamoured of clearness and precision, he found the mixture of motives untrue to nature, and Goethe admitted that his criticisms were original and keen, and 'we could wish that we had more of them.' The interview lasted an hour, and it is clear that there was no courtier—

* Belschowskeys—Life of Goethe, Vol. II, p. 411.

like sycophancy in Goethe's appreciation of the emperor's conversation. Five days later, Goethe had another conversation with Napoleon in this time at a Ball. "You ought to write the Death of Caesar, but in grander style than Voltair's, said Napoleon." "The world should be shown how Caesar would have made it happy if he had been given time to realize his high minded plans. You come to Paris. I demand it of you, by all means. There you will have a broader view of the world. You will then find an over-abundance of material for your poems."

The Emperor also conversed with Wieland who has left his own account of the interview. Both poets were fascinated by the magic personality of Napoleon, and both have left some record of their conversation with the man who at this period was in very truth a ruler of kings.

"I had been but a few minutes in the room" Wieland says, when Napoleon crossed it to come to us. I was presented by the Dutches of Weimer. He paid me some compliment in an affable tone, fixing his eye piercingly upon me. Few men have appeared to me to possess, in the same degree, the power of penetrating at a glance the thoughts of others. I have never beheld anyone more calm, more simple, more mild or less ostentatious in appearance. Nothing about him indicated the feeling of power in a great monarch. He spoke to me as an old acquaintance would speak to an equal. What was more extra-ordinary on his part, he conversed with me exclusively for an hour and a half, to the great surprise of the assembly. He appeared to have no relish for anything gay. In spite of the pre-possessing amiability of his manners, he seemed to me to be bronze. Towards midnight I began to feel that it was improper to detain him so long, and I took the liberty to request permission to retire. 'Go then' said he in a friendly tone—Good night.

A little later, both poets received the cross of the Legion of Honour.

"I have never seen a calmer, simpler, gentler and less assuming man" declared Wieland. **"The Greatest understanding the world has ever seen"** was Goethe's verdict to Boisserce in 1815—after

Napoleon had fallen. "I will gladly confess" he wrote to his friend Cotta at the time "that nothing higher and more pleasing could have happened to me in all my life than to have stood before the French Emperor on such a footing."

Goethe said **"What a compendium of the world!"** He was something, and he looked what he was—that was all*.

Napoleon conquered Goethe for all the remaining years of his long life by sheer personal magnetism added to genuine cultivation of mind. He had, we see, a mentality fully able to cope with that of the greatest imaginative writer since Shakespeare. No wonder that Goethe's biographer says: **"Napoleon did not speak (to the poet) as a General and Statesman, but as a literary critic, an historian, a philosopher. And with what sagacity what discrimination, what originality?"** ** **!!**

Napoleon had always been a great reader, though he declared that in his public life he only read what was of direct use for his purpose. When he was a scholar at Birenne, the frequency of his demands for books was the torment of the College librarian. When he was a lieutenant in garrison at Valence he read ravenously and indiscriminately everything he could lay his hands on. "When I was a lieutenant of artillery," he said before the collected princes at Erfurt, "I was for three years in garrison at Valence. I spent that time in reading and re-reading the library there." Later, we read of his tearing along to join his armies, his coach full of books and pamphlets which would be flung out of the window when he had run through them. When he travelled with Josephine, all the newest books were put into the carriage for her to read to him. And though he declared that his reading was purely practical, he always had a travelling library of general literature, with which he took great pains. He had planned a portable collection of three thousand choice volumes which should be printed for him,. But when he found, it would take six years, and a quarter of a million sterling to complete, he wisely abandoned the project. Even to Waterloo

---

* Goethe's conversation with Eckermannn Feb. 16, 1826.

** The life of Goethe by Albert Belschowscky, Vol. II.

he was accompanied by a travelling library of 800 volumes in six cases— the Bible, Homer, Ossian, Bossuet, and all the seventy volumes of Votaire. "Three days after his final abdication, we find him writing for a library from Malmaison, books on America, his chosen destination, books on himself and his campaigns, a collection of the Moniteur, the best dictionaries and encyclopaedias. Now, in his solitude, he devoured them—history, philosophy, strategy, and memoirs. Of these last alone he read seventy-two volumes in twelve months. Nor was he by any means a passive reader. He would scribble on margins, he would dictate notes or criticisms. The one pleasure of the Napoleon's life at St. Helena was, on the arrival of books. Then, he would shut himself up with them for days together—bathing in them, revelling in them and feasting on them."

Napoleon's range of reading was very exhaustive. It included Homer, Virgil, Tasso, and novels of all countries, histories of all times, Mathematics, legislation and theology. He praises Homer and Ossian, he was never wearied of sounding 'Read again" he said to an officer on board the "Bellerophon"—"read again the poetry of Achilles, devour Ossian". **"These are the poets who lift up the soul, and give the man a colossal greatness."**

Bonrrienna gives the list of books that Napoleon took with him to Egypt. It was in Bonaparte's own hand writing. It includes: Plutarch's 'lives', Homer and Virgil, four volumes of Voltair's and four of Rousseau's, Tacitus and Thucidides, La Sage's works in ten volumes, forty volumes of English Novels and above all Ossian.

Napoleon lays great stress for public instruction, and further believes in the study of Geometry and history. He calls history "the basis of the moral sciences, this torch of truth, this destroyer of prejudices"—Mathematics and history will enable the governors of the future ideal state to perfect their logic and guide peoples in the search for truth.

As said earlier,

Napoleon was from the very beginning of his career an exceptionally well-read man, **and to have read wisely the best**

works of every country is the highest form of culture. It is probable that in the whole history of modern world, no other man of action was ever so keenly interested in books. Young Bonaparte had read everything that he could lay his hands as in those days of studentship. At 18, he had devoured the works of Rousseau (of whom he said that without him, the French Revolution would not have been), of Voltaire and a large number of French authors. He was familiar with the 'Arabian Nights', 'Don Quixote' 'Clarissa Harlowe" and much else of the light literature of Europe, before, he commenced in earnest, his career as a man of action. He had read the Greek and Latin historians, and his favourite books was **Piutarch's "Lives". When he ascended the throne of France, he was not only the best read monarch in Europe, but probably by far the best endowed of all European monarchs since time began, not even Frederik the Great.**

Bonaparte at 27, became Commander-in-Chief of the Army in Italy covering himself with glory having served his apprenticeship alike to literature and to war. Henceforth for 18 years there is a continuous career of activity with extra-ordinary achievements in war and peace. We recall a succession of memorable victories in the battlefield, we recall triumphs of administrative activity scarcely less memorable; nor do we forget the compilation of that civil code *(code Napoleon)* which no nation that received it, has cared to abandon. The civil code became law in 1804. After undergoing slight modifications and additions, it was in 1807 re-named *code Napoleon.* Its provision had already in 1806, been adopted in Italy. In 1810 Holland and the newly annexed coast line of the North Sea as far as Hamburg, and even Lubeck on the Baltic, received it as the basis of their laws, as did the Grand Duchy of Berg in 1811. Indirectly, it has also exerted an immense influence on the legislation of Central and Southern Germany, Prussia, Switzerland, and Spain; while many of the Central and Southern American states also have borrowed its salient features. The *'Code Napoleon'* was prepared by single man Napoleon with devoted energy. Napoleon owed much of his success in legislation to the arduous self-culture of his early years.

As a man of letters:

Napoleon as a man of letters is at his highest point in his Proclamations*, his despatches, his correspondence.

Santa Beuva compares his writings with that of Pascal and tells us that it offers a worthy pendant in the most perfect styles of antiquity, and is comparable, of its kind to Xenophon and Caesar. The greatest of European literary critics do not fail of quotations to support his position. One recalls the proclamation* with which he took command of the army in Italy—that phenomenal opportunity which "made" him. Here I quote from his address in 1796.

"Soldiers! You are ill-fed and almost naked; the Government owes you much, but can do nothing for you. Your patience, your courage do you honour, but bring you neither advantage nor glory. I am about to lead you into the most fertile plains of the world. Rich provinces, great cities will be in your power. There you will find honour, and fame, and wealth. Soldiers of the Army of Italy, will you be found wanting in courage?"

Thus Napoleon addressed the half-starved and dejected legions who had been struggling for two years on the Maritime Alps against the Austrians and Sardinians in an apparently impossible attempt to gain a footing in Northern Italy. The army was little more than a mob of malcontents, lacking even the common necessaries of life. Forty thousand outcasts, if you will, undisciplined, many of them without boots, more of them in all of them with scarcely a ray of hope; soldiers in name rather than in reality. Brave men and heroes there were, order and subordination there were not. To introduce cohesion and discipline into these unruly forces was the almost superhuman task Napoleon had undertaken.

And then the continuous flow of letters, commands, exhortations. There has never been anything like it.

Carlyle called Napoleon "Europe's last great man." "Only those who knew Napoleon in the intercourse of private life render

* See Annexure IV.

justice to his character. For my own part, I know him, as it were, by heart; and in proportion as time separates us, he appears to me like a beautiful dream. And would you believe that in any recollections of Napoleon, that which seems to me to approach most nearly to ideal excellence is not the hero, filling the world with his gigantic fame, but the man viewed in the relations of private life?"

Napoleon's Humanism

"If people come to know that their king is a kind man, his administration is a utter failure.".

—Napoleon

Men of sterling character have the courage to speak the truth. They are bound to speak the truth in the love of it. It is the courageous man, infact, who can best afford to be generous, or rather, it is his nature to be so. It was characteristic of Napoleon, when visiting works of mechanical excellence to pay great respect to the inventor, and on his taking leave, to salute him with a low bow. Once at St. Helena, when walking with Mrs. Balcombe, some servants came along carrying a load. The lady in an angry tone, ordered them out of the way **on which Napoleon interposed saying "Respect the burden Madam."**

The brave man is magnanimous as well as gentle. He does not take even an enemy at a disadvantage, nor strike a man when he is down, and unable to defend himself. Even in the midst of deadly strife, such instances of generosity have not been uncommon.

On one occasion when the revolutionary government of France were celebrating the 21st January with great pubiic rejoicing at the anniversary of the execution of the king, they urged Napoleon to honour the festival by his presence and to take a conspicuous part in the festivities... Napoleon promptly declined. "This fete" said he, "commemorates a melancholy event, a tragedy, and can be agreeable to but few people. It is proper to celebrate victories, but victims left upon the field of battle are to be lamentated. To celebrate the anniversary of a king's death by execution, is an act unworthy of a Government; it irritates instead of adding to their strength."

❖ ❖ ❖

Abbot in his book on 'the life of Napoleon Bonaparte' describes many such incidents as cited above. It seems, every person who had any intercourse "with this extra-ordinary man (Napoleon) either as a companion in arms, in the cabinet, or as a servant, glows with excitement when speaking of the exalted intellect, and the kindly heart of their adored master."

One day, Napoleon was traversing the camp, attended by two officers, when he met a very pretty sutler woman, weeping bitterly, and leading by the hand a little boy about five years old. The Emperor, who happened to be unknown to the woman, reined up his horse, and inquired into the cause of her grief. The woman, much disconcerted, made no reply, but the child frankly answered.

"My mother is crying, Sir , because my father has beaten her."

"And where is your father?"

"He is close by. He is a sentinal on duty with the baggage."

Napoleon again addressed himself to the woman, and inquired the name of her husband. She refused to tell, being fearful that the Captain, as she supposed the Emperor to be, would cause him to be punished.

"Your husband has been beating you," Napoleon said, "You are weeping, and yet you are so afraid of getting him into trouble that you will not even tell me his name. This is very inconsistent. May it not be that you are a little at fault yourself?"

"Alas! Captain", the forgiving wife replied, "he has a thousand good qualities, though he had one very bad one. He is jealous, terribly jealous; and when he gets into a passion he can not restrain his violence. And I love him, for he is my lawful husband and the father of my dear boy." So saying, she fondly kissed her child, who, by the way in which he returned her caresses, proved his affection for his mother.

Napoleon was deeply touched by this little domestic drama. Burdened as he was with the cares of empire, he could turn aside from them to dry up the fountain of sorrow in the heart of this humble follower of the camp. Addressing the woman again, he said: "Whether you and your husband love each other or not, I do not choose that he should beat you. Tell me your husband's name, and I will mention the affair to the Emperor."

"If you were the Emperor himself", she replied, "I would not tell it you, for I know that he would be punished."

"Silly woman!" Napoleon rejoined, "All that I want is to teach him to behave well to you, and to treat you with the respect you deserve." Then, shrugging his shoulders, he made some further remark upon female obstinacy, and galloped away.

"Well gentlemen," said he to his companions, "what do you think of that affectionate creature? There are not many such women at the Tuileries. A wife like that is a treasure to her husband." Immediately he despatched an officer to desire the commander of the escort to come to him. He inquired very particularly respecting the woman, her husband, and the child.

"He is", said the officer, "One of the best behaved men in the company. He is very jealous of his wife, but without reason. The woman's conduct is irreproachable."

"Try and ascertain", said Napoleon, "if he has ever seen me; if he has not, bring him here."

It appeared that Napoleon had never been seen by the grenadier, who was a fine-looking young man of about five and twenty, who had recently joined the army. When he was conducted to Napoleon, the latter said, in a familiar tone, "What is the reason, my lad, that you beat your wife? She is a young and pretty woman, and a better wife than you are a husband. Such conduct is disgraceful in a French grenadier."

"If women are to be believed", the man replied, "they are never in the wrong. I have forbidden my wife to talk to any man whatever; and yet, in spite of my commands, I find her constantly gossiping with one or another of my comrades." On hearing this Napoleon said:

"Now, there is your mistake. You want to prevent a woman from talking; you might as well try to turn the course of the Danube. Take my advice: do not be jealous. Let your wife gossip and be merry. If she was doing wrong, it is likely she would be sad instead of gay. I desire that you do not strike your wife again. If my order be not obeyed, the Emperor shall hear of it. Suppose His Majesty were to give you a reprimand, what would you say then?"

The man, not a little irritated at this interference with his marital privileges, replied, "My wife is mine, General, and I may beat her if I choose; I should say to the Emperor, 'Look you to the enemy, and leave me to manage my wife'."

Napoleon laughed and said, "My good fellow you are now speaking to the Emperor."

The word fell upon the soldier's heart like magic. Much confused, he hung his head lowered his voice, and said, "Oh, sire! that quite alters the case. Since your Majesty Commands, I, of course, obey."

"That is right", Napoleon replied, "I hear an excellent character of your wife; everybody speaks well of her; she braved my displeasure rather than expose you to punishment; reward her by kind treatment. I promote you to the rank of sergeant. Apply to the Grand Marshal, and he will give you five hundred francs; with that you can furnish you sutler's stores, which will enable your wife to carry on a profitable business. Your son is a fine boy, and at some future time he shall be provided for. But, mind! Never let me hear of your beating your wife again. If you do, you shall find that I can deal hard blows as well as you."

Several years after this, the Emperor was with the army in another campaign. Napoleon, who had a wonderful power of recollecting the countenances of persons whom he had once seen, met the "daughter of the regiment" and her son, and immediately rode up to her, saying, "Well, my good woman, how do you do? Has your husband kept the promise he made me?"

The affectionate wife burst into tears, and, throwing herself at the Emperor's feet, exclaimed, "Oh, sire! since my good star led into the presence of your Majesty, I have been the happiest of women."

"Then reward me", said Napoleon "by being the most virtuous of wives", With these words he tossed a few pieces of gold into her hands and rode away, while the whole battalion raised an enthusiastic shout of "Vive l' Emperor!"

❖ ❖ ❖

Baron Langon says: "The present generation whose Thrones filled by men of the ordinary stamp, are unable to comprehend the state of feeling with which the Emperor inspired us." Providence has not granted them the favour which must ever be our pride and glory, to have been face to face with Napoleon, to have heard his voice vibrate through our ears and hearts, and to have gazed upon his placid and majestic Countenance, "To us, **Napoleon** was not a mere Emperor, he was a being of higher order—one of those sublime creations that perhaps help to exalt our ideas of the Creator." 'Napoleon was our father, our master, in some degree our idol.' 'We young men cherished for him the affection and duty of sons.' "There existed between him and ourselves a positive sympathy, which made us regard as a sacred and family duty that which the present generation of young Frenchmen would pronounce to be servility and base vassalage."

Here is an example of Napoleon' magnanimity

Napoleon once related the following incident to his minister of war:

"As I was passing through Givet, a detachment of English prisoners set to work to repair the flying bridge. I remarked especially the zeal and activity of eight or ten of them, who threw themselves into a little boat. Give orders for a list to be made of the ten men who most distinguished themselves upon this occasion; let them receive a new suit of clothes and five Napoleons each, with an order to go to Morlaix, where they must be handed over to the Transport Office, making known the cause of their release.... There is an English clergyman there who asked my permission to spend three months in England; grant this to him. He might take charge of others I also send you a petition handed to me under the same circumstances by an English lady; send me a report upon this demand."

There are innumerable instances required to be quoted. But I confine to only two or three which I reproduce.

To CANOVA, Sculptor at Rome

"Milan, 6th August, 1797."

"I have learned through one of your friends that you have been deprived of the pension you enjoyed at Venice. The French Republic takes a particular interest in the great talent which distinguishes you. As a celebrated artist you have a right to the special protection of the army of Italy. I have given orders for your pension to be paid at once. I beg you will let me know that this order has been executed, and believe in the pleasure I experience in being agreeable to you.

"Bonaparte".

Yet another instance of humanism

TO GENERAL SAVARY (MINISTER OF POLICE)

"St. Cloud, 20th November, 1811."

"You have committed a breach of duty in prosecuting an individual simply because he made some complaints against you; this was all the more unjust, because he told me things which I did not know and which I ought to have known. Taking this man from the present moment under my special protection, no measures must be adopted against him without my special authorisation. I hope that you will not fall again into the same error. All French citizens have the right of appealing to me against no matter who...

"Napoleon".

Example of Fairness

TO GENERAL BERTHIER

"Cairo, 6th October, 1798."

"You will order General Manscourt to send the merchants of the Mamelukes who have arrived at Alexandria, to Cairo. An inquiry will be held to find out if these merchants have received any advances.

"You will also order the General to seize the property of Hassan-Allah, in order that we may repay ourselves the 40,000 medins he owes to Koraim. As for the brother of **Koraim, his property should not be confiscated, as he is not yet accused of anything.**

"Bonaparte".

Respect for Values

When Napoleon returned from Elba secretly, Louis the XVIII heard of Napoleon's landing, and his advance to Genoble. The Count of Artois (afterwards Charles X) had been despatched to Lyons to concentrate there all the available forces of the kingdom, and to crush the Emperor. He entered the city but a few hours before Napoleon appeared at its gates. Two regiments of the line-one infantry and Cavalry—were in the place. Other regiments were advancing by rapid marches. The local national guard, well armed, and well disciplined amounted to twenty thousand men. But the Count of Artois was received coldly by the troops, and still more coldly by the inhabitants. The count accompanied by a guard of a gentlemen who were his personal friends, and who were pledged for his protection. When they saw the universal enthusiasm in favour of Napoleon, believing the Barabon cause irretrievably lost, they also perfediously abandoned the Prince and turned to the Emperor. The Count was compelled to flee from the city, accompanied by only one guard. **And here again appeared the grandeur of character which was instinctive with Napoleon. He sent the cross of the Legion of Honour as a reward to this man for his fidelity to the Barabon Prince. It was accompanied with the characteristics words:**

"I never leave a noble action without a reward."

And when the treacherous comrades presented themselves to the Emperor, tendering to him their services, he dismissed them with contempt saying:

"Your conduct towards the Count of Artois, sufficiently proves, how you would act by me, were fortune foresake me. I thank you for your offer. You will retire immediately to your homes."

The Barabons had been forced by foreign bayonets upon the army and the nation, and could claim from them no debt of loyalty. But the personal followers of the Prince were traitors to abandon him in misfortune.

❖ ❖ ❖

Here is an instance of the loyalty of Napoleon's soldier, and the generosity of the Czar Alexander Emperor of Russia.

Marshal Lefebvre had remained faithfully with Napoleon at Fountainbleau until after his abdication. He then went to Paris where he was presented to Alexander.

"You were not, then, under the walks of Paris" said the Czar Alexander "When we arrived?"

"No Sire", Lefebvre replied, "We had the misfortune to unable to reach here in time."

"The misfortune!" rejoined the Emperor Czar Alexander smilingly; "you are then sorry to see me here?"

"Sire" replied the honest and noble hearted Marshal, "I behold with **admiration a warrior who, in youth has learned to use victory with moderation, but it is with deepest grief that I see a conqueror within my country."**

"I respect your sentiment Monsieur Marshal", the Emperor Czar replied, "and they only add to my esteem for you."

❖ ❖ ❖

Aristotle drew of the magnanimous man two thousand years ago. He said "The magnanimous man will behave with moderation under both good fortune and bad. He will know how to be exalted and how to be abased. He will neither be delighted with success nor grieved by failure. He will neither shun danger nor seek it; for there are few things which comes for. He is reticent and somewhat slow of speech, but speaks his mind openly and boldly when occasion calls for it. He is apt to admire for, nothing is great to him. He overlooks injuries. He is not given to talk about himself or about others, for, he does not care that he himself should be praised or that other people should be blamed. He does not cry out about trifles and craves help from none." **Napoleon's life speaks of Aristotelian concept of magnanimity.**

It is therefore, the righteous cause, the determined man stands for. Everywhere, it is the main spring of what is called force of character and the sustaining power of all great actions. It is the strong and courageous man who leads and guides and rules the world. **Napoleon's** example is remembered and appealed to, and his thoughts, his spirit, his courage and his convict ions continue to inspire the succeeding generation. It is energy—the central element of which is the will—that produces miracles of enthusiasm in all ages.

He was no doubt *'Par Excellence!'*

His Views on the Right of Property

"What is the right of property?" It is not only the right of using, but again of abusing it.... One must always keep in mind the advantage of owning property. The best protection to the owner of property is the interest of the individual; one may always rely on his activity.... Legislation should favour the proprietor.... He must be allowed great freedom of action because whatever interferes with the use of property, displeases the citizens... A government makes a great mistake in trying to be too paternal—

Liberty and property are both ruined by over solicitude. If the government prescribes the way in which property should be used, it no longer exists. It is indispensable the courts should supervise, stop expropriation, receive complaints of, and guarantee property owners against the enterprises of our prefacts, our prefacture councils and all other agents—Expropriation is a judicial proceeding.

Napoleon's Views on Democracy

Democracy can succeed only where the great mass of the people is perpetually energized by self-confidence, self-respect, and hope. The people that falters is lost.

It is the bane of democracy that persuasive speakers come to the front too easily, leaving far behind, the sage administrator, the able man of action. That has been so from the age of Cleon onwards. True, that risks of this peculiar system are lessened by the permanent officials, the secret prompters of the political stage. Nevertheless, the fortunes of great people have been determined very largely by men whose first recommendation has been elegance; and only after sad experience has the balance turned in favour of the man of action.

As Bonaparte remarked, "One hundred men do nothing but talk, and three hundred nothing but vote without speaking a word. Futile dream of a mediocre intelligence.

By the same token, Sir Mohd. Iqbal—the great Indian philosopher viewed democracy as a system in which the heads are counted but not weight. In a satirical way, he wrote:

"Beware the system of democracy and follow the lead of men of ripe experience, because the brain of two hundred donkeys can not produce the understanding of one human being."

—Iqbal.

More than any other form of Government, democracy requires certain optimism concerning mankind. The best argument for democracy is, therefore, the existence of men who justify that optimism. It follows, therefore, that one of the best ways to serve 'democracy' is to be that kind of man. Unfortunately, people have very little knowledge or judgement or self-control, and are therefore, not fit to be trusted with the task of ruling themselves, not even with the task of choosing the rulers.

"A good government may indeed, redress the grievances of an injured people; but strong people can alone build up a great nation. To be strong, a people must be self-reliant, self-ruled and self-sustained. The dependence of one people upon another, even for the benefits of legislation, is the deepest source of national weakness."

—Napoleon.

Napoleon's Views on Religion

France during his days had been corrupt, and that her paramount needs was morality. But how could there be morality without religion? When Roederer ventured to suggest that religion must serve and not dominate the state, Bonaparte assented, adding these curious words.

"How can you have order in a state without religion?" Society can not exist without inequality of fortunes, which can not endure apart from religion. When one man is dying of hunger near another who is ill of surfeit, he can not resign himself to this difference, unless there is an authority which declares:

"God wills it thus": "there must be poor and rich in the world: but hereafter, and during all eternity the division of things will take place differently." Secondly, in every religious system, "discipline and rites" depend upon faith, for, it is faith alone which suggests or prescribes these; they are the outcome and expressions of this, it attains its ends through these, and manifests itself by them; they the exterior of which it is the interior, thus let these be affected, and it is in distress; the living, palpitating flesh suffers through the sensitive epiderm.

Although Bonaparte was born in the Catholic religion, he was not happy with Christianity "which set up a body, which divides the allegiance of the citizen, and may even oppose the government." "True Christianity", he said "tends to make men happy"; but so does the government, and "the two processes may clash". But we must admit that certain tendencies of the present age justify his forecast; for, the modern state seeks to regulate domains of life which formerly pertained solely to the church. His prophecy is, therefore remarkable.

At St. Helena he said to Gourgaud (8th June 1816)

"Everything proclaims the existence of a God: that is beyond a doubt; but all our religions are clearly the outcome of men. A man can swear to nothing that he will do in his last moments; yet undoubtedly my belief is that I shall die without a confessor, nevertheless there is one (pointing to one of us) who perhaps will confess me. Assuredly, I am far from being an atheist; yet I cannot believe all that is taught contrary to reason, without being dishonest and a hypocrite. Under the Empire, and particularly after the marriage with Marie Louise, very great efforts were made to induce me to go to Notre Dame in full state to receive the communion after the manner of our kings. I refused absolutely. My faith was not strong enough for it to be a benefit to me, and yet was too great to commit a sacrilege in cold blood... To know whence I come, what I am, whither I go, is beyond me; and yet all that is a reality. I am the watch that exists but does not understand itself... I can appear before God's tribunal, I can await His judgement without fear. He will not detect in me the idea of murder, poisoning, unjust or premeditated death so common in careers like mine. I willed only the glory, the power, the splendour of France. To that all my faculties, my efforts, my time were given. That could not be a crime. To me those efforts appeared a virtue."

During his campaign in Italy Bonaparte for a time desired to over throw the temporal power of the Papacy, because the church was hostile and meddling with the affair of the Government. He wrote to the General Rusca on 7th January 1797 from Milan. I reproduce the letter here.

TO GENERAL RUSCA

Milan, 7th January, 1797.

"Some unfortunate people have allowed themselves to be seduced by perfidious agents, who excite them to revolt and draw down upon them the horrors of war. You will march to Catelnovo and shoot the chief of the rebels, and send twenty hostages to Milan; you will destroy the house of the confessor of the Duke of Modena, who is the author of this rebellion, and on the ruins you will cause a pyramid to be erected with this inscription: Punishment of an infuriated priest who misused his position as a minister to preach revolt and assassination. You will assemble the magistrates, the heads of the various convents, and the cure's, and tell them from me that as long as they are animated by the true principles of religion, like Cardinal Mattei and the bishops of Modena and Pavia,

I shall respect them and their property; but if they become instruments of civil war, I shall have their convents destroyed, and I shall cause the cure's of revolted villages to be personally punished...

—Bonaparte

Again he wrote to The Archbishop of Genoa:

TO THE ARCHBISHOP OF GENOA

Passariano, 10th September, 1797.

"I have just received you pastoral letter of the 5th. I thought I was listening to one of the twelve apostles. It was thus that St. Paul spoke. How respectable is religion when it has ministers like you! True apostle of the Evangelists, you oblige your enemies to esteem and to admire you; you convert even the incredulous.

"How comes it that the Church which has a chief like you, should contain miserable Sabaltans who have neither charity nor peace?" And Napoleon went on to say that priests like these, with haggard eye, who preached revolt, murder and blood, who were paid with the gold of the rich, who betrayed the people like Judas, should be driven from the Church, which should call down upon them the anathemas and maledictions of Heaven. "The sovereignty of the people, liberty, this", said the General-in-Chief, " is the political code of Gospel."

—Bonaparte

Finally, Napoleon arrested the Pope and imprisoned him in Paris. However, Napoleon wanted to speedily settle affairs with Rome. With this intension, the emperor addressed a long letter to the captive Pope in which he said:—

"Most Holy Father—I send you the Bishops of Milan to inform you of my desire to see concord re-established between your Holiness and myself. I do not wish your Holiness to entertain any doubt with regard to my principles or my intentions. Your Holiness fargot the prenciples of justice and charity when you fulminated your bull of excommunication; it was to bless and strengthen thrones that Jesus Christ laid down His life. But this excommunication must have been obtained from you Holiness by surprise by wicked men. I appeal to the Church and to your Holiness, who is now better informed. I despise this and only consider it as the work of evil-doers and the enemies of religion. It is based too, upon false assertions. Not only have I not neglected to execute the Concordat, but, far from that, I have ameliorated more and more the situation of the Catholic religion, and every day I bless the God of our fathers for having selected me to restore His worship and His altars, and to cause Him to be honoured in France, Italy, Germany and Poland. Your Holiness also bases your excommunication on temporal reasons; and here I must acquaint you with all I think on this subject. In re-establishing worship in France, I desired to restore to my people true religion and the salutary influence of its spiritual chief, and not to re-establish the intolerable pretensions of Gregory VII. I intended to give my people a chief pastor, and not to subject them to a foreign sovereign. **My throne is from God, and I am accountable only to Him.** I recognize the spiritual power of your Holiness, but I will not, and cannot, recognize any temporal influence. The triple tiara is a monstrous production of pride ambition, entirely contrary to the humility of the Vicar of Christ. The irresistable passions of the persons who surround your Holiness would have done great harm, if God had no granted me calmness and the true knowledge of the sublime principles of our religion. Neither France, nor Italy will ever recognise the influence of a foreign sovereign, but they will always recognise the salutary authority of the Vicar of Jesus Christ, the chief pastor, having charge of souls, like St. Peter and the first Pontiffs. I execrate the principles of Julius, of Boniface, and Gregory, which caused half the Christian world to separate itself from the Catholic religion, and they are now rendering account to God for all the souls which were damned in consequence of their mad ambition. It is for your Holiness to choose; France and I have chosen. We desire the religion of St. Peter, of St. Paul, and of St. Bernard, founded on the principles of the Gallican Church. We recognise the principles and utility of the unity and influence of the Chair of St. Peter, the rock upon which Jesus Christ permitted His Church to be built, but we are determined not to submit to a sovereign who governs territory, men, and temporal matters. If your Holiness desires to preserve this temporal influence and to meddle with the affairs of the world; if you consider yourself the king of kings, we shall oppose you with the Scriptures, and shall look upon you as the enemy of religion; we shall appeal to a general council. If, on the contrary, your Holiness desires cnly the inheritance of Jesus Christ and of St. Peter; if you are satisfied with the care of souls; if you are animated with the true spirit of the Gospel; if you preach union and the principles of morality and charity, we are ready to be reconciled to you. If, like Jesus Christ, your Holiness considers that your Kingdom is not this world; if you have no other thoughts but those concerning another life, we shall recognise your spiritual authority, and support it with all the force of our sceptre, for we shall look upon it as the firmest support of our throne and of the prosperity of your people.

"We do not address your Holiness in dubious or insidious language. Religion is clear; Jesus Christ and His apostles preached it on the house-tops so that it might be known to all. Do you desire to be Pope, the Vicar of Jesus Christ, the successor of St. Peter? We shall receive you in triumph, and fold you in our arms. But if you are dominated by the pride and ostentation of the world, think that our throne ought to serve you as a footstool, and that we shall place our crown under the dust of your feet? We shall consider you only as the work of the demon; as spoiled by pride and worldly interest, and as the enemy of religion, of our throne, and of our people. **Your influence is powerful and your empire is great, when you remain within the limits traced by Jesus Christ: but your power becomes ridiculous and despicable when you wish to march with the potentates of the earth, surrounded by pride, menaces, and force.** You are nothing when your empire is of this world; you are everything when your empire is not of this world. But now Rome irrevocably forms part of my Empire, you have enough to do when confining yourself to spiritual affairs and the care of souls. My mission is to govern the West; do not meddle with me; and if your Holiness had been occupied with nothing else but the salvation of souls, the Church of Germany would not be in its present state of disorganisation. For a long time the Roman Pontiffs have meddled with matters which do not concern them, neglecting the true interests of the Church. **I recognise you for my spiritual chief, but I am your Emperor."**

Mohammedan Religion

On several occasions he declared that the morality of the Christian religion was merely that of Socrates and Plato. Sometimes he expressed doubts whether Jesus Christ ever existed; and he declared emphatically his preference of Mohammedanism to Christianity.

When he was in Egypt, he was fascinated by the Mohammedan religion. He attended the fete of the Prophet, and listened to the reading of several Arab poems in praise of the Prophet and the Koran, and said his prayers in the grand mosque of Cairo. He was called Sultan Kabir by the Ulema and Sheiks of Cairo.

He issued the following order:

ORDER

Cairo, 16th August, 1799.

"The commanders of the provinces will make known in an Arabic circular, to be sent to all the villages, the pomp with which the fete of the Prophet has been celebrated at Cairo. No celebration within the memory of man was so brilliant. All the troops in Cairo, lighted by a great number of torches, went to visit the Sheik El-Bekry. The General-in-Chief dined with him, as also Mustapha Pasha, and all the principal officers captured at Aboukir. The General-in-Chief was present at the reading of several Arab poems written in honour of the Prophet; after which, in the midst of the grand sheiks, he said prayers and heard the genealogy of the Prophet recited. The Pasha and the Turkish prisoners were overcome with surprise at the respect shown by the French for Islamism and the law of the most holy of Prophets.

—*Bonaparte.*

Here is another letter to General Marmont.

TO GENERAL MARMONT

Cairo, 28th August, 1798.

"I have received your letter of the 7th Fructidor. I flatter myself that you will be able to send us the greater portion of our artillery... You may remember our bàtteries of Toulon, and how little dangerous the English are by land. Artillery, with red-hot cannon balls, served with sand froid, is terrible against vessels.

"Our affair here are improving every day. Go and see the Sheik El-Messiri on my behalf; tell him among other things of the manner in which we celebrated the fete of the Prophet; that three of four times a day I hold conferences with the chiefs of the law and the principal Cherifs of Cairo, and that no one more than myself is persuaded of the purity and sanctity of the Mohammedan religion.

—*Bonaparte.*

At St. Helena, Napoleon's conversations were duly recorded by Gourgaud who was a devout Roman Catholic, one of the chief topics was religion.

On one occasion he reads up the books of Sammuel and Kings to see what is their testimony in favour of legitimate monarchy. But on other occasions the Bible is read with no such object; and he was, we are told, a great admirer of St. Paul. His thoughts, indeed, in this dark hour, turn much to questions of faith, not altogether to edification. We have, of course, often heard anecdotes in which he is represented as pointing to the firmament, and declaiming a vague Deism. Newman, too, in a noble passage, has given from tradition the final judgment passed on Christianity by Napoleon at St. Helena: wherein Napoleon is reported to have compared the shadowy fame of Caesar and Alexander with the living force of Christ, and to have summed up with, "Can he be less than divine?"

But the real Napoleon talked in very different fashion. Gourgaud talks of the stars and their Creator in the way attributed to Napoleon, but the latter snubs him. **"Briefly, Napoleon's real leaning seems to be to Mohammedanism.** His objection to Christianity is that it is not sufficiently ancient. Had it existed, he says, since the beginning of the world, he could believe it. But it had not; nor could it have sustained itself till now without the crucificaiton and the Crown of Thorns, for mankind is thus constituted, nor can he accept that form of religion which would damn Socrates, Plato, and he courteously adds the English: Why in any case punishment be eternal?" "Besides", he continued, "Mohammed conquered half the known world in ten years, a task which Christianity accomplished in three centuries, or again he declared his admiration to Mohammad in declaring a holy war. Moreover, he declares that he was much disturbed by the arguments of the Sheiks in Egypt, who contended that those who worshipped three deities must necessarily be pagans."

"Mahometanism on the other hand, is more simple; and, he characteristically adds, is superior to Christianity." Another time he declares Mahometanism to be the most beautiful of all religions. And once he even says "We Mahometans." (See Annexures V, VI, VII).

"But as he proceeds, he becomes more hostile to Christianity. "As for me," he breaks out on one occasion, "My opinion is that (the divine?) Christ never existed. He was put to death like any other fanatic who professed to be a prophet or a Messiah. There were constantly people of this kind. Then I look back from the New Testament to the old—I find one able man—Moses, but the Jews are cowardly and cruel." And he ends by returning to the Bible with a map and declaring that he will write the campaign of Moses.

So slight is his belief in **Christ** that he mentions as an extra-ordinary fact that Pope Pius VII did actually believe in Christ.

As a man, he proclaims himself a materialist. Sometimes he thinks that man was created in some particular temperature of the air, sometimes that he was produced from clay, "as Herodotus narrates that Nile mud was transformed into rats," that he was warmed by the sun, and combined with electric fluids. "Say what you like, everything is matter, more or less organised. When out hunting, I had the deer cut open, and saw that their interior was the same as that of man. A man is only a more perfect being than a dog or a tree, and living better. The plant is the first link in a chain of which man is the last. I know that this is all contrary to religion, but it is my opinion that we are all matter." Again: "What are electricity, galvanism, magnetism? In these lies the great secret of nature. Galavanism works in silence. I think myself that man is the product of these fluids and of the atmosphere, that the brain pumps up these fluids and imparts life, and that the soul is composed of these fluids, which after death return into the atmosphere, whence they are pumped into other brains." (Theory of evolution).

Again: "When we are dead my dear Gourgaud, we are altogether dead." What is a soul? Where is the soul of a sleeper or of a madman or of a babe?

Another time he breaks out: "Were I obliged to have a religion, I would worship the sun—the source of all life—the real God of the earth."

Often he is only thinking aloud in the bitterness of his heart—as when he says, that he cannot believe in a just God punishing and rewarding, for, good people are always unfortunate and scoundrels are always lucky: "Look at Talleyrand, he is sure to die in his bed."

Bertrand thinks, says Geourgaud, that the Emperor "has religion," and we certainly think that Napoleon was more religious than these conversation represent. But he had much lee-way to make up. He was the child of that Revolution which abjured religion. And yet there was strength in him to perform the most courageous acts of his life, the restoration of the French Church, the conclusion of the Concordat, and the compelling his scoffing companions in arms to follow him to Church.

Whatever may have been his motives, they must have been potent to make him break with the traditions of his man-hood. For religious faith had observance which still lurked timidly in the civil life of France, had disappeared from among its soldiers. "The French army at this time," says Count Lavalletee of the army of Egypt, "was remarkably free from any feeling of religion."

His life of camps, his revolutionary associations, his conflict with the Papacy, kept Napoleon aloof from the faith in which he was born. All that we can safely gather from his conversation at St. Helena, is that his mind turns greatly on these questions of religion.

He ponders and struggles. A remark which he lets fall at St. Helena explains probably his normal state of mind. "Only a fool," he says one day, "say that he will die without a religion. There is so much that one does not know, that one cannot explain." And as he spoke of the mysteries of religion, we may speak of his frame of mind with regard to them. "There is so much that one does not know, that one cannot explain."

Maulvi Abdul Karim in his book on "Prophet of Islam and his Teachings" (published in 1937 at Calcutta) had this to say, I quote from his book:

"Mr. Ripley—well-known throughout the world for his 'Believe it or not' series of films, who made a careful study of Napoleon's life stated in the 'Express' that he had no doubt, Napoleon in Egypt embraced Islam and lived and died a Muslim. In one of his despatches Napoleon wrote: "I hope the time is not far off when I shall be able to establish a uniform regime based upon the principles of Quran which alone are true and which alone can lead man to happiness." In an assembly of Savants, Governors and nobles at Cairo, Napoleon declared:—

"Surely I have told you on different occasions and I have intimated to you by various discourses that I am a unitarian Musalman and I glorify Prophet Mohammad." That Napoleon's profession of Islam was not a matter of political expediency as some people think, has been clearly shown by J. D. Jenkins in the course of a learned article on the 'Religious faith of Napoleon in which reference has been made to Napoleon's journal at St. Helena edited by General Gourgaud, who was a devout Roman Catholic."

In sum, the religious policy of Napoleon is confusing. His belief form an entrancing, though a difficult subject of enquiry. He was no doubt, a believer, but whether, he continued to remain a Roman Catholic or a Muhammadan seems very confusing. Basically, he was a Christian, but he strictly followed the Mohammadan belief; whether he embraced Islam or not requires a thorough research. He once said: "Religion is an affair of Conscience." However, it is immaterial whether he remained a Christian or a Muslim or a Sun worshipper or an Atheist. He was a great humanist who had thoughtfulness for others woes. He respected all religions and was concerned with the plight of the poor fellow human beings; and 'God loves those who love their fellow men'. His respect for values, his belief in the oneness of God, and his "throne accountable only to God alone" for what all he did, and his dedication to work, and his generosity towards the vanquished etc., are the qualities which pleases the Lord. He was therefore Great indeed. The Nineteenth century has not produced a like of him.

He was Par Excellence.

Conclusion

We may now pause before that splendid prodigy whose personality had its own magnificence.

A mind bold, independent and decisive—a strong will—an energy that distanced expedition, a conscience pliable to every touch of interest, marked the outline of this extra-ordinary character— the most extra-ordinary perhaps, that, in the annals of this world, ever rose or reigned or fell.

Flung into life, in the midst of a revolution that quickened every energy of a people who acknowledged no superior, he commenced his course, a stranger by birth and a scholar by charity!

With no friend but his sword, and no fortune but his talents, he rushed into the lists where rank and wealth, and genius had arrayed themselves, and competition fled from him as from the glance of destiny. He knew no motive but interest—he acknowledged no criterion but success—he worshipped no God but ambition, and with eastern devotion he knelt at the shrine of his idolatry.

At his touch, crowns crumbled, artisans reigned, humblest of the humble who had talents were raised to become Marshals and Dukes, the wildest theories took the colour of his whim, and all that was venerable, and all that was novel, changed placed with the rapidity of his drama. Even apparent defeat assumed the appearances of victory—His proclamations inspired his soldiers.

But if his fortune was great, his genius was transcendent; decisions flashed upon his counsels; and it was the same to decide and to perform. To inferior intellects, his combinations appeared perfectly impossible; his plans perfectly impracticable; but in his hands, simplicity marked their development, and success vindicated their adoption.

His person partook the character of his mind—if the one never yielded in the cabinet, the other never bent in the field. He said "God gave to me a mind which has not been mortgaged to the opinion of any person or set of persons: a mind I was to use and not to surrender."

Nature had no obstacles that he did not surmount—space no opposition that he did not spurn; and whether amidst Alpine rocks, Arabian sands, or Polar snows, he seemed proof against peril, and empowered with obiquity! The whole continent of Europe trembled at beholding his designs of unification, and the miracle of their execution. Skepticism bowed to the prodigies of his performances; romances assumed the air of history, nor was there aught too incredible for belief, or too fanciful for expectation, when the world saw a subaltern of Corsica waving his imperial flag over her most ancient capitals. All the visions of antiquity became common places in his contemplation; kings were his people—nations were his outposts; and he disposed of courts and crowns, and camps and churches, and Cabinets, as if they were titular dignitaries of the chess board. Because he believed in the equality of privileges and unification, he was just, fair and honest.

Cradled in the camp, he was to the last hour the Darling of the army; and whether in the camp or the cabinet, he never foresook a friend or forgot a favour. Of all his soldiers, not one abandoned him.

His affection of literature must not be omitted. He affected the patronage of letters—the proscribers of books, he encouraged philosophy and sent his academic prize to the philosopher of England.

His life, his fall, baffled all speculation. In short his whole history was like a dream to the world, and no man can tell how or why he was awakened from the reverie.

Such in short is the picture of Napoleon Bonaparte, the first and the last emperor of the French. Let the present day kings, Head of States and Governments learn from him the lesson that the interest of his people and the nation was supreme, and for the sake of his people and his country, he gave his life at St. Helena.— Supreme sacrifice indeed.

List of Readings

1. Abbot, Hoseph S.C., *The Life of Napoleon Bonaparte Ward.*, Lock & Co., London & Melbourne, 1897.
2. Adair, John, *Great leaders*, The Talbott Adair Press, Newlands, Pewley Hill Guild Ford, Surrey, England, 1989.
3. Arton, Guido, *Napoleon is dead in Russia*, Translated by Munial Prindrod, London. George Allen & Unwin Ltd., Ruskin House, 1970.
4. Balcombe (Mrs. Abell Betsey Balcombe), *Recollections of the Emperor Napoleon at St. Helena,* London, 1844.
5. Bingha, D.A., A Selection from letters and despatches of the First Napoleon in three volumes, Vol. I, II, & III, London, Chapman & Hall Ltd., 1884.
6. Browning, Oscar, *Napoleon the First Phase,* Some chapters on the boyhood, and youth of Bonaparte, 1769-1793. John Lane, The Bodlay Head, London, N. York, M.D. ccccr 1903.
7. Bryant, Arthur, *The Letter of Napoleon to Maria*—Lousia Hutchinson & Co. Publishers Ltd., London.
8. Bellschowskey, Albert, *The life of Goethe*, Vol. II.
9. Christopher, Herold, *Bonaparte in Egypt,* Hamirh Hamilton.
10. Conol O'Riordan, *Napoleon Passess.* Anaw Smith, London, 1933.
11. Calebo Alfred, *History of Modern France*, Vol. II, Janathan Cape, Thirty Bedford square, London, 1957.
12. Fisher H.A.L., *Napoleon*, Oxford University Press, London, 1912.
13. Geyl, Pieter, *Napoleon—For and Against.* New Haven, Yale University Press, 1949.

14. Gourgaud, Baron Gen. *St. Helena's Journal of Gourgaud, 1815-1818*, London, John Lane, The Bodley Head Ltd. (Being a diary written at St. Helena during a part of Napoleon's Captivity, England edition First published 1932.
15. Hassal, Arthur, *The Life of Napoleon, Matheun* & Co., 36, Essex St. W.I.C., London, 1911.
16. Henry, Lachoque, *The last days of Napoleon's empire from Waterloo to St. Helena,* Translated by Lovett F. Edwards, George Allen & Unwin Ltd., Ruskin House, London, 1965.
17.
Hotman, Robert B., *Napoleon's Propaganda*, Lousiana, Street University Press, Batan Rouge, 1950.
18. Macdonnel, A.J. *Napoleon and his Marshals*, McMillan & Co. Ltd., N.Y. St. Martin Press, 1960.
19. Maitland, *Narrative of Capt. Maitland*, New Ed., London, 1904.
20. Madelin, Louis, *The Consulate and the Empire,* Vol. I, 1789-1809, London, William Heineman & Co. Ltd., 1934 (Translated).
21. Madelin, Louis, *The Consulate and the Empire, 1809-1815*, Vol. II, Translated from E.F. Bucklay, London, William Haiman Ltd.
22. Mourois, Ande, *Napoleon*, Pictorial Biography, Thames and Hudson, London, 1963.
23. Nair, R.M.C. *Wilson, The Mind of Napoleon*. (A study of Napoleon, Roosvelt and the money power), Gerore Routledge & Sons, London, 1931.
24. Naylor, John, *Waterloo*, London, B.T. Batsford Ltd., 1960.
25. Plutarch, *Plutarch's Lives of Themistocles, Pericles, Aristides, Acibiades, Coriolams, Demosthenes and Cicero, Ceasar and Antony,* The Harvard Classics Gorolives Enterprises Co., Danbury, Connecticut 1909.
26. Rabiquet, Jean, *Daily Life in France under Napoleon*. Translated French George, Allen & Unwin, London, 1962.
27. Rose J., Holland, *Life of Napoleon*, Vol. I, London, George Sell & Co., 1903.
28. Rose, J. Holland, *Memoirs of Lord Keith,* 1904, Napoleonic Studies, London, 1906.
29. Rose, Holland J., *The Personality of Napoleon*, London, Bell & Sons Ltd., 1929.

30. Roserbery, Lord, *Napoleon—the Last Phase*, Arthur & Humphrey's London, 1900.
31. Saunders, Edith, *The Hundred Days,* Longmans, 1964.
32. Shorter, Clemant, *Napoleon in his Defence,* Cassel & Co. Ltd., London, N.Y. 1910.
    (Being the reprint of certain letters written by Napoleon from St. Helena to Lady Clavering, and a reply by Theodore Hook Cassel & Co., London, 1910.
33. Strokoe, Dr. John, *Memoirs of Dr. John Strokoe*, Naval Surgeon. Translated from French of Paul, Count by Edith S, Strokoe, John Lane, The publisher Bodley Head, London and N.York, 1905.
34. Taina, H.A., *Modern Regime*, Translated from French by John Durand, Vol. Samson Ltd., Marston Searle & Rivinston Ltd., Fleet Street, 89, London, 1891.
35. Usher Sir Thomas, *Napoleon Last Voyages* (Being the Diaries of Admiral Usher on board, the 'Undaunted' and John. R. Gloves. Secretary to the Rear Admiral Cockburn on board the 'Northemberland' London, T. Fisher, Unwin Adelphin Terrace, MCM VI.
36. Vachee, Col. and Frederic Lees, Napoleon at work, Translated from the French by Frederik Lees, London Adam & Charge, Black, 1914.
37. Violet, M. McDonnel, *Daily Life of Napoleon*. Translated Ruskin House, George, Allen & Unwin, Ltd., Museum St., London, 1962.
38. Wilson, McNair R., *The Mind of Napoleon. A study of Napoleon, Roosevelt and the money power.* George Routledge and Sons Ltd., Broad Way House, Caster Lane, E.C., London, 1931.
39. Le Petit Homme Rouge, *Court of the Tuileries 1852-70,* Translated. London, Chatto & Winders, 1907.
40. Jervis, W.H., A History of France from the Earliest times to the fall of the second empire in 1870, revised and rewritten by Arthur Hassalls, London, John Murray, Alberamalie, St. W.I. 1918.
41. Thomas Carlyle, The French Revolutions, A History, Vol. I & II, London, J.M. Dent & Co. Everyman's library edited by Ernest Rhys., 1906.

Annexure-I

Reasons for Napoleon's Leaving Elba

Why Napoleon left Elba to join his people in France after his abdication? The reason being, it was agreed in the Treaty of abdication to Elba that he would receive an income on the Great Book of France of two million Francs; that his family should receive an income of two million and a half Francs; that his son should have as his inheritance the Duchies of Parma, Pia Cenza, and Guastalle, and should at once assume the title of Prince of these states. Not one of these stipulations which were the compensation for his abdication, had been observed when Napoleon left Elba. Neither he, nor his relatives ever received a Franc. Although the emperors of Russia and Austria, as well as Castlereagh of England urged Talleyram the execution of the Treaty. They insisted on it as a question of honour and good faith. To them Talleyrand could answer confusedly that there was danger in supplying what might be used as the means of intrigue. It is a tale of ignominy and broken faith, but neither lie with Napoleon. The application on his behalf for the payment of subsidy when due was not even answered by the French Government. Napoleon at St. Helena detailed no less than ten capital and obvious breaches of this treaty committed by the Allies. The Barabons who were in power in France were made it a policy to drive 'Napoleon to some act of despair. His family was plundered.' Not only the stipulated income not paid to him, but the ministry boasted of the breach of faith. Projects for his assassination were formally considered. It was the Allies, and not Napoleon that broke the Treaty of Fountainbleau. That, on the contrary, he himself observed the Treaty until, on its non fulfilment being flagrant, he quited Elba–rather he was starved out of Elba.

On the 26th of February 1815 Napoleon embarked on board his own armed Corvette, 'The Inconstant' with 400 grenadiers of his guard, commanded by his faithful generals Drouet, Bertrand and Cambranne. Some of the small vessels followed, conveying troops collected in Corsica and elsewhere, the whole amounting to about 1000 men. On the 1st of March 1815 Napoleon landed on the beach—a short distance from the town of Cannes. On the 7th of March 1815, he encountered for the first time detachment of the Royal troops, which threatened to bar his passage at the small town at La Mura. The emperor advanced alone, with a firm and calm countenance, to the head of the column, and exclaimed in a loud voice, "Soldiers, if there is one among you who desires to kill his general—his Emperor, he can do so here I am!" The effect of his words and presence was electrical; the soldiers joyfully thronged around him, fraternized with their Comrades of his guard, and marched with him to Grenoble. From that place to Lyons his march was a continued triumph.

Marshal Navy proffered his services to their king, and on being, placed in command of a 'Corps d' armee' assembled at Besancon, had engaged to bring back the Corsican to Paris in an iron cage. But a personal appeal from the Emperor, awakened all the Marshals most cherished and flattering reminiscences; he forgot his oaths and promises to Louis XVIII the king, and rejoined his ancient Sovereign on the 17th of March at Auxere. His troops instantly followed his example, and that success of Napoleon's enterprise was assured. The king having issued a proclamation, quitted the Palace in the night between 19th and 20th March, and made his way under the protection of his household troops to Lilla, and afterwards to Ghent where he remained during the brief period of Napoleon's second reign. The emperor entered Paris in the evening of 20th having thus accomplished his perilous undertaking without encountering the smallest serious opposition, or shedding a single drop of French blood. His reception at the Tuileries was a scene defying all description. He was literally carried up to the grand staircase in the arms of his excited followers, into the state apartments, were a vast and brilliant crowd of all the notabilities of the empire had assembled to welcome him. Thus, during their return from Elba, the full extent of his strength was made manifest. **Even his enemies recognized that his throne had been built upon the hearts of his people. The Pope himself came to Paris and consecrated the new emperor at a moment when coalition of all the European powers (viz.) Austria, England, Prusia, Russia etc. was being formed for his destruction.**

Napoleon, at St. Helena said (Gourgaud reporting), that had the stipulated income been paid, he could have kept **Open house for the learned men of Europe, for whom he would have formed a centre. He would have built a Palace for them, and led a country house life, surrounded by men of mark.** He would, too have enriched the island by throwing open its little ports.

It is all destiny.

Annexure-II

Captain Maitland*

Napoleon Bounaparte, when he came on board the *Bellorophon,* on the 15th of July 1815, wanted exactly one month of completing his forty-sixth year, being born the 15th August 1769. He was then a remarkably strong, well-built man, about five feet seven inches high, his limbs particularly will formed, with a fine ankle and very small foot, of which he seemed rather vain, as he always wore while on board the ship, silk stockings, and shoes. His hands were also very small, and had the plumpness of a woman's rather than the robustness of a man's. His eyes light grey, teeth good: and when he smiled, the expression of his countenance was highly pleasing; when under the influence of disappointment, however, it assumed a dark gloomy cast. His hair was of a very dark brown, nearly approaching to black, and though a little thin on the top and front, had not a grey hair amongst it. His complexion was a very uncommon one, being of a light sallow colour, differing from almost any other ever met with. From his having become corpulent, he had lost much of his personal activity, and if we are to give credit to those who attended him, a very considerable portion of his mental energy was also gone... His general appearance was that of a man rather older than he, then was. His manners were extremely pleasing and affable, and endeavoured, in every way, to promote good humour: he even admitted his attendants to great familiarity, and I

*Captain of the ship 'the Bellorophon'.

saw one or two instances so their contradicting him in the most direct terms, though they generally treated him with much respect. He possessed, to a wonderful degree, a facility in making a favourable impression upon those with whom he entered into conversation: this appeared to me to be accomplished by turning the subject to matters he supposed the person he was addressing was well acquainted with, and on which he could show himself to advantage.

Annexure-III

Bathurst

Lord Roseberry in his book 'Napoleon—the last phase (London, Arthur L. Humphreys. 1900)' in the Chapter IX under the Caption 'Lord Bathurst' clearly states the wickedness of the ministers of the British Government for sending Napoleon on exile to St. Helena, although the people of Great Britain and the opposition leaders like Lord Holland and the Duke were raising protests at the House of Commons regarding the treatment of Napoleon at St. Helena. The common man of Britain was all praise and love for Napoleon.

Napoleon said: **"I have however, no longer to learn that it is not fair to judge of a people by the conduct of the Government."**

I herewith reproduce the whole Chapter IX under the Caption 'Bathurst' from Lord Rose berry's Book 'Napoleon—the last phase which is self-explanatory.'

Lord Bathurst

"Nothing," wrote the Russian Commissioner to his Government after nearly three years' experience at St. Helena, "Can be more absurd, more impolite, less generous and less delicate than the conduct of the English to Napoleon." It would not be fair or just, however, to debit Lowe or Cockburn with the responsibility for these ignominies, or for the general principle of the Emperor's treatment. They were only the somewhat narrow and coarse agents of a sordid and brutal policy. It was the British Ministry which was answerable jointly and severally for the treatment of Napoleon; and which, strangely enough, was equally condemned by the partisans of Lowe. "Worst of all," says the governor's most efficient advocate, "... was the conduct of the British Government, which, viewed in itself, was utterly undignified: viewed from Sir Hudson Lowe's standpoint was unfair and teacherous." When, however, we remember who and what these ministers were we cease to marvel. Vandal, in one of the most eloquent passage to his noble history, points out that the eventual victory of Great Britain over Napoleon was the victory of persistency over genius. "The men who governed in London, flung by the illness of George III into a chaos of difficulties, placed between a mad King and a discredited Regent, exposed to the virulent attacks of the Opposition, to the revolt of injured interests, to the complaints of the City, face to face with a people without bread and with on almost ruined commerce... sometimes despair of even maintaining Wellington at Lisbon. But in their extreme peril, none of them think of yielding—of asking or even accepting peace—or of sacrificing the British cause or British pride." Rarely, he continues, have men displayed more admirable proofs of cool and obstinate courage. **"Yet, who are these men? Among them there is not a single minister of great renown, of a glorious past, of a superior intelligence.** The successors of Pitt... have only inherited his constancy, his tenacity, his hatred. But knowing that they bear the destinies of their country and of the world , they derive from that consciousness a virtue of energy and patience which makes them equal to the greatest." **Liverpool, Eldon, Bathurst, Castlereagh, and Sidmouth were men whose names can scarcely be said to glow in history.** They had, however, felt doggedly that they must fight it out to the bitter end; and, supported throughout by the victories of their navy and the grim patience of their people, as well as, lately, by military success, had pulled through and emerged victorious. **But victory had not taught them magnanimity.** They had caught their great enemy: their first wish was to get somebody else to shoot him or hang him: failing which, they were determined to lock him up like a pickpocket. All that they saw clearly was that he had cost them a great deal of trouble and a great deal of money, so that he must cost them as little more as possible. They were honest men acting up to their lights: **We can only regret that the men were dull and the lights were dim.**

The Minister charged with carrying out this policy was Lord Bathurst, Secretary of State for the joint department of War and the Colonies.

Who was Bathurst?

It is difficult to say, he was, we know, grandson of that secular Lord Bathurst, who, sixty years after his first elevation to the peerage was created an Earl, and in who, in the last months of his life, in his ninety-first year, was the subject of a famous apostrophe by Burke. He was, we know, son of that second Lord Bathurst, who was the least capable of Chancellors. He himself was one of those strange children of our political system who fill the most dazzling offices with the most complete obscurity. He had presided over the Foreign Office. He was now, and was for a term of fifteen years, a Secretary of State. Yet even our most microscopic Biographical Dictionary may be searched in vain for more than a dry recital of the offices that he filled, the date of his birth, and the date of his death.

He was now in charge of Napoleon. He tersely instructed Lowe, that the Emperor was to be treated till further orders as a prisoner of war, but that he was to be allowed **"every indulgence which may be consistent with the entire security of his person."** He then passed through Parliament an act of Draconian but perhaps necessary severity. **Any British subject who should assist in Napoleon's escape, or, after his escape, assist him on the high seas, was to be punished with death without benefit of clergy.** Lowe, by the bye, used to allude to this act in delicate raillery of the Commissioners. "After all, I cannot hang you," he would say. Meanwhile Bathurst was tightening the screw. £8000 was to be the limit of Napoleon's expenditure on table and household; he was to pay all his own followers and servants, and the household was at once to be reduced by the magical number of four: no names or degree were specified, so that it was clearly an economy of four mouths that was aimed at. The remainder were to be persuaded to leave him, as their residence in the island added greatly to the expense. It may be presumed, therefore, that the "indulgence, consistent" after all, "with the entire security of his person"—of intercourse with few fellow-countrymen and of the attendance of his old servants was to be, if practicable, withdrawn. Lowe moreover, was to draw the bonds more straitly than Cockburn. No communication was to reach Napoleon except through Lowe. The fecility accorded to Bertrand by the Admiral of giving cards of admission which would enable visitors to Napoleon to pass the sentries was withdrawn. A declaration was to be signed by all the French courtiers and servants of the Emperor that they would submit to all regulations imposed on their master, and so forth. He attached great importance to enclosing Napoleon in a sort of area railing which he despatched from England, and which should add the final precaution to security. "We consider it," he writes, "a very essential point particularly until the iron railing shall arrive, to ascertain, late in the evening and early in the morning, that he is safe." But it seems to have been found inexpedient to carry constraint too far. For the interest in the captive was intense. Every scrape of news from St. Helena was eagerly devoured by the public. The craving for each fragment of intelligence was so great, that is was scarcely possible to preserve from the avidity of the press the most private letters written from St. Helena. A lad who came from there in 1817 narrates how, on landing at Portsmouth, persons of all ranks seemed ready to tear the passengers in pieces for information about the captive. And, as soon as they reached the hotel, strangers brought portraits of Napoleon to have the likeness attested. Warden's worthless book was for the same reason extremely popular. Santini's not less worthless book was not less popular. It went through seven editions in a fortnight. So, at least, its author declares.

The opposition leader, Lord Holland, too, raised in the House of Lords a debate on the treatment of Napoleon. And from his time forth there reigns a blender tone in the regulations of Bathurst. His next letter to Lowe, written a month after the debate, is couched in a spirit that may almost be deemed urbane. "You may assure him of your disposition to make his situation more comfortable by a supply of the publications of the day... I think it right also to add that there exists in this country no indisposition to allow his, the gratification of the table—more especially of wine." And later on in the same year he expands the limit of even $12,000 a year, if that sum be inadequate for "such an establishment as would be requisite for a general officer of distinction." (Napoleon, it will be observed, has gradually risen from a "general not in employ" to "a general officer of distinction").

Bathurst seems to have been in all respects as worthy of Lowe, as Lowe of Bathurst, and to both there was a common standard of tact and taste. Take the following specimen. Rats are the curse of St. Helena, and on this subject the Secretary of State writes to the Governor: "You will also receive a private letter from Mr. Goulburn on the great inconvenience to which he (Napoleon) is said to be exposed by the quantity of rats with which his house is infested. There is something so ludicrous in a fallen leader's complaint on such a subject, and is one so little in unison with the animal's alleged sagacity, that it is not a topic likely from choice to be brought forward as a grievance: but the number of these animals may amount to be a real one; and though I have reason to believe that the increase is owing to the negligence of his servants," in which he is very willing to encourage them, "yet it is fit on every account that the subject should be examined and a proper remedy applied." We cannot call to mind any complaint of Napoleon's on the subject, though his house was overrun with these disgusting vermin. But the graceful allusions of the Secretary of State which we have italicised lose none of their point from this circumstances: though he may be held to be going a little far when he hints that the Emperor, always scrupulously dainty in such things, wilfully encouraged the negligence of his servants in order to promote the increase of rats.

When Napoleon is dying, Bathurst touches a note which is almost sublime. "If he be really ill," writes the Secretary of State, "he may derive some consolation by knowing that the repeated accounts which have of late been transmitted of his declining health have not been received with indifference. You will therefore communicate to General Bonaparte the great interest which His Majesty has taken in the recent accounts of his indisposition, and the anxiety which His Majesty feels to afford him every relief of which his situation admit. You will assure General Bonaparte that there is no alleviation which can be derived from additional medical assistance, nor any arrangement consistent with the safe custody of his person at St. Helena (and His Majesty cannot now hold out any expectation of his removal) which His Majesty is not most anxious to afford," and so forth. The force of Bathurst could no further go. Fortunately before this precious effusion was received at St. Helena, its prisoner was where the sympathy of George IV, strained through Bathurst, could not reach him. Scott thinks that it would have been solace to him. Comment on such an opinion seems unnecessary.

The whole correspondence, so far as we know it, is sordid and pitiful enough. Making all allowances for the cost and exhaustion of the war and for the natural anxiety that the great disturber of peace should not escape, it appears, to us, at the end of the century in which it passed, a humiliating compound of meanness and panic. But the responsibility for this ignominious episode, this policy of petty cheeseparing and petty police, must rest not with the instruments, but with the principals; with the Liverpools and Bathursts at home, not with the Cockburns and Lowes at St. Helena: although the Ministers, as we have seen, tried to dissociate themselves from the sinister reputation of Lowe by extending a conspicuously cold shoulder to him on his return.

Annexure-IV

Proclamations of Napoleon

(i)

To the Army in Italy*

(1796)

Born in 1769, died in 1821; served in Corsica and Toulon in 1793; went to Italy in 1794: to Egypt in 1798; executed coup d'etat of Brumaire in 1799, won the Battle of Marengo in 1800; made Counsul for life in 1802; Emperor in 1804; won the Battle of Austerlitz in 1805, Jena and Friedland in 1807; fled from Moscow in 1812; lost the Battle of Leipsig in 1813; abdicated April 11, 1814; escaped from Elba in February 1815; defeated at Waterloo in June, 1815, exiled to St. Helena in October of the same year.

Soldiers, you have, in fifteen days, gained six victories, taken twenty-one stand of colours, fifty pieces of cannon, several fortified palaces, made fifteen hundred prisoners, and killed or wounded over ten thousand men. You are the equals of the conquerors of Holland and of the Rhine.

Destitute of everything, you have supplied yourselves with everything. You have won battles without cannon, crossed rivers without bridges, made forced marches without shoes, bivouacked without spirituous liquor, and often without bread. The Republican

---

* Delivered early in May, 1796, or soon after he had taken command in Italy. He had relieved Schere in March. The Battle of Lodi was won a few days later (May 10), and Arcote on November 15-17. Napoleon's speeches, with a few exceptions, were proclamations; but in form and spirit, they were orations. This speech was translated "by a member of the New York Bar, "for Cormenin's "Eminent Orators of France.".

phalanxes—the soldiers of liberty, were alone capable of enduring what you have suffered.

Thanks to you, soldiers! Your country has a right to expect of you great things. You have still battles to fight, cities to take, rivers to pass. Is there one among you whose courage flags? One who would prefer returning to the sterile summits of the Apennines and the Alps, to undergo patiently the insults of that slavish soldiery? No, there is not one such among the victors of Montenotte, of Millesimo, of Diego, and of Mondovi!

(ii)
To the Army of Italy Again*
(1796)

Soldiers! You have precipitated yourselves like a torrent from the Apennines. You have overwhelmed or swept before you all that opposed your march. Piedmont, delivered from Austrian oppression, has returned to her natural sentiments of peace and friendship toward France. Milan is yours, and overall Lombardy floats the flag of the Republic.

To your generosity only do the Dukes of Parma and of Modena now owe their political existence. The army which proudly threatened you finds no remaining barrier of defence against your courage. The Po, the Tessino, the Adda, could not stop you a single day. Those vaunted ramparts of Italy proved insufficient; you traversed them as rapidly as you did the Apennines. Success so numerous and brilliant have carried joy to the heart of your country! Your representatives have decreed a festival, to be celebrated in all the communes of the Republic, in honor of your victories. There will your fathers, mothers, wives, sisters, all who hold you dear, rejoice over your triumphs, and boast that you belong to them.

Yes, soldiers, you have done much, but much still remains for you to do. Shall it be said of us that we knew how to conquer,

---

* Delivered on May 15, 1796, a few days after the battle of Lodi. The translation was made for "Sargent's Standard Speaker" (1932).

but not to profit by victory? Shall posterity reproach us with having found a Capua in Lombardy? Nay, fellow soldiers! I see you already eager to cry "To arms!" Inaction fatigues you! and days lost of glory are to you days lost to happiness.

Let us, then, begone! We have yet many forced marches to make, enemies to vanquish, laurels to gather and injuries to avenge! Let those who have sharpened the poniards of civil war in France, who have pusillanimously assassinated our ministers, who have burned our vessels at Toulon—let them now tremble! The hour of vengeance has knolled! But let not the people be disquieted. We are the friends of every people: and more especially of the descendants of the Brutuses, the Scipios, and other great men to whom we look as bright exemplars. To reestablish the Capital; to place there with honor the statues of the heroes who made it memorable; to rouse the Roman people, unnerved by many centuries of oppression—such will be some of the fruits of our victories. They will constitute an epoch for posterity.

To you, soldiers, will belong the immortal honor of redeeming the fairest portion of Europe. The French people free and respected by the whole world, shall give to Europe a glorious peace, which shall indemnify it for all the sacrifices which it has borne the last six years. Then, by your own firesides you shall repose; and your fellow citizens, when they point out any one of you, shall say; "He belonged to the army of Italy!"

(iii)
Speech of the Directory*
(1797)

Citizens, the French people, in order to be free, had kings to combat. To obtain a Constitution founded on reason, it had the prejudices

---

* Delivered on December 10, 1797, soon after his arrival in Paris, victorious from Italy and bringing the Treaty of Campo Formio. The Moniteur of Paris, in its report of this speech, said the speaker's "sample and modest countenance contrasted with his great reputation." According to St. Amand, the speech "delivered in a jerky voice with a tone of command, produced a deeper impression that would have done the voice of the most famous orators of the century." The translation was made for Theirs' "History of the French Revolution."

of eighteen centuries to overcome. The constitution of the year 3 and you have triumphed over all obstacles. Religion, feudalism, royalty have successively for twenty centuries past governed Europe; but from the peace which you have just concluded dates the era of republican Governments.

You have succeeded in organizing the great nation whose vast territory is circumscribed only because Nature herself has fixed its limits. You have done more. The two finest countries in Europe, formerly so renowned for the arts, the sciences, and the great men whose cradle they were, see with the greatest hopes, genius and freedom issuing from the tomb of their ancestors. These are two pedestals on which the destinies are about to place two powerful nations.

I have the honor to deliver to you the treaty signed at Campo Formio, and ratified by his majesty, the emperor. Peace insures the liberty, prosperity, and the glory of the Republic. When the happiness of the French people shall be seated on better organic laws, all Europe shall become free.

(iv)
During the Egyptian Campaign*
(1798)

Soldiers, you are a wing of the army of England! You are master of the modes of warfare appropriate to mountains, to plains, to sledges. Naval war remains to complete your experience. The Roman legions whom you have sometimes imitated, but not as yet equalled, fought Carthage successively upon this sea and upon the plains of Zama. Victory never forsook them, because they were constantly brave, patient of fatigue, well disciplined, resolute. But, soldiers, Europe has her eyes upon you! You have great destinies to fulfil, battles to fight, fatigues to surmount!

* Translated "by a member of the New York Bar."

Frenchmen, you are about to undertake a conquest of which the effects upon the civilization and commerce of the world are incalculable. The first city you are to meet was founded by Alexander.

Cadis, Sheiks, Imams, Chorbadgys, you will be told that I came to destroy your religion; do not believe it. Let your answer be that I come to re-establish your rights and punish your usurpers, and that I have more respect than the Mamelukes for your God, His Prophet, and the Koran.

Tell your people that all men are equal before God. Wisdom, talent, and virtue make the only difference between them.

But, is there a fine country? It is appropriated by the Mamelukes. Is there a beautiful slave, a fine horse, a fine house? All this belongs to the Mamelukes. If Egypt be their farm, let them show the lease which God has given them of it! But God is just and merciful to the people. The Egyptians will be called to fill the public stations. Let the wisest, the most enlightened, the, most virtuous govern, and the people will be happy.

You had formerly large cities, great canals, a flourishing commerce. What has ruined them all if not the avarice, the injustice, and the tyranny of the Mamelukes?

Cadis, Sheiks, Imams, Chorbadgys, tell the people that we, too, are true Mussulmans. Is it not we who demolished the Pope, the great enemy of the Mussulmans? Are we not the friends of the grand seignior?

Thrice happy those who shall be found on our side! They will prosper in fortune and rank. Happy those who shall remain neutral! They will have time to know the result, and then will join us.

But woe, eternal woe, to those who take arms in favour of the Mamelukes and fight against us! There will be no hope for them; they will perish!

Sheiks, Ulema, believers of Mohammad, make known to the people that those who have been enemies to me will find no refuge either in this world or the other. Is there a man so blind as not to see that Destiny itself directs my operations.*

(v)

On the Anniversary of Austerlitz**
(1806)

Soldiers, it is this day a year ago, at this very hour, that we were upon the memorable plain of Austerlitz. The Russian battalion fled appalled. Their allies are no more. Their fortresses, their capitals, their magazines, their arsenals, two hundred and eighty stand of colours, seven hundred field-pieces, five grand strongholds are in our power.

The Oder, the Wasta, the Polish deserts, the inclement weather, nothing has been able to arrest your course—all have fled before you. The French eagle hovers over the Vistula. The brave and unfortunate Poles imagine they behold again the legations of Sobieski.

Soldiers, we shall not lay down our arms until a general peace has restored to our commerce, its freedom and its colonies. We have conquered on the Elba and the Oder, Pondichery, our Indian establishments, the Cape of Good Hope, and the Spanish colonies. Who should give the Russians the hope of balancing the destinies? Are not they and we the soldiers of Austerlitz?

---

* Napoleon's famous remarks at the Pyramids was not part of any of these speeches. As theirs relates the incident, the army on its march suddenly came within sight of "the gigantic Pyramids gilded by the sun," and then "halted as if seized with curiosity and admiration." With his face "beaming with enthusiasm," Napoleon "began to gallop before the ranks of the soldiers," and pointing to the Pyramids exclaimed "consider that from the summits of these Pyramids forth centuries have their eyes fixed upon you." Theirs given only these words.

** Translated "by a member of the New York Bar."

(vi)

To His Soldiers At Fontainebleau*

(1814)

Soldiers, I bid you farewell. For twenty years that we have been together your conduct has left me nothing to desire. I have always found you on the road to glory. All the powers of Europe have combined in arms against me.

A few of my generals have proved untrue to their duty and to France. France herself has desired other destinies; with you and the brave men who still are faithful, I might have carried on a civil war; but France would be unhappy. Be faithfull then to your new king, be obedient to vour new commanders, and desert not our beloved country.

Do not lament my lot. I will be happy when I know that you are so. I might have died; if I consent to live, it is still to promote your glory. I will write the great things that we have achieved.

I can not embrace you all, but I embrace your general. Come, General Petit, that I may press you to my heart! Bring me the eagle, that I may embrace it also. Ah: dear eagle, may this kiss which I give thee find an echo to the latest posterity! Adieu, my children; the best wishes of my heart shall be always with you: do no forget me!

(vii)

After the Return from Elba**

(1815)

Soldiers, behold the officers of battalion who have accompanied me in my misfortune: they are all my friends; they are dear to my heart. Every time I saw them, they represented to me the several regiments of the army. Among these six hundred brave men, there

---

* Spoken at the Tuileries the day after his arrival. Translated "by a member of the New York Bar."

** Spoken at the Tuileries, the day after his arrival. Translated "by a member of the New York Bar."

are soldiers of every regiment; all brought me back those great days whose memory is so dear to me, for all were covered with honourable scars received in those memorable battles. In loving them, it is you all, soldiers of the French army, that I loved.

They bring you back these eagles, let them be your rallying-point. In giving them to the Guard, I give them to the whole army. Treachery and untoward circumstances had wrapped them in shroud, but, thanks to the French people and to you, they reappear resplendant in all their glory. Swear that they shall always be found when and wherever the interest of the country may call them! Let the traitors and those who would invade our territory, be never able to endure their gaze.

Annexure-V

St. Helena, May 12th, 1821*

Before this letter can reach you, you will have heard that Bonaparte died on the evening of the 5th inst. This event has produced no small sensation here. For some weeks past, it was known that he was indisposed, but on the morning of the 4th I was thunderstruck on being abruptly told by Sir Hudson Lowe that Bonaparte was dying. On the night of the 5th I received a notification from the governor that dissolution had taken place and that my attendance was desired at Longwood the following morning at 6 o'clock precisely to view the body. I was overtaken on the road about daybreak by the governor and his staff, and in a short time we were joined by the Marquis de Montchenu, Admiral Lambert, General Coffin, Mr. Greentree, some of the captains of the navy, the commanding officer of artillery, and the head of the commissariat department; six medical gentlemen were also in attendance. Our whole party, consisting of about twenty persons, was ushered into the room where the body was laid. The only alteration I could observe in the face since I had seen it in life was that it was not quite so full, but a fine face I never saw. The expression was calm, and placid, and a crucifix was deposited on the breast, and in adjoining room was an altar with decorations and his priest; upon a table near the foot of the bed stood a picture of young Napoleon and on another table a bust. The bedstead was the same one he had used in his campaigns. After remaining long enough to be perfectly

---

* Letter from Mr. T.H. Brooke from St. Helena after Napoleon's Death

satisfied as to the identity of the corpse we withdrew. In the afternoon of the same day it was publicly announced that the body might be seen by any respectable person between the hours of 4 and 6, and amongst the crowds who were eager to avail themselves of the sight were Mrs. Brooke, Agnes, Captain Power, and myself a second time. Some new arrangements had taken place since the morning. The body had been removed to another chamber hung and floored with black cloth. At the head of the room stood the altar highly decorated. Over the body was suspended a glass chandelier, and the priest stood on one side near the head, and on the other side was Count Bertrand.

Madame Bertrand and her daughter stood next the priest, and Count Montholon was at the foot of the corpse which was dressed in the full uniform of the French National Guards, the hat, boots, and spurs on, and the sword lying by left side. The crucifix was still on the breast, the hands were exposed to view, and so uncommonly beautiful as to be the subject of general remark, and sometimes even of exclamation. The face had sunk since I had seen it in the morning, but still retained its placid expression, and had acquired somewhat the appearance of a smile. We bowed respectfully to the French party as we approached the corpse, and the salutation was returned in a solemn but very affable manner, and our exit was made through a different door to make way for the crowd that was pressing in. During the day the body had been opened and the intestines taken out. After 6 that evening such of the soldiers as desired were permitted to see it, and during several hours the following day all restrictions were removed from those who had any curiosity, and I understand that the French people were rather gratified at the numbers who crowded for the purpose. His death, I understand, was caused by ulcers of a cancerous nature in his stomach. He said his father had died of the same disorder.

He was aware of his situation, and appeared quite sensible although speechless the morning he died. He lay quietly on his back. At one time his hands were observed tremulously approaching each other and as soon as the fingers touched he clasped them together, and remained some time in that position. He has made a will. The 10th instant was fixed for his burial, the spot for which was one he had mentioned as the place he should desire to be laid in were he to be interred here. You may recollect a cottage that belonged to led Sampell in a valley between the Hutt's gate and Dr. Kay's house. It is in sight of the road leading to Longwood, an is the property of Torbett, the shopkeeper. A little above this cottage is a remarkable fine spring of water, shaded by willow trees, and it was from thence that water was daily supplied in two silver vases for the special use of Bonaparte. Here men were employed night and day in excavating a tomb eleven feet deep faced with masonry.

At ten in the morning of the 10th, the troops formed on one side of the road from Longwood gate, nearest to which was the 20th Regiment forming the right of the line, next the marines of the fleet, on their left again was posted the 66th Regiment, and on the left line the St. Helena volunteers. About half a mile farther on the Royal Artillery, were posted with eleven field pieces, the whole of the troops under arms mustering about 1,800 men. At 12 o'clock, the governor, the French commissioner, the admiral, members of the council, the staff, naval and medical officers, and some others assembled at Longwood House.

The French people celebrated high mass in their chapel whilst we remained on the lawn. This being over, Count Montholon made his appearance and requested the company to walk in. We were received in the drawing-room by Madame Bertrand and the whole French party, except the priest, who remained with the body. Twelve grenadiers of the 20th Regiment, who had been kept in waiting, were then called in, passed through the drawing-room, and proceeded to the apartment where the body was laid. The company then arranged themselves on each side of the drawing-room, whilst the corpse was carried out, preceded by the priest in a rich canonical dress, with a silver censer in one hand and a book in the other, repeating a prayer. Young Bertrand followed with a vase of holy water. The French party followed immediately after the corpse, and the British functionaries after, the governor the admiral, and the French commissioner bringing up the rear. The body of Buonaparte's carriage had been taken off the spring and replaced by a stage surmounted by a canopy so as to form a hearse; then followed Madame Bertrand and her daughter in a phaeton covered with black cloth. After them such midshipmen and lieutenants of the navy as attended the funeral, then staff and medical officers and naval captains according to rank, juniors first on horseback, the rear brought up by members of the council, General Coffin, the admiral the Marquis de Montchenu and the governor. In passing the troops the band of each corps played a funeral dirge or dead march. When the procession had passed the left of the line the troops then followed, left in front, until the hearse reached the path which branches off from the high road down to the tomb. The body was then carried by a party consisting of three men from each corps. Upon its being lowered into the tomb three salvoes were fired from the pieces, which, together with the infantry, were disposed in line upon the road above. After this the priest again repeated some prayers and sprinkled something out of the censer, which concluded the ceremony.

—T.H. Brooke.

Annexure-VI

A few sayings of Napoleon Bonaparte:

1. Good taste is the highest attainment of civilization.
2. A useless life is a heavy burden. I cannot long support it.
3. Madness is the last stage of human degradation. It is the abdication of humanity. Better to die a thousand times.
4. Love ought to be a pleasure, and not a torment.
5. To be worthy of your destiny, pass only laws that are wise and moderate. Carry them out with force and energy. Encourage the spread of intelligence and respect religion.
6. Liberty and property are both ruined by over solicitude.
7. Do you know what that is, which pierces the heart most deeply? It is the ingratitude of mankind, kills man surely, than steel or poison.
8. Destinies of great men are unpredictable. One must always obey ones destiny—all is written above.
9. Rest is mental friction, and retirement mere boredom.
10. Man is governed by imagination only, without imagination, he is a brute.
11. Love must be the occupation of idlemen, the temporary distraction of the warrior, and the chief peril of the sovereign.

12. Love will replace both greed and fear as the basis of association, and the gifts to God to men will be made available for use, instead of destruction.
13. If the people come to know that their sovereign is a kind man, his administration is utter failure.

4

Ralph Waldo Emerson

American Thinker & Philosopher

Love is only the reflection of man's
own worthiness from other men.
The whole human family is bathed
with an element of love like a fine ether.

—Emerson.

Ralph Waldo Emerson

A.D. 1803 – A.D. 1882

American Thinker and Philosopher

'I am defeated all the time, yet to victory I am born.

Emerson.

The Romans call a man who is wise and prudent CATUS. I feel, Emerson deserves to be called CATUS. Mens characters are revealed much more by the speech than, as some think by their looks. Emerson was both a good speaker, thinker and a very handsome man. He attained the heights of excellence by virtue of his learning, thinking and speaking out the truth of God.

Descended from the founder of Concord, Massachussetts through generations of scholars and preachers, Ralph Waldo Emerson was born on the Twenty fifth day of May 1803 at Boston. Son of Reverend William Emerson and Ruth Haskins Emerson he was a unitarian clergyman and a friend of the arts. He inherited the profession of divinity which had attracted all his ancestors in direct line from the puritan days. His mother was strongly Anglican. Orphaned of his father in 1811, he grew up under the strong influence of his aunt Mary Moody Emerson. ***His ancestors prayed that none of Emerson's family should be rich, but educated.*** Ralph joined the Boston Latin school in 1812 where his literary gifts were recognized. Enrolled at the Harvard College in 1817 and graduated in 1821 by helping to support himself as a messenger, waiter and tutor. He taught in a school while preparing for a part time study in the Harvard Divinity school. From his junior year at the college, he noted his ideas and sensations which served through life as the quarry from which he drew his lectures. *Emerson felt that his strength lay in the exercise of moral imagination rather than reasoning and the defence of the Church dogma.* In 1829, he became the minister of the second church at Boston and refused to administer the Lord's supper in the accepted traditional manner. The trammels of ecclesiastical systems, the crystallizations of formal creeds, the limitations of outward observances, of time honoured expressions he threw off, and sought truth in which all men can unite because he felt truth was beyond parts or church, that he spoke in favour of unity of heart among men of all religions. He was a moral and intellectual preacher for a free platform. He advocated a practical application of the Sermon on the Mount rather than a conventional adherence to the ceremonies of the church. Indeed he objected to some of the ceremonies – specially the one dealing with the sacrement of the Lord's Supper. "The Kingdom of God is not meat and drink but righteousness and peace". This, however, was not palatable to the church, and Emerson had to break with the ministry. His interpretation of religion was too unorthodox for the rigid formulas of the established church. "Christianity as I see it has its object simply to make man good and wise. Its institutions, then, should be as flexible as the wants of men." He was thus the awakener and quickener of intellectual and moral life among young men. He was an inspiring seer of the highest value to his time and country. His legacy to the world is not a system, not a creed, not an observance, but a stimulues; an impulse to a perfect life.

In severing himself from his church he attacked no institution, no man. He merely observed that since he was unable to see eye to eye with his congregation, it would be best for them to get another Pastor. To many of the reactions, his iconoclasm was anything but tender. His own sermons from the first time had been unusually free of traditional doctrine and were instead, eternal exploration of the uses of spirit, showing an idealistic tendency, and announcing his personal doctrine of self-reliance and self-sufficiency. His sermons indeed divested christianity of all external or historical support. He believed in the universal moral law and its tests, a life of virtuous accomplishments. "I think truth and therefore I am true." His attitude towards prayer, down with vain regrets, he cries down with begging for private ends. "Commune God and let your work, thought, expression, all be true prayer. Be self-reliant and all doors are open to you, all honour and love are yours." The unitarianism had little appeal to him now. When Emerson left his pulpit, he went out to search for the meaning of life. He took long walks and tried to attune his ear and his heart to the music of Nature. He learnt that the heart of Nature was beating in unison with his own heart. When he reflected upon the intimate relationship between himself and the rest of the world, his whole being was electrified with a surge of power, an over mastering confidence in himself and in his fellowmen. This power was infinite, and he could teach others to draw upon the same power within themselves. He said "We are forever on the verge of all that is great." "Trust in yourself, claim your share of the greatness of life. Assert your relationship to the Divine. Surrender yourself to the power within you–not the power to enslave but the power to liberate, to help." 'dare to become the master of your own fate and teach all and sundry to dare likewise. *Emerson thus, became a teacher of man of the science of joy'*.

In 1832 after resigning from the ministry, he set off on a journey to Italy, England and Scotland where he met Cloreidge, Wordsworth and Carlyle. His sojourn to Europe brought him into direct contact with men and ideas which stimulated his reason and imagination. Here, German idealism and Goethean as well as English transcendentalism provided material and incentives for his future work. These thoughts together with the insights derived from Montaigne, Plato and Swedenborg turned Emerson's attention to a deliberate observation of nature.

He published his first book on 'Nature' which is the fundamental document of his philosophy. They were not a course of lectures, but a series of genuine essays thought out for years. Nature ranks now as his nearest approach to a system of philosophy put forth in successive chapters. Its insistence that a new existence was possible for man, if he would but awake his instincts and discipline his life drew Emerson into New England transcendentalists circle (Viz.) Henry David Thoreau, Amos Browson Alcot, Nathaniel Hawthorne and others who sought a new vision in life. Standing at the conflex of time, he has at his disposal, the social heritage of the past, and before him future bounded in its possibility only by his own creative imagination. Doctrines such as this, shot like lightning through the down calvanist atmosphere of New England. It fitted the mood of the Pioneer society in the West, its easy harmonies were welcome in a country threatened by social struggle; there were even aspects of its that could be found to meet the needs of an emerging industrial society. The concept of society was dynamic and experimental which is the most permanent valuable element in his social thought – that at every moment society must start fresh with a clear field, and no shakling traditions. His emphasis on the sovereignty of the individual has strengthened the ballot and democracy. His ethical individualism has furnished a basis for economic individualism. His doctrine of self-reliance and opportunity are excellent homilies on the prevailing virtues of a capitalist economy. The denial of the existence of evil and the principles of compensation can be used to bridge inequality of income and social status.

His *Phi Beta Kappa* oration (The American Scholar of 1837) at the Harvard University (see Annexure-I) attracted attention and praise. His Divinity school address (see Annexure-II) with its bold appeal to preachers to revise their theology and meet their hearers with original truth instead of traditional form of religion aroused the native intolerance of New England which was found revolutionary to protest on uncharitable attacks. About this time, men surrounding him began to recognize his intellectual and social forces. Many intellectuals including his own family members started dealing with the young, due to their insight and eloquence. Emerson began to draw a circle of friends and a school of thought in Concord, Boston, Plymouth, Salem and the New England towns. This movement was called transcendentalist philosophy.

Transcendentalism is a naturalistic interpretation of the world, is founded on the conception of moral law. Moral law is manifestedly grounded, not on a naturalistic experience of the world, but much more neatly on positive ethical decrees 'intuited' independently of experience. At the heart of Emersonian transcendentalism lie neither science nor ineffable mystic ecstasy, but timeless moral imperatives. These transcendentalists were infact idealists of various shades of thought. Their organ 'the Dial' became a open forum for much youthful literature, and many earnest essays on the reformation of the society in Education, morals and politics. At about the same time Emerson identified himself with the still unpopular cause of emancipation of Negro slaves with advanced ideas of Alcott in the field of Education, and with several schemes for social reforms which the conservationists of the period viewed with dislike or scornful indifference. In the civil war of 1861-65 Emerson wrote articles in the 'Dial' and spoke of the movement as the progress of revolution, and such is proved indeed to be. "Those who share it have no external organisations, no badge, no creed, no name." They do not vote or print or even meet together. They are united only in a common love of truth and love its work...Without concert or proclamation of any kind, they have silently given in their several adhesion to a new hope. The intellectuals of Boston and Cambridge did not like his ideas. But the common people understood his simple teaching. One woman, it seems, said "We understood Emerson because he speaks directly to our hearts."

Ralph's poetic genius was given public recognition at the time of his death in every part of the globe, and along with this appreciation, went the perception that a distinct Emersonian School of thought had arisen which influenced the striking personalities who had gathered round him in early or late in his career. They were a group called Concord authors or the concord school of philosophy. Among them were Henry David Thoreau, George William Curtis, William Torry Haris, Benjamin Franklin, Sanborn etc. etc. They were influenced in varying degrees by his stimulating mind and gentle social attraction. His aunt Mary Moody Emerson had more to do with his intellectual and spiritual training than any of his early instructors.

If Emerson lacked what he calls animal spirit, he was certainly deficient in either ardour or cheerfulness. "What is a man good for, without enthusiasm? He was a prophet of joy, respecting the Pursuit of happiness far beyond most mordists, and he is said to have rebuked Ruskin himself for his pessimism. He discerned no special gift for suffering in his own make up; neither was he anxious to cultivate it. For him, the spiritual world was in harmony with human aspirations; to doubt this would be to blaspheme life itself.

His philosophy and his thinking inspired the teeming millions of the world. It is indeed an honour to be associated with his thinking and his philosophy, and ethical and moral values which has stimulated the young men of America to make the nation great. Therefore, it is worthwhile for the youth to reflect on what this great American social thinker and philosopher had said, and more so, his philosophy of individual liberty and friendship. What he said nearly two centuries ago, is true even today to the present day India which is experiencing the imitation technology, and losing its individual liberty, ethical individualism and the 'Sovereignty of the living individual." Although Emerson was not a systematic philosopher, yet, his wisdom do sum up to a philosophy and his automistic utterances cohere somehow into a well defined point of view.

I, therefore, thought it wise to include in this series 'In Quest of Excellence' Emerson–the great social thinker and philosopher so that the youngmen and women may reflect over his philosophy of ethical individualism and friendship and shape their personalities.

Emerson As a Social Thinker and Philosopher

'The mark of the man of the world is absence of pretentions.'

—Emerson.

The first American thinker who exerted a wide and deep influence both at home and abroad was Ralph Waldo Emerson. Gifted with powers of original thought and exalted literary expression, he said:

'Every man I meet is my superior in some way.'

Being a Staunch follower of universal tolerance, he proclaimed the doctrine of individual liberty.

He believed in the simplicity of energy of the Higher law – the Oneness of mankind. Placing the ethical code of humanity upon a practical basis – **'to live, let live and help live'**, he laid emphasis on the dignity of the common man, and appealed to his countrymen to liberate themselves from the philosophy of resignation, and accept the gospel of aspiration, and further, urging every man to assert himself–not his isolated self, but his inclusive self. "Surrender yourself to the power within you – not the power to enslave, but the power to liberate, to help." 'Dare to become the master of your own fate, and teach all and sundry to dare likewise.'

Insisting his people to unshackle their minds, he appealed to them to learn to know themselves for the man that they are destined to become. He said **'the eyes of man are in his forehead and not**

in his hind head', and exhorted the people to cast off their foolish outer garments of servitude, psychophancy and humiliation, prejudice and hate, and to standforth as free men. He wanted every young man (American) to be a builder of his own life, to become founders and leaders, and not leaners. "Let us stop imitating our brothers of the Old World, for, what is imitation but the backward travelling of the mind. Our houses are built with foreign tastes, our shelves are garnished with foreign ornaments, our opinions, our tastes, our faculties lean, and follow the past and the distant. Therefore, stop being followers and leaners, become founders and builders. Build your own world, build your own life. ***The Private life of one man can be made more illustrious than any kingdom in history."*** **In the words of William James, this intellectual and ethical individualism is called the 'Sovereignty of the Living Individual.' "The individual must choose his own calling, guide his own conduct, form his own opinion, construct his own history. Nothing is sacred except his own mind; nothing is important except as it is relevant to his purposes."** Thus, Emerson's philosophy pointed out the nobility of the common place. "Know whoever you are, that the world exists for you. In each and every man there is an angel in disguise who plays the fool." It was to these angels Emerson spoke when he addressed his audience exhorting them to stand forth in all their divine splendour as free men. His doctrine of self-sufficiency and self-reliance springs from his view that the individual need only look into his own heart for the spiritual guidance that has hitherto been the province of the established churches. The individual must have the courage to be himself, and to trust the innerforce within him, he lives his life according to his intuitively derived precepts.

His *Phi Beta Kappa* oration (the American scholar of 1837) attracted attention and praise mingled with surprise. Subsequently, he wrote many essays 'on Nature', 'on Friendship', 'On the conduct of life etc. etc. He was, therefore, widely acclaimed as an edifying essayist and later, he came to be valued for his incisive and pattern breaking poetry. **But his chief importance is as a thinker.** Although, he was not a systematic philosopher, yet, his wisdom do sum up to a philosophy and his automistic utterances cohere somehow into a well defined point of view. His chief weakness as a social thinker lay in his over estimate of the role of the individual in the social process, and his under estimate of the place of the institutions. Throughout his thinking, one feels that his world was not a society, but a collection of individuals. However, his philosophy, his stress on the importance of moral and ethical values stimulated the youngmen of America to make the nation great.

Expanding the Horizon of Thought Through Reading and Writing

From his childhood, Emerson confessed that a day spent without books was impoverished; in later years, he testified that reading was the one pleasure which did not grow stale with the time; **when he read a book which opened up a new field, he said, he wished he might live 3000 years.** Books destroy time and space, enable us to move with the speed of thought and established communications with great minds, as Southey in his 'The Scholar' has expressed. I quote:

My days among the Dead are passed,
Around me, I behold,
Where'er these casual eyes are cast,
The mighty minds of old.
My never failing friends are they,
With whom I converse day by day,
With them I take delight in weal,
And seek relief in woe;
And while I understand and feel,
How much to them I owe,
My cheeks have often been bedew'd
With tears of thoughtful gratitude.
My thoughts are with the Dead, with them
I live in long-past years,
Their virtuous love, their faults condemn,
Partake their hopes and fears,
And from their lessons seek and find

Instructions with an humble mind.
My hopes are with the Dead; anon
my place with them will be,
And I with them shall travel on
Through all Futurity;
Yet leaving here a name, I trust
That will not perish in the dust.

—*R. Southey*

In the highest civilization, reading was still the highest delight fortifying its devotees against calamity; after his father's death, reconciliation with life began to approach him first through reading. In 1817, Emerson began working his way through Harvard, serving as 'President's freshman' and waiting on tables. It is not surprise then, that he should have considered some books as important to us as parents and lovers and passionate experiences, nor that a man's library should be a kind of harem to him. ***He even felt that those who loved the same books would be likely to love one another.*** The significance and importance of reading is summed up in a pleasant little piece:

"When shall I be tired of reading?
When the moon is tired of waxing and waning,
When the cloud is tired of raining,
When the sea is ebbing and flowing,
When the planets tire of going, And
When Death is sick of feeling,
Then I shall be tired of reading".

—*Emerson.*

Emerson's Varacity as a reader is well established even outside the literary field. He read science, philosophy and multitudinous, miscelaneous periodicals, and even Government reports. When he first visited Europe, he read Goethe in Naples, and Manzoni in Florence, and carried Byron in his pocket through the continent. If he had an hour or part of a day to spare, he sought the nearest reading room for Newspapers and Journals. He also valued foreign literature which helped break subservience to conventions with which we are familiar. ***He always felt privileged to stay in a house in which scholarly reference books were available.***

He said, books serve their highest function when they set us free from themselves, and he does not shrink from the thought of outgrowing Montaigne, Shakespeare, Plutarch and Plotinus; or of seeing Homer and Milton reduced to 'tinpans' in time. He said 'imitation even of Shakespeare is ruinous'. He read literature mainly for its inspirational power, learning to 'read one' in all books, and seeking 'the one incorruptible text of truth.' He admired often Leigh Hunt's Abu Ben Adam as the most durable of Victorian poems. I give below the poetic verses of Leigh Hunts' Abu Ben Adam.

Abu Ben Adam (may his tribe increase!)
Awoke one night from a deep dream of Peace,
And saw, with in the moonlight in his room,
Making it rich, and like a lilly in bloom,
An angel writing in a book of gold:
Exceeding peace had made Ben Adam bold,
And to the presence in the room he said,
'What writest thou?'...The vision rais'd its head,
And with a look made of all sweet accord,
Answered, "The names of those who love the Lord!
'And is mine one?' said Abu 'Nay, not so'.
Replied the angel. Abu spoke more low,
But cheerly still; and said, 'I pray thee, then,
Write me as one that loves his fellow men.'
The angel wrote, and vanish'd. The next night
It came again with a great wakening light,
And show'd the names whom love of God had blest,
And lo! Ben Adhem's name led all the rest.

—*Leigh Hunt.*

He mentions Homer more often than any other classical poet (generally in connection with *'Illiad'*). Once he lists Homer, Herodotus, Acschylus, Plato, Plutarch as the five Greeks 'we could not spare'. Lucretius gets only a passing nod, but Virgil, Horace, Livy, Cicero, Caesar are mentioned with reasonable frequency. He loved 'Pultarch's lives and morals' for, he could not think of him 'without a tingling of the blood.' He says, ***"If the books of the world were on fire, he would as soon fly to rescue Plutarch".*** Was equally it seems fond of Dante "as his imagination is the nearest to hands and feet that we have seen". Again, Emerson loved oriental literature specially the **'Vishnu Purana' and Bhagwat Gita.** If the orient interested Emerson as a Philosophical Thinker, it also interested him as a litterateur most of all the **Persians Hafiz and Sa'di (the Divan-i-Hafiz and Gulistan and Bostan)** who became to him a kind of type of the ideal poet. He pays rich tribute to **Sa'di** in the following poem :

"Be thou ware where Sa'di dwells;
Wisdom of the gods is he -
Entertain it reverently,
Gladly round that Golden lamp
Sylvan deities encamp,
And simple maids and noble youth
Are welcome to the man of truth,
Most welcome they who need him most,
They feed the spring which they exhaust.

For greater need
Draws better deed; -
But critic, spare thy vanity
Nor – show thy pompous parts,
To vex with odious subtlety
The cheerer of man's heart."

—Emerson.

About the 17th century victorian prose and non fiction writers, Macaulay's learning and vivacity, and prodigious talent appealed to him. He felt, novels have certain usefulness–"if they teach you the secret that the best life is conversation; and the greatest success is confidence, or perfect understanding between sincere people."

His views on Writing and Speaking :

Emerson called writing 'The greatest of arts' 'the subtlest and of most miraculus effect'. *'The man is only half himself' he says, 'the other half is his expression.'* Since Emerson himself was a writer, in his eyes the writer was not wholly the creator of this work, it would have less value if he were. ***The good writer "Writes for the love of truth and beauty and not with ulterior ends."*** A writer has indeed a double dependence upon the eternal varieties whence he draws his inspiration and upon the community which he addresses. The best writing is a kind of communal composition, and it is Shakespeare's greatness that he has no peculiarities, curiosities, egotism, or importunate topics; 'he is wise without emphasis or assertion, he is strong as nature is strong; and when Emerson compared himself with others as an individual, he was humble, but when he remembered that he was an immortal child of God receiving his endowments from God, and with an immortal destiny, he could perceive no reason why he should bow his head before any man.

By the same token, Emerson feels that speaking too is an art, oratory a great art and the combination of all the qualities of the artist in the orator. The reason why Athenian orators were the greatest because in Athens oratory was given highest encouragement and importance. Speaking involved more action than writing, and thinking on his feet apparently seemed greater thing to him than thinking in his study. He even perceived a heroic quality in speaking, for, the speaker stands before his audience as a challenger, and must keep himself a little ahead of them, the communication was the key to peace among men. Public speaking seems a more direct form of communication than writing. As a preacher, Emerson knew from the beginning that preaching involves a meeting of minds, and that where this does not occur, there is no preaching , however beautiful a composition may be exhibited. He praised the oratory of ancient Greece as an art of most finished beauty and practical application.

His Essays on Friendship

Emerson writes that the beauty of friendship lies in the recognition of the ultimate relationship that exists between man and man. To him, the life of a man is a quest for friendship, a striving for the class–reunion of the human soul. True friendship is not merely a passion, but it is also an action of the soul. It is a divine game of give and take. The only way to have a friend is to be one. "We must learn to grasp heroic hands in heroic hands." **To Emerson, the active and heroic concept of friendship is the only solid thing in a world of shadows.** He proclaims loudly to cultivate the art of friendship which makes one to come close to the heart of reality." "You stop looking at the rainbow, and you begin to see the true light." **If man could be inspired with a tender kindness to the souls of men, and should come to feel that every man was another self, then this feeling would cause the most striking changes of external things. He, therefore, said 'Every man' I meet, I consider him superior in some way."**

Man is one because his soul is a part of the soul of God.

Association with the Humble

Emerson greatly enjoyed the society of the humble. **"I much prefer the company of plough boys and time-peddlers to the silken and perfumed amity which celebrates its days of encounter by a frivolous display by rides in a curricle and drivers at the best taverns. He confessed he liked low company. "The society of gypsies was more attractive than that of the Bishops."** He complained of the arrogant contempt learned men feel for the unlearned, a contempt which has certainly not lessened with the years and which has helped to polarize our society so dangerously. **Human beings are potentially divine, but in the present stage of development, they often look and behave very much like fools. In every age, imbecility predominates in the vast majority.** ***There are vast number of malefactors, but of benefactors, only a handful.*** The survival from either poor or rich, black or white must depend on fitness to survive. Napolean was of the same opinion, and he chose a labourer who was quite fit, and made him a Duke or a Marshall. The English Oligarchy was against this, and they believed in 'Divine Rights.' It is because of this, war against Napolean was declared, and armies began to march. Emerson said "providence has given every race its own talents, and ordains that only that race which combines perfectly with the virtues of all shall endure."

His Essays on Society and Solitude

Talking of society ***Emerson believed that ordinary social calls should not exceed 10 minutes, unless extension is asked or granted.*** In practice Emerson always recognized the need for a judicious balance between society and solitude, fearing the excess of both. Michael Angelo lived alone, and never or very rarely took meals with any person. ***The most valued friend is he to whom one can say anything discussing all topics without fear of offence, and such a friendship doubles the value of life.*** There are people in the world in whose presence we rise with ease above the plane we commonly inhabit. "We are easily greet with the loved and honoured associates."

Emerson praised clubs which are refuge against "the vulgarities of the street and the tavern." He even thought, he wanted a kind of coffee house in which writers could meet instead of merely encountering each other. In social intercourse, there is no more important element than conversation, which Emerson fully recognized. He said (quoted elsewhere in this essay) **"the man is only half himself, the other half is his expression."** ***He disliked ridicule and sarcasm.*** *He always wanted to go to the best hotels and restaurants available, for, though they cost more, they do not cost much more and there is a good company, and the best information. He says he did not want disciples, and admits that to meet young men who showed vital interest in his ideas was stimulating and refreshing, and he was responsive to such,* even when they sometime become over enthusiastic and showered him with burdensome letters.

On the Conduct of Life

The art of living is the art of learning to skate on surfaces, and the equestrian in the circus, throwing himself from horse to horse, balancing first on one foot and then on the other, achieve what we must all achieve in other ways. Man is his own balancing point, "where of everything may be affirmed and desired with equal reason." Every act, be it only the writing of a sentence imposes limitations, and commits to choice. Through excess wisdom, the wiseman becomes a fool if he fastens his attention upon one idea and neglect the others, the truth will turn to falsehood. Both rationalists and mystics have their place; one brings us closer to experience, the other to God. True skepticism is not unbelief, denial, scoffing, nor profligate jeering, for the doubter must always doubt his own doubts. Emerson, therefore, praised Montaigne for occupying a middle ground between the abstractions and the materialists, finding "both wrong by being in extremes" and striving to take up his own ground on the beam of the balance.

The Emersonion ideal is that of the man who is free to do as he likes but who chooses to do what is right and in harmony with the will of God. His fundamental quarrells with the reformers was that they had lost the sense of the whole, and that none of their recommendations went to the heart of the matter. He praises Goethe because he combined genius and common sense, thus reconciling the idea with common things and meet the needs of common men. *He blamed Savants (learned men) for being out of touch with actuality, and philosophers for failing to see the beauty of common life.* ***He felt that "to interpret Christ, it needs Christ in the heart." The real religion of the day is reverence for character.*** **The heart of Emerson's religion was his insistence upon the necessity of a direct *and immediate apprehension of spiritual reality. The perfect man (al-insan-al-Kamil)*** knew both poetry and mathematics joined *a hunger for beauty with a high devotional spirit, loved justice and possessed beautiful manners.* Therefore, ***Emerson's ideal man was not pure spirit, but a balance between spirit and matter, reason and understanding.*** *He was a spiritual Man not because he despised the senses but because he wished to live a complete life.*

Mathew Arnold said of Emerson, "He is the friend and aider of those who live in the spirit." **He believed that unless life can be lived spontaneously and fully and gladly, there is no hope for the future of the world. "It is not enough God spoke to Moses, He must speak to me and to you." "It is not enough that Shakespeare and Micheal Angelo created great art; you and I must create also." And if we cannot do this ourselves, we must recognize its value in those of our contemporaries who can.**

Intuition and Inspiration

Whereas other poets were inspired by emotions, Ralph was inspired by ideas. Basically, he liked his poems better than his prose, because it seemed to him that, in them, he had achieved great universality of utterances. In other words, it was as true of Emerson the writer as it was for the man that the more he lost his life, the more completely he found it.

If intuition was the source of Emersonian man's spiritual perceptions, and consequently of his self-reliance, this was a natural gift, and nature, by any definition, or his relationship to nature was a powerful factor in it. Another important source of nourishment was art, and if you were a writer, as Emerson was, then art also becomes your own medium of expression. But the artist was a man as well as a writer–'not a writer' said Emerson, but 'a man in writing'– and a man lives with other men and women in society at large, and in the world of closer personal relations.

Art delights in carrying thought in to action, whereas literature is the conversion of action in the thought. Every work of art is an expression of an ideal. The only difference is that, for realists, the ideal is immediately provoked by the spectacle of the real; whereas for others, it is to a great extent the product of an internal elaboration. The artists mental process, or for that matter those of a person experiencing aesthetic pleasure, are in their internal make up identical at every point to the process that give rise to great act of devotion and sacrifice. The man who gives himself wholly to the beauty that he contemplates is at one with it, as the man who gives himself to a group of which he is a part, wholly identifying himself with it, is at once with that group. For instance, the first acquaintance with a great work of art has usually proved to be an important event in every young artist's life. When Correggio first gazed on Raphael's 'Saint Cicilia', he felt within himself an awakened power, and exclaimed. "And I too am a painter!"

Great achievement in art and in religion comes not 'from vain or shallow thought' but from inspiration, love and passion. Whatever Emerson admired, inspired him with the desire to do it himself. Yet the incentives which inspire the ambitions of most men passed him by. Power did not attract him. He aspired eminance as an orator and writer, but even here he had no desire to dominate men's minds. What he wanted to do was to awaken their own powers and inspire them to think themselves. Nor was he, ever interested in the accumulation of money. He thought any man who respected himself must wish to be 'self-sustained'. **In his eyes, poverty was demoralizing, and "to spend without earning was the doctrine of the snake." A man must earn a living because it was incumbent upon him to be a producer as well as a consumer. Success consists in close appliance to the laws of the world, and since those laws are intellectual and moral, an intellectual and moral obedience.** In his eyes a rich man is he, who is capable of helping and assisting the needy. I used to tell my friends that a rich man is one who has thoughtfulness for others woes, and a desire to help the needy.

From the above it is clear that Emerson was indeed a great social thinker.

On Nature

Emerson says **"all human beings are faulty (friends such as we desire are dreams and fables).** Again, on love, Emerson comments that love transforms life, character, and the world; and through it boys and girls–learn how to respect personality. In a marriage both intellect and the heart are refined and purified year after year. An admirer of nature, he was fascinated by the beauty of the human body. He said "we go to the gymnasium and swimming pool to see the power and beauty of the body". **A beautiful body**

was a pledge of wholeness, a symbol of perfection and goodness, and no degradation to which it might be subjected could quite destroy its dignity. Primitive people recognized this when they gave even the Deity a human form. Emerson was, therefore, very sensitive to beauty in men, women and children.

In Sum

Emerson's thoughts appealed to me most. It has some realism. But Emerson's real ambition was for spiritual insight. **"I have a power in my soul which enables me to perceive God."** It would not have disturbed him to be told that his own perceptions have been influenced not only by the Bible and the Christian traditions upon which he had been reared, but by oriental seers, medieval and 12th century mystics like Sa'di and Hafiz, and a variety of contemporary and near contemporary philosophers who emphasised dynamism and organisms, eclecticism and experimental philosophy. Nothing can have any meaning for us until we have felt its truth and reality within ourselves. Moreover, there can be no perception without consanguinity between perceiver and perceived; that is why, the existence of a spiritually minded man makes it necessary for us to believe that the universe is spiritual also. The children of God never argue that Jesus 'simply affirmed', and that truth itself cease to be truth when stated politically?

Emerson's most mature works reveal a developed humanism together with a full awarness of man's limitations. He gave direction to a religious philosophy and ethical movement that above all stressed belief in the spiritual potential of every man.

To a certain extent we may say that his philosophy may perhaps be described as a pragmatic mysticism. It is dualistic in that, it looks both ways from its position on the bridge between the soul and nature. It is monistic in that it maintains that this bridge is the only reality. But is pragmatic in that it tests all truths (including the mystical belief in the value of life) by experience. Emerson used all these lines of approach but committed himself to none of them. He was deeply impressed by the thought that men who have thought deeply and truly are in fundamental agreement with one another; he stressed this agreement and thus become a powerful force towards conciliation.

His work is analytical of things as he thought they were; it stands or falls by our consent to agree to recognize their pertinence. His success is measured by the number of true things a reader hears him saying. He has spoken exciting truth and he is both sensible and inspired. This combination is rare.

It is the universal nature which gives worth to particular men and things. This is reflected in the following poem:

> "There is no great and no small;
> To the soul that maketh all;
> And where it cometh, all things are:
> And it cometh everywhere.
> I am the owner of the sphere;
> Of the seven stars and the solar year;
> Of Caesar's hand, and Plato's brain;
> Of Lord Christ's heart and Shakespeare's strain."

His legacy to the world is not a system, nor a creed, nor an observance but a stimulus, an impulse to a perfect life. Indeed Emerson was *Par-Excellence.*

Reading List

1. Abbe. Effende — Emerson R.W. American Scholar Cornell University Press 1955
2. Cook. Reginald L. — Emerson. Selected Prose & Poetry edited. N.Y. Rinehart 1950
3. Doren. Mark Van — The Portable Emerson. The Viking Press The Colonial Press Incorp. USA 1959
4. Emerson. Ralph Waldo — Complete Prose Works Ward Lock & Co. Ltd. London 1918
5. Emerson. R.W. — Conduct of Life. New York. Doubleday
6. Emerson. R.W. — Essays.

New York. Crowells, 1963

7. Emerson. R.W. — Emerson on Shakespeare
for his essays on Representative man
London. De La More Press, 1904

8. Emerson, R.W. — Emerson's Works
1905

9. Emerson, R.W. — Essays
Carlton House, New York

10. Emerson, R.W. — Essays and English Traits
The Harvard Classics.
Groher Enterprises Corp.
Danberry Connecticut, 1980

11. Konvitz, Milton R. & Whicher, Stephen E. — Emerson–a collection of critical essays. Edited.
Prentice Hall Incorp.
Englewood Cliffs, New Jersey, 1962

12. Nagenknecht, Edward — Portrait of a Balanced Soul.
N.Y. Oxford University Press 1924

13. Perry, Bliss — The heart of Emerson's journals
Edited
Dover Publishers Incorp. N. Y. 1958

14. Porte, Joel — Emerson and Thoreau–
Transcendentalist in conflict.
Lalvani Publishing House.
Bombay 1969

15. Rusk, Ralph L. — The Life of Ralph Waldo Emerson
N.Y. Charles Scribners and Sons.
1949

16. *Encyclopedias*
(i) Concise Dictionary of American Biography
(ii) Encyclopedia of Social Sciences
(iii) Encyclopedia Britannica
(iv) Encyclopedia Americana

Annexure-I

The American Scholar

An Oration Delivered before the Phi Beta Kappa Society, at Cambridge, August 3, 1837

Mr. President and Gentlemen, I greet you on the recommencement of our literary year. Our anniversary is one of hope, and, perhaps, not enough of labour. We do not meet for games of strength or skill, for the recitation of histories, tragedies, and odes, like the ancient Greeks; for parliaments of love and poesy, like the Troubadours; nor for the advancement of science, like our contemporaries in the British and European capitals. Thus far, our holiday has been simply a friendly sign of the survival of the love of letters amongst a people too busy to give to letters any more. As such it is precious as the sign of an indestructible instinct. Perhaps the time is already come when it ought to be, and will be, something else; when the sluggard intellect of this continent will look from under its iron lids and fill the postponed expectation of the world with something better than the exertions of mechanical skill. Our day of dependence, our long apprenticeship to the learning of other lands, draws to a close. The millions that around us are rushing into life, cannot always be fed on the sere remains of foreign harvests. Events, actions arise, that must be sung, that will sing themselves. Who can doubt that poetry will revive and lead in a new age, as the star in the constellation Harp, now flames in our zenith, astronomers announce, shall one day be the polestar for a thousand years?

In this hope I accept the topic which not only usage but the nature of our association seem to prescribe to this day – the AMERICAN SCHOLAR. Year by year we come up hither to read one more chapter of his biography. Let us inquire what light new days and events have thrown on his character and his hopes.

It is one of those fables which out of an unknown antiquity convey an unlooked-for wisdom, that the gods, in the beginning, divided Man into men, that he might be more helpful to himself; just as the hand was divided into fingers, the better to answer its end.

The old fables covers a doctrine ever new and sublime; that there is One Man–present to all particular men only partially, or through one faculty; and that you must take the whole society to find the whole man. Man is not a farmer, or a professor, or an engineer, but he is all. Man is priest, and scholar, and statesman, and producer, and soldier. In the *divided* or social state these functions are parcelled out to individuals, each of whom aims to do his stint of the joint work, whilst each other performs his. The fable implies that the individual, to possess himself, must sometimes return from his own labour to embrace all the other labourers. But, unfortunately, this original unit, this fountain of power, has been so distributed to multitudes, has been so minutely subdivided and peddled out, that it is spilled into drops, and cannot be gathered. The state of society is one in which the members have suffered amputation from the trunk, and strut about so many walking monsters – a good finger, a neck, a stomach, an elbow, but never a man.

Man is thus metamorphosed into a thing, into many things. The planter, who is Man sent out into the field to gather food, is seldom cheered by any idea of the true dignity of his ministry. He sees his bushel and his cart, and nothing beyond, and sinks into the farmer instead of Man on the farm. The tradesman scarcely ever gives an ideal worth to his work, but is ridden by the routine of his craft, and the soul is subject to dollars. The priest becomes a form; the attorney a statute-book; the mechanic a machine; the sailor a rope of the ship.

In this distribution of functions the scholar is the delegated intellect. In the right state he is *Man Thinking*. In the degenerate state, when the victim of society, he tends to become a mere thinker, or still worse, the parrot of other men's thinking.

In this view of him, as *Man Thinking*, the theory of his office is contained. Him Nature solicits with all her placid, all her monitory pictures; him the past instructs; him the future invites. Is not indeed every man a student, and do not all things exist for the student's behoof? And, finally, is not the true scholar the only true master? But the old oracle said, "All things have two handles: beware of the wrong one." In life, too often, the scholar errs with mankind and forfeits his privilege. Let us see him in his school, and consider him in reference to the main influences he receives.

I

The first in time and the first in importance of the influences upon the mind is that of nature. Every day, the sun; and, after sunset, Night and her stars. Ever the winds blow; ever the grass grows. Every day, men and women, conversing, beholding and beholden. The scholar is he of all men whom this spectacle most engages. He must settle its value in his mind. What is nature to Him? There is never a beginning, there is never an end, to the inexplicable continuity of this web of God, but always circular power returning into itself. Therein it resembles his own spirit, whose beginning, whose ending, he never can find–so entire, so boundless. Far too as her splendours shine, system on system shooting like rays, upward, downward, without centre, without circumference–in the mass and in the particle, Nature hastens to render account of herself to the mind. Classification begins. To the young mind everything is individual, stands by itself. By and by, it finds how to join two things and see in them one nature; then three, then three thousand; and so, tyrannized over by its own unifying instinct, it goes on tying things together, diminishing anomalies, discovering roots running under ground whereby contrary and remote things cohere and flower out from one stem. It presently learns that since the dawn of history there has been a constant accumulation and classifying of facts. But what is classification but the perceiving that these objects are not chaotic, and are not foreign, but have a law which is also a law of the human mind? The astronomer discovers that geometry, a pure abstraction of the human mind, is the measure of planetary motion. The chemist finds proportions and intelligible method throughout matter; and science is nothing but the finding of analogy, identity, in the most remote parts. The ambitious soul sits down before each refractory fact: one after another reduces all strange constitutions, all new powers, to their class and their law, and goes on forever to animate the last fibre of organization, the outskirts of nature, by insight.

Thus to him, to this school-boy under the bending dome of day, is suggested that he and it proceed from one root; one is leaf and one is flower; relation, sympathy, stirring in every vein. And what is that root? Is not that the soul of his soul? A thought too bold; a dream too wild. Yet when this spiritual light shall have revealed the law of more earthly natures—when he has learned to worship the soul, and to see that the natural philosophy that now is, is only the first gropings of its gigantic hand, he shall look forward to an ever expanding knowledge as to a becoming creator. He shall see that nature is the opposite of the soul, answering to it part for part. One is seal and one is print. Its beauty is the beauty of his own mind. Its laws are the laws of his own mind. Nature then becomes to him the measure of his attainments. So much of nature as he is ignorant of, so much of his own mind does he not yet possess. And, in fine, the ancient precept, "Know thyself," and the modern precept, "Study nature," become at last one maxim.

II

The next great influence into the spirit of the scholar is the mind of the past-in whatever form, whether of literature, of art, of institutions, that mind is inscribed. Books are the best type of the influence of the past, and perhaps we shall get at the truth–learn the amount of this influence more conveniently—by considering their value alone.

The theory of books is noble. The scholar of the first age received into him the world around; brooded thereon; gave it the new arrangement of this own mind, and uttered it again. It came into him life; it went out from him truth. It came to him short-lived actions; it went out from him immortal thoughts. It came to him business; it went from him poetry. It was dead fact; now, it is quick thought. It can stand, and it can go. It now endures, it now flies, it now inspires. Precisely in proportion to the depth of mind from which it issued, so high does it soar, so long does it sing.

Or, I might say, it depends on how far the process had gone, of the distillation, so will the purity and imperishableness of the product be. But none is quite perfect. As no air-pump can by any means make a perfect vacuum, so neither can any artist entirely exclude the conventional, the local, the perishable from his book, or write a book of pure thought, that shall be as efficient, in all respects, to a remote posterity, as to contemporaries, or rather to the second age. Each age, it is found, must write its own books; or rather, each generation for the next succeeding. The books of an older period will not fit this.

Yet hence arises a grave mischief. The sacredness which attaches to the act of creation, the act of thought, is transferred to the record. The poet chanting was felt to be a divine man: henceforth the chant is divine also. The writer was a just and wise spirit: henceforward it is settled the book is perfect; as love of the hero corrupts into worship of his statue. Instantly the book becomes noxious: the guide is a tyrant. The sluggish and perverted mind of the multitude, slow to open to the incursions of Reason, having once so opened, having once received this book, stands upon it, and makes an outery if it is disparaged. Colleges are built on it. Books are written on it by thinkers, not by Man Thinking; by men of talent, that is, who start wrong, who set out from accepted dogmas, not from their own sight of principles. Meek young men grow up in libraries, believing it their duty to accept the views which Cicero, which Locke, which Bacon, have given; forgetful that Cicero, Locke and Bacon were only young men in libraries when they wrote these books.

Hence, instead of Man Thinking, we have the book worm. Hence the book-learned class, who value books, as such; not as related to nature and the human constitution, but as making a sort of Third Estate with the world and the soul. Hence the restorers of readings, the emendators, the bibliomaniacs of all degrees.

Books are the best of things, well used; abused, among the worst. What is the right use? Then where is the one and which all means go is effect. They are for nothing but to inspire. I had better never see a book than to be warped by its attraction clean out of my own orbit, and made a satellite instead of a system. The one thing in the world, of value, is the active soul. This every man is entitled to ; this every man contains within him, although in almost all men obstructed, and as yet unborn. The soul active sees absolute truth and utters truth, or creates. In this action it is genius; not the privilege of here and there a favorite, but the sound estate of every man. In its essence it is progressive. The book, the college, the school of art, the institution of any kind, stop with some past utterance of genius. This is good, say they, – let us hold by this. They pin me down. They look backward and not forward. But genius looks forward: the eyes of man are set in his forehead, not in his hindhead: man hopes: genius creates. Whatever talents may be, if the man create not, the pure efflux of the Deity is not his – cinders and smoke there may be, but not yet flame. There are creative manners, there are creative actions, and creative words; manners, actions words, that is, indicative of no custom or authority, but springing spontaneous from the mind's own sense of good and fair.

On the other part, instead of being its own seer, let it receive from another mind its truth, though it were in torrents of light, without periods of solitude, inquest, and self-recovery, and a fatal disservice is done. Genius is always sufficiently the enemy of genius by over-influence. The literature of every nation bears me witness. The English dramatic poets have Shakespearized now for two hundred years.

Undoubtedly there is a right way of reading, so it be sternly subordinated. Man Thinking must not be subdued by his instruments. Books are for the scholar's idle times. When he can read God directly, the hour is too precious to be wasted in other men's transcripts of their readings. But when the intervals of darkness come, as come they must – when the sun is hid and the stars withdraw their shining – we repair to the lamps which were kindled by their ray, to guide our steps to the East again, where the dawn is. We hear, that we may speak. The Arabian proverb says, "A fig tree, looking on a fig tree, becometh fruitful."

It is remarkable, the character of the pleasure we derive from the best books. They impress us with the conviction that one nature wrote and the same reads. We read the verses of one of the great English poets, of Chaucer, of Marvell, of Dryden, with the most modern joy – with a pleasure, I mean, which is in great part caused by the abstraction of all time from their verses. There is some awe mixed with the joy of our surprise, when this poet, who lived in some past world, two or three hundred years ago, says that which lies close to my own soul, that which I also had well-nigh thought and said. But for the evidence thence afforded to the philosophical doctrine of the identity of all minds, we should suppose some pre-established harmony, some foresight of souls that were to be, and some preparation of stores for their future wants, like the fact observed in insects, who lay up food before death for the young grub they shall never see.

I would not be hurried by any love of system, by any exaggeration of instincts, to underrate the Book. We all know, that as the human body can be nourished on any food, though it were boiled grass and the broth of shoes, so the human mind can be fed by any knowledge. And great and heroic men have existed who had almost no other information than by the printed page. I only would say that it needs a strong head to bear that diet. One must be an inventor to read well. As the proverb says, "He that would bring home the wealth of the Indies, must carry out the wealth of the Indies." There is then creative reading as well as creative writing. When the mind is braced by labour and invention, the page of whatever book we read becomes luminous with manifold allusion. Every sentence is doubly significant, and the sense of our author is as broad as the world. We then see what is always true, that as the seer's hour of vision is short and rare among heavy days and months, so is its record, perchance, the least part of his volume. The discerning will read, in his Plato or Shakespeare, only that least part—only the authentic utterances of the oracle – all the rest he rejects, were it never so many times Plato's and Shakespeare's.

Of course, there is a portion of reading quite indispensable to a wise man. History and exact science he must learn by laborious reading. Colleges, in like manner, have their indispensable office – to teach elements. But they can only highly serve us when they aim not to drill, but to create; when they gather from far every ray of various genius to their hospitable halls, and by the concentrated fires, set the hearts of their youth on flame. Thought and knowledge are natures in which apparatus and pretension avail nothing. Gowns and pecuniary foundations, though of towns of gold, can never countervail the least sentence or syllable of wit. Forget this, and our American colleges will recede in their public importance, whilst they grow richer every year.

III

There goes in the world a notion that the scholar should be a recluse, a valetudinarian – as unfit for any handiwork or public labour as a penknife for an ax. The so-called "practical men" sneer at speculative men, as if, because they speculate or see, they could do nothing. I have heard it said that the clergy – who are always, more universally than any other class, the scholars of their day–are addressed as women; that the rough, spontaneous conversation of men they do not hear, but only a mincing and diluted speech. They are often virtually disfranchised; and indeed there are advocates for their celibacy. As far as this is true of the studious classes, it is not just and wise. Action is with the scholar subordinate, but it is essential. Without it he is not yet man. Without it thought can never ripen into truth. Whilst the world hangs before the eye as a cloud of beauty, we cannot even see its beauty. Inaction is cowardice, but there can be no scholar without the heroic mind. The preamble of thought, the transition through which it passes from the unconscious to the conscious, is action. Only so much do I know, as I have lived. Instantly we know whose words are loaded with life, and whose not.

The world – this shadow of the soul, or other me, lies wide around. Its attractions are the keys which unlock my thoughts and make me acquainted with myself. I run eagerly into this resounding tumult. I grasp the hands of those next to me and take my place in the ring to suffer and to work, taught by an instinct that so shall the dumb abyss be vocal with speech. I pierce its order; I dissipate its fear; I dispose of it within the circuit of my expanding life. So much only of life as I know by experience, so much of the wilderness have I vanquished and planted, or so far have I extended my being, my dominion. I do not see how any man can afford, for the sake of his nerves and his nap, to spare any action in which he can partake. It is pearls and rubies to his discourse. Drudgery, calamity, exasperation, want, are instructors in eloquence and wisdom. The true scholar grudges every opportunity of action past by, as a loss of power.

It is the raw material out of which the intellect moulds her splendid products. A strange process too, this by which experience is converted into thought, as a mulberry leaf is converted into satin. The manufacture goes forward at all hours.

The actions and events of our childhood and youth are now matters of calmest observation. They lie like fair pictures in the air. Not so with our recent actions–with the business which we now have inhand. On this we are quite unable to speculate. Our affections as yet circulate through it. We no more feel or know it than we feel the feet, or the hand, or the brain of our body. The new deed is yet a part of life – remains for a time immersed in our unconscious life. In some contemplative hour it detaches itself from the life like a ripe fruit, to become a thought of the mind. Instantly it is raised, transfigured; the corruptible has put on incorruption. Henceforth it is an object of beauty, however base its origin and neighbourhood. Observe too the impossibility of attending this act. In its grub state, it cannot fly, it cannot shine, it is a dull grub. But suddenly, without observation, the selfsame thing unfurls beautiful wings, and is an angel of wisdom. So is there no fact, no event, in our private history which shall not sooner or later lose its adhesive, inert form, and astonish us by soaring from our body into the empyrean. Cradle and infancy, school and playground, the fear of boys, and dogs, and ferules, the love of little maids and berries, and many another fact that once filled the whole sky, are gone already; friend and relative, profession and party, town and country, nation and world, must also soar and sing.

Of course, he who has put forth his total strength in fit actions has the richest return of wisdom. I will not shut myself out of this globe of action, and transplant an oak into a flower-pot, there to hunger and pine; nor trust the revenue of some single faculty, and exhaust one vein of thought, much like those Savoyards, who, getting their livelihood by carving shepherds, shepherdesses, and smoking Dutchmen, for all Europe, went out one day to the mountain to find stock, and discovered that they had whittled up the last of their pine trees. Authors we have, in numbers, who have written out their vein, and who, moved by a commendable prudence, sail for Greece or Palestine, follow the trapper into the Prairie, or remble round Algiers, to replenish their merchantable stock.

If it were only for a vocabulary, the scholar would be covetous of action. Life is our dictionary. Years are well spent in country labours; in town; in the insight into trades and manufactures; in frank intercourse with many men and women; in science; in art; to the one end of mastering in all their facts a language by which to illustrate and embody our perceptions. I learn immediately from any speaker how much he has already lived through the poverty or the splendour of his speech. Life lies behind us as the quarry from whence we get tiles and copestones for the masonry of today. This is the way to learn grammar. Colleges and books only copy the language which the field and the work-yard made.

But the final value of action, like that of books, and better than books, is that it is a resource. That great principle of Undulation in nature, that shows itself in the inspiring and expiring of the breath; in desire and satiety; in the ebb and flow of the sea; in day and night; in heat and cold; and, as yet more deeply ingrained in every atom and every fluid, is known to us under the name of Polarity – these "fits of easy transmission and reflection," as Newton called them–are the law of nature because they are the law of spirit.

The mind now thinks, now acts, and each fit reproduces the other. When the artist has exhausted his materials, when the fancy no longer paints, when thoughts are no longer apprehended and books are a weariness–he has always the resource to live. Character is higher than intellect. Thinking is the function. Living is the functionary. The stream retreats to its source. A great soul will be strong to live, as well as strong to think. Does he lack organ or medium to impart his truth? He can still fall back on this elemental force of living them. This is a total act. Thinking is a partial act. Let the grandeur of justice shine in his affairs. Let the beauty of affection cheer his lowly roof. Those "far from fame," who dwell and act with him, will feel the force of his constitution in the doings and passages of the day better than it can be measured by any public and designed display. Time shall teach him that the scholar loses no hour which the man lives. Herein he unfolds the sacred germ of his instinct, screened from influence. What is lost in seemliness is gained in strength. Not out of those on whom systems of education have exhausted their culture, comes the helpful giant to destroy the old or to build the new, but out of unhandselled savage nature; out of terrible Druids and Berserkers come at last Alfred and Shakespeare.

I hear therefore with joy whatever is beginning to be said of the dignity and necessity of labour to every citizen. There is virtue yet in the hoe and the spade, for learned as well as for unlearned hands. And labour is everywhere welcome; always we are invited to work; only be this limitation observed, that a man shall not for the sake of wider activity sacrifice any opinion to the popular judgments and modes of action.

I have now spoken of the education of the scholar by nature, by books, and by action. It remains to say somewhat of his duties.

They are such as become Man Thinking. They may all be comprised in self-trust. The office of the scholar is to cheer, to raise, and to guide men by showing them facts amidst appearances. He plies the slow, unhonored, and unpaid task of observation. Flamsteed and Herschel, in their glazed observatories, may catalogue the stars with the praise of all men, and the results being splendid and useful, honor is sure. But he, in his private observatory, cataloguing obscure and nebulous stars of the human mind, which as yet no man has thought of as such–watching days and months sometimes for a few facts; correcting still his old records–must relinquish display and immediate fame. In the long period of his preparation he must betray often an ignorance and shiftlessness in popular arts, incurring the disdain of the able who shoulder him aside. Long he must stammer in his speech; often forego the living for the dead. Worse yet, he must accept – how often! poverty and solitude. For the ease and pleasure of treading the old road, accepting the fashions, the education, the religion of society, he takes the cross of making his own, and, of course, the self-accusation, the faint heart, the frequent uncertainty and loss of time, which are the nettles and tangling vines in the way of the self-relying and self-directed; and the state of virtual hostility in which he seems to stand to society, and especially to educated society. For all this loss and scorn, what offset? He is to find consolation in exercising the highest functions of human nature. He is one who raises himself from private considerations and breathes and lives on public and illustrious thoughts. He is the world's eye. He is the world's heart. He is to resist the vulgar prosperity that retrogrades ever to barbarism, by preserving and communicating heroic sentiments, noble biographies, melodious verse, and the conclusions of history. Whatsoever oracles the human heart, in all emergencies, in all solemn hours, has uttered as its commentary on the world of actions–these he shall receive and impart. And whatsoever new verdict Reason from her inviolable seat pronounces on the passing men and events of today – this he shall hear and promulgate.

These being his function, it becomes him to feel all confidence in himself, and to defer never to the popular cry. He and he only knows the world. The world of any moment is the merest appearance. Some great decorum. Some fetish of a government, some ephemeral trade, or war, or man, is cried up by half mankind and cried down by the other half, as if all depended on this particular up or down. The odds are that the whole question is not worth the poorest thought which the scholar has lost in listening to the controversy. Let him not quit his belief that a popgun is a popgun, though the ancient and honourable of the earth affirm it to be the crack of doom. In silence, in steadiness, in severe abstraction, let him hold by himself; add observation to observation, patient of neglect, patient of reproach, and bide his own time – happy enough if he can satisfy himself alone that this day he has seen something truly. Success treads on every right step. For the instinct is sure, that prompts him to tell his brother what he thinks. He then learns that in going down into the secrets of his own mind he has descended into the secrets of all minds. He learns that he who has mastered any law in his private thoughts, is master to that extent of all men whose language he speaks, and of all into whose language his own can be translated. The poet, in utter solitude remembering his spontaneous thoguths and recording them, is found to have recorded that which men in crowded cities find true for them also. The orator distrusts at first the fitness of his frank confessions, his want of knowledge of the persons he addresses, until he finds that he is the complement of his hearers–that they drink his words because he fulfils for them their own nature; the deeper he dives into his privatest, secretest presentiment, to his wonder he finds this is the most acceptable, most public, and universally true. The people delight in it; the better part of every man feels, This is my music; this is myself.

In self-trust all the virtues are comprehended. Free should the scholar be–free and brave. Free even to the definition of freedom, "without any hindrance that does not arise out of his own constitution." Brave; for fear is a thing which a scholar by his very function puts behind him. **Fear always springs from ignorance.** It is a shame to him if his tranquily, amid dangerous times, arise from the presumption that like children and women his is a protected class; or if he seek a temporary peace by the diversion of his thoughts from politics or vexed question, hiding his head like an ostrich in the flowering bushes, peeping into microscopes, and turning rhymes, as a boy whistles to keep his courage up. So is the danger a danger still; so is the fear worse. Manlike let him turn and face it. Let him look into its eye and search its nature, inspect its origin—

see the whelping of this lion–which lies no great way back; he will then find in himself a perfect comprehension of its nature and extent; he will have made his hands meet on the other side, and can henceforth defy it and pass on superior. The world is his who can see through its pretension. What deafness, what stone-blind custom, what overgrown error you behold is there only by sufferance–by your sufferance. See it to be a lie, and you have already dealt it its mortal blow.

Yes, we are the cowed–we the trustless. It is a mischievous notion that we are come late into nature; that the world was finished a long time ago. As the world was plastic and fluid in the hands of God, so it is ever to so much of his attributes as we bring to it. To ignorance and sin, it is flint. They adapt themselves to it as they may; but in proportion as a man has anything in him divine, the firmament flows before him and takes his signet and form. **Not he is great who can alter matter, but he who can alter my state of mind.** They are the kings of the world who give colour of their present thought to all nature and all art, and persuade men by the cheerful serenity of their carrying the matter, that this thing which they do is the apple which the ages have desired to pluck, now at last ripe, and inviting nation to the harvest. **The great man makes the great thing.** Wherever Macdonald sits, there is the head of the table. Linnaeus makes botany the most alluring of studies, and wins it from the farmer and the herb-woman; Davy, chemistry; and Cuvier, fossils. The day is always his who works in it with serenity and great aims. The unstable estimates of men crowd to him whose mind is filled with a truth, as the heaped waves of the Atlantic follow the moon.

For this self-trust, the reason is deeper than can be fathomed – darker than can be enlightened. I might not carry with me the feeling of my audience in stating my own belief. But I have already shown the ground of my hope, in adverting to the doctrine that man is one. I believe man has been wronged; he has wronged himself. He has almost lost the light that can lead him back to his prerogatives. Men are become of no account. Men in history, men in the world of today, are bugs, are spawn, and are called "the mass" and "the herd." In a century, in a millennium, one or two men; that is to say, one or two approximations to the right state of every man. All the rest behold in the hero or the poet their own green and crude being – ripened; yes, and are content to be less, so that may attoin to its full stature. What a testimony, full of grandeur, full of pity, is borne to the demands of his own nature, by the poor clansman, the poor partisan, who rejoices in the glory of his chief. The poor and the low find some amends to their immense moral capacity, for their acquiescence in a political and social inferiority. They are content to be brushed like flies the path of a great peoms, so that gintice shell be done from by him to that common nature which it is the dearest desire of all to see enlarged and glorified. They sun themselves in the great man's light, and feel it to be their own element. They cast the dignity of man from their downtrod selves upon the shoulders of a hero, and will perish to add one drop of blood to make that great heart beat, those giant sinews combat and conquer. He lives for us, and we live in him.

Man such as they are, very naturally seek money or power; and power because it is as good as money – the "spoils," so called, "of office." And why not? For they aspire to the highest, and this, in their sleep-walking, they dream is higher. Wake then and they shall quis the false good and leap to the true, and leave governments to clerks and desks. This revolution is to be wrought by the gradual domestication of the idea of Culture. The main enterprise of the world for splendour, for extent, is the upbuilding of a man. Here are the materials strewn along the ground. **The private life of one man shall be a more illustrious monarchy, more formidable to its enemy, more sweet and serene in its influence to its friend, than any kingdom in history.** For a man, rightly viewed, comprehendeth the particular natures of all men. Each philosopher, each bard, each actor has only done for me, as by a delegate, what one day I can do for myself. The books which once we valued more than the apple of the eye, we have quite exhausted. What is that but saying that we have come up with the point of view which the universal mind took through the eyes of one scribe; we have been that man and have passed on. First, one, then another, we drain all cisterns and waxing greater by all these supplies, we crave a better and more abundant food. The man has never lived that can feed us ever. The human mind cannot be enshrined in a person who shall set a barrier on any one side to this unbounded, unboundable empire. It is one central fire, which, flaming now out of the lips of Etna, lightens the capes of Sicily, and now out of the throat of Vesuvius, illuminates the towers and vineyards of Naples. It is one light which beams out of a thousand stars. It is one soul which animates all men.

But I have dwelt perhaps tediously upon this abstraction of the scholar. I ought not to delay longer to add what I have to say of near reference to the time and to this country.

Historically, there is thought to be a difference in ideas which predominate over successive epochs, and there are data for marking the genius of the Classic, of the Romantic, and now of the Reflective or Philosophical age. With the views I have intimated of the oneness of the identity of the mind through all individuals, I do not much dwell on these differences. In fact, I believe each individual passes through all three. **The boy is a Greek; the youth, romantic; the adult, reflective.** I deny not however that a revolution in the leading idea may be distinctly enough traced.

Our age is bewailed as the age of Introversion. Must that needs be evil? We, it seems, are critical; we are embarrassed with second thoughts; we cannot enjoy any thing for hankering to know whereof the pleasure consists; we are lined with eyes; we see with our feet; the time is infected with Hamlet's unhappiness–

Sicklied o'er with the pale cast of thought.

It is so bad then? Sight is the last thing to be pitied. Would we be blind? Do we fear lest we should outsee nature and God, and drink truth dry? I look upon the discontent of the literary class as a mere announcement of the fact that they find themselves not in the state of mind of their fathers, and regret the coming state as untried; as a boy dreads the water before he has learned that he can swim. If there is any period one would desire to be born in, is it not the age of Revolution; when the old and the new stand side by side and admit of being compared; when the energies of all men are searched by fear and by hope; when the historic glories of the old can be compensated by the rich possibilities of the new era? This time, like all times, is a very good one, if we but know what to do with it.

I read with some joy of the auspicious signs of the coming days, as they glimmer already through poetry and art, through philosophy and science, through church and state.

One of these signs is the fact that the same movement which effected the elevation of what was called the lowest class in the state, assumed in literature a very marked and as benign an aspect. Instead of the sublime and beautiful, the near, the low, the common, was explored and poetized. That which had been negligently trodden under foot by those who were harnessing and provisioning themselves for long journeys into far countries, is suddenly found to be richer than all foreign parts. The literature of the poor, the feelings of the child, the philosophy of the street, the meaning of household life, are the topics of the time. It is a great stride. It is a sign–is it not? of new vigour when the extremities are made active, when currents of warm life run into the hands and the feet. I ask for the great, the remote, the romantic; what is doing in Italy or Arabia; what is Greek art, or Provencal minstrelsy; I embrace the common, I explore and sit at the feet of the familiar, the low. Give me insight into today, and you may have the antique and future worlds. What would we really know the meaning of? The meal in the firkin; the milk in the pan; the ballad in the street; the news of the boat; the glance of the eye; the form and the gait of the body–show me the ultimate reason of these matters; show me the sublime presence of the highest spiritual cause lurking, as always it does lurk, in these suburbs and extremities of nature, let me see every trifle bristling with the polarity that ranges it instantly on an eternal law; and the shop, the plough, and the ledger referred to the like cause by which light undulates and poets sing–and the world likes no longer a dull miscellany and lumber-room, but has form and order; there is no trifle, there is no puzzle, but one design unites and animates the farthest pinnacle and the lowest trench.

This idea has inspired the genius of Goldsmith, Burns, Cowper, and, in a newer time, of Goethe, Wordsorth, and Carlyle. This idea they have differently followed and with various success. In contrast with their writing, the style of Pope, of Johnson, of Gibbon, looks cold and pedantic. This writing is blood-warm. Man is surprised to find that things near are not less beautiful and wondrous than things remote. The near explains the far. The drop is a small ocean. A man is related to all nature. This perception of the worth of the vulgar is fruitful is discoveries. Goethe, in this very thing the most modern of the moderns, has shown us, as none ever did, the genius of the ancients.

There is one man of genius who has done much for this philosophy of life, whose literary value has never yet been rightly estimated–I mean Emanuel Sweden borg. The most imaginative of men, yet writing with the precision of a mathematician, he endeavored to engraft a purely philosophical Ethics on the popular Christianity of his time. Such as attempt of course must have difficulty which no genius could surmount. But he saw and showed the connection between nature and the affections of the soul. He pierced the emblematic or spiritual character of the visible, audible, tangible world. Especially did his shade-loving muse hover over and interpret the lower parts of nature; he showed the mysterious bond that allies moral evil to the foul material forms, and has given in epical parables a theory of insanity, of beasts, of unclean and fearful things.

Another sign of our times, also marked by an analogous political movement, is the new importance given to the single person. Everything that tends to insulate the individual–to surround him with barriers of natural respect, so that each man shall feel the world is his, and man shall treat with man as a sovereign state with a sovereign state—tends to true union as well as greatness. "I learned," said the melancholy Pestalozzi, "that no man in God's wide earth is either willing or able to help any other man." Help must come from the bosom alone. **The scholar is that man who must take up into himself all the ability of the time, all the contributions of the past, all the hopes of the future.** He must be an university of knowledges. If there be one lesson more than another which should pierce his ear, it is, the world is nothing, the man is all; in yourself is the law of all nature, and you know not yet how a globule of sap ascends; in yourself slumbers the whole of

Reason; it is for you to know all; it is for you to dare all. Mr. President and Gentlemen, this confidence in the unsearched might of man belongs, by all motives, by all prophecy, by all preparation, to the American Scholar. We have listened too long to the courtly muses of Europe. The spirit of the American freeman is already suspected to be timid, imitative, tame. Public and private avarice make the air we breathe thick and fat. The scholar is decent, indolent, complaisant. See already the tragic consequence. The mind of this country, taught to aim at low objects, eats upon itself. There is no work for any but the decorous and the complaisant. Young men of the fairest promise, who begin life upon our shores, inflated by the mountain winds, shined upon by all the stars of God, find the earth below not in unison with these, but are hindered from action by the disgust which the principles on which business is managed inspire, and turn drudges, or die of disgust, some of them suicides. What is the remedy? They did not yet see, and thousands of young men as hopeful now crowding to the barriers for the career do not yet see, that if the single man plant himself indomitably on his instincts, and there abide, the huge world will come round to him. Patience–patience; with the shades of all the good and great for company; and for solace the perspective of your own infinite life; and for work the study and the communication of principles, the making those instincts prevalent, the conversion of the world. Is it not the chief disgrace in the world, not to be an unit–not to be reckoned one character–not to yield that peculiar fruit which each man was created to bear, but to be reckoned in the gross, in the hundred, or the thousand, of the party, the section, to which we belong; and our opinion predicted geographically, as the north, or the south? Not so, brothers and friends – please God, ours shall not be so. We will walk on our own feet; we will work with our own hands; we will speak our own minds. The study of letters shall be no longer a name for pity, for doubt, and for sensual indulgence. The dread of man and the love of man shall be a wall of defence and a wreath of joy around all. A nation of men will for the first time exist, because each believes himself inspired by the Divine Soul which also inspires all men.

Annexure-II

An Address

Delivered before the Senior Class in Divinity College, Cambridge, Sunday Evening, July 15, 1838

In this refulgent summer, it has been a luxury to draw the breadth of life. The grass grows, the buds burst, the meadow is spotted with fire and gold in the tint of flowers. The air is full of birds, and sweet with the breadth of the pine, the balm-of-Gilead, and the new hay. Night brings on gloom to the heart with its welcome shade. Through the transparent darkness the stars pour their almost spiritual rays. Man under them seems a young child, and his huge globe a toy. The cool night bathes the world as with a river, and prepares his eyes again for the crimson dawn. The mystery of nature was never displayed marc happily. The corn and the wine have been freely dealt to all creatures, and the never-broken silence with which the old bounty goes forward has not yielded yet one word of explanation. One is constrained to respect the perfection of this world in which our senses converse. How wide; how rich; what invitation from every property it gives to every faculty of man! In its fruitful soils; in its navigable sea; in its mountains of metal and stone; in its forests of all woods; in its animals; in its chemical ingredients; in the powers and path of light, heat, attraction and life, it is well worth the pith and heart of great men to subdue and enjoy it. The planters, the mechanics, the inventors, the astronomers, the builders of cities, and the captains, history delights to honour.

But when the mind opens and reveals the laws which traverse

the universe and make things what they are, then shrinks the great world at once into a mere illustration and fable of this mind. What am I? and What is? asks the human spirit with a curiosity new-kindled, but never to be quenched. Behold these outrunning laws, which our imperfect apprehension can see tend this way and that, but not come full circle. Behold these infinite relations, so like, so unlike, many, yet one. I would study, I would know, I would admire forever. These works of thought have been the entertainments of the human spirit in all ages.

A more secret, sweet and overpowering beauty appears to man when his heart and mind open to the sentiment of virtue. Then he is instructed in what is above him. He learns that his being is without bound; that to the good, to the perfect, he is born, low as he now lies in evil and weakness. That which he venerates is still his own, though he has not realized it yet. He ought. He knows the sense of that grand word, though his analysis fails to render account of it. When in innocency or when by intellectual perception he attains to say–"I love the Right; Truth is beautiful within and without forevermore. Virtue, I am thine; save me; use me; thee will I serve, day and night, in great, in small, that I may be not virtuous, but virtue"–then is the end of the creation answered, and God is well pleased.

The sentiment of virtue is a reverence and delight in the presence of certain divine laws. It perceives that this homely game of life we play, covers, under what seem foolish details, principles that astonish. The child amidst his baubles is learning the action of light, motion, gravity, muscular force; and in the game of human life, love, fear, justice, appetite, man, and God, interact. These laws refuse to be adequately stated. They will not be written out on paper, or spoken by the tongue. They elude our persevering thought; yet we read them hourly in each other's faces, in each other's actions, in our own remorse. The moral traits which are all globed into every virtuous act and thought – in speech we must sever, and describe or suggest by painful enumeration of many particulars. Yet, as this sentiment is the essence of all religion, let me guide your eye to the precise objects of the sentiment, by an enumeration of some of those classes of facts in which this element is conspicuous.

The intuition of the moral sentiment is an insight of the perfection of the laws of the soul. These laws execute themselves. They are out of time, out of space, and not subject to circumstance. Thus in the soul of man there is a justice whose retributions are instant and entire. He who does a good is instantly en-nobled. He who does a mean deed is by the action itself contracted. He who puts off impurity, thereby puts on purity. It a man is at heart just, then in so far is he God; the safety of God, the immortality of God, the majesty of God do enter into that man with justice. If a man dissemble, deceive, he deceives himself, and goes out of acquaintance with his own being. A man in the view of absolute goodness, adores, with total humility. Every step so downward, is a step upward. The man who renounces himself, comes to himself.

See how this rapid intrinsic energy worketh everywhere, righting wrongs, correcting, appearances, and bringing up facts to a harmony with thoughts. Its operation in life, though slow to the senses, is at last as sure as in the soul. By it a man is made the Providence to himself, dispensing good to his goodness, and evil to his sin. Character is always known. Thefts never enrich; alms never impoverish; murder will speak out of stone walls. The least admixture of a lie–for example, the taint of vanity, any attempt to make a good impression, a favourable appearance – will instantly vitiate the effect. But speak the truth, and all nature and all spirits help you with unexpected furtherance. Speak the truth, and all things alive or brute are vouchers, and the very roots of the grass underground there do seem to stir and move the bear you witness. See again the perfection of the Law as it applies itself to the affections, and becomes the law of society. As we are, so we associate. The good, by affinity, seek the good; the vile, by affinity, the vile. Thus of their own volition, soul proceed into heaven, into hell.

These facts have always suggested to man the sublime creed that the world is not the product of manifold power, but of one will, of one mind; and that one mind is everywhere active, in each ray of the star, in each wavelet of the pool; and whatever opposes that will is everywhere balked and baffled, because things are made so, and not otherwise. Good is positive. Evil is merely privative, not absolute: it is like cold, which is the privation of heat. All evil is so much death or nonentity. Benevolence is absolute and real. So much benevolence as a man hath, so much life hath he. For all things proceed out of this same spirit, which is differently named love, justice, temperance, in its different applications, just as the ocean receives different names on the several shores which it washes. All things proceed out of the same spirit, and all things conspire with it. Whilst a man seek good ends, he is strong by the whole strength of nature. Insofar as he roves from these ends, he bereaves himself of power, or auxiliaries; his being shrinks out of all remote channels, he becomes less and less, a mote, a point until absolute badness is absolute death.

The perception of this law of laws awakens in the mind a sentiment which we call the religious sentiment, and which makes our highest happiness. wonderful is its power to charm and to command. It is a mountain air. It is the embalmer of the world. It is myrrh and storax, and chlorine and rosemary. It makes the sky and the hills sublime, and the silent song of the stars is it. By it is the universe made safe and habitable, not by science or power. Thought may work cold and intransitive in things, and find no end or unity; but the dawn of the sentiment of virtue on the heart, gives and is the assurance that Law is sovereign over all natures; and the worlds, time. space, eternity, do seem to break out into joy.

This sentiment is divine and deifying. It is the beatitude of man. It makes him illimitable. Through it, the soul first knows itself. It corrects the capital mistake of the infant man, who seeks to be great by following the great, and hopes to derive advantages from another – by showing the fountain of all good to be in himself, and that he, equally with every man, is an inlet into the deeps of Reason. When he says, "I ought"; when love warms him; when he chooses, warned from on high, the good and great deed; then, deep melodies wander through his soul from Supreme Wisdom. Then he can worship, and be enlarged by his worship; for he can never go behind this sentiment. It the sublimest flights of the soul rectitude is never surmounted, love is never outgrown.

This sentiment lies at the foundation of society, and successively creates all forms of worship. The principle of veneration never dies out. Man fallen into superstition, into sensuality, is never quite without the visions of the moral sentiment. In like manner, all the expressions of this sentiment are sacred and permanent in proportion to their purity. The expressions of this sentiment affect us more than all other compositions. The sentence of the oldest time, which ejaculate this piety, are still fresh and fragrant. This thought dwelled always deepest in the minds of men the devout and contemplative East; not alone in Palestine, where it reached its purest expression, but in Egypt, in Persia, in India, in China. Europe has always owed to Oriental genius its divine impulses. What these holy bards said, all sane men found agreeable and true. And the unique impression of Jesus upon mankind, whose name is not so much written as ploughed into the history of this world, is proof of the subtle virtue of this infusion.

Meantime, whilst the doors of the temple stand open, night and day, before every man, and the oracles of this truth cease never, it is guarded by one stern condition; this, namely; it is an intuition. It cannot be received at second hand. Truly speaking, it is not instruction, but provocation, that I can receive from another soul. What he announces, I must find true in me, or reject; and on his word, or as his second, be he who he may, I can accept nothing. On the contrary, the absence of this primary faith is the presence of the degradation. As is the flood so is the ebb. Let this faith depart, and the very words it spake and the things it made, become false and hurtful. Then falls the church, the state, art, letters, life. The doctrine of the divine nature being forgotten, a sickness infects and dwarfs the constitution. Once man was all; now he is an appendage, a nuisance. And because the indwelling Supreme Spirit cannot wholly be got rid of, the doctrine of it suffers this perversion, that the divine nature is attributed to one or two persons, and denied to all the rest, and denied with fury. The doctrine of inspiration is lost; the base doctrine of the majority of voices usurps the place of the doctrine of the soul. Miracles, prophecy, poetry, the ideal life, the holy life, exist as ancient history merely; they are not in the belief, nor in the aspiration of society; but when suggested, seem ridiculous. Life is comic or pitiful as soon as the high ends of being fade out of sight, and man becomes near-sighted, and can only attend to what addresses the senses.

These general views, which, whilst they are general, none will contest, find abundant illustration in the history of religion, and especially in the history of the Christian church. In that, all of us have had our birth and nurture. The truth contained in that, you, my young friends, are now setting forth to teach. As the Cultus, or established worship of the civilized world, it has great historical interest for us. Of its blessed words, which have been the consolation of humanity, you need not that I should speak. I shall endeavour to discharge my duty to you on this occasion, by pointing out two errors in its administration, which daily appear more gross from the point of view we have just now taken.

Jesus Christ belonged to the true race of prophets. He saw with open eye the mystery of the soul. Drawn by its severe harmony, ravished with its beauty, he lived in it, and had his being there. Along in all history he estimated the greatness of man. One man was true to what is in you and me. He saw that God incarnates himself in man, and evermore goes forth anew to possession of his World. He said, in this jubilee of sublime emotion, "I am divine, Through me, God acts; through me, speaks. Would you see God, see me; or see thee, when thou also thinkest as I now think." But what a distortion did his doctrine and memory suffer in the same, in the next, and the following ages! There is no doctrine of the Reason which will bear to be taught by the Understanding. The understanding caught this high chant from the poet's lips, and said, in the next age, "This was Jehovah come down out of heaven. I will kill you, if you say he was a man." The idioms of his language and the figures of his rhetoric have usurped the place of his truth; and churches are not built on his principles, but on his tropes. Christianity became a Mythus, a poetic teaching of Greece and Egypt, before. He spoke of miracles; for he felt that man's life was a miracle, and all that man doth, and he knew that this daily miracle shines as the character ascends. But the word Miracle, as pronounced by Christian churches gives a false impression; it is Monster. It is not one with the blowing clover and the falling rain.

He felt respect for Moses and the prophets, but no unfit tenderness at postponing their initial revelations to the hour and the man that now is: to the eternal revelation in the heart. Thus was he a true man. Having seen that the law in us is commanding, he would not suffer it to be commanded. Boldly, with hand, and heart, and life, he declared it was God. Thus is he, as I think, the only soul in history who appreciated the worth of man.

1. In this point of view we become sensible of the first defect of historical Christianity. Historical Christianity has fallen into the error that corrupts all attempts to communicate religion. As it appears to us, and as it has appeared for ages, it is not the doctrine of the soul, but an exaggeration of the personal, the positive, the ritual. It has dwelt, it dwells, with noxious exaggeration about the person of Jesus. The soul knows no persons. It invites every man to expand to the full circle of the universe, and will have no preferences but those of spontaneous love. But by this eastern monarchy of a Christianity, which indolence and fear have built, the friend of man is made the injurer of man. The manner in which his name is surrounded with expressions which were once sallies of admiration and love, but are now petrified into official titles, kills all generous sympathy and liking. All who hear me, feel that the language that describes Christ to Europe and America is not the style of friendship and enthusiasm to a good and noble heart, but is appropriated and formal– paints a demigod, as the Orientals or the Greeks would describe Osiris or Apollo. Accept the injurious impositions of our early catechetical instruction, and even honesty and self-denial were but splended sins, if they did not wear the Christian name. One would rather be.

A pagan, suckled in a creed outworn, 11 than to be defrauded of his manly right in coming into nature and finding not names and places, not land and professions, but even virtue and truth foreclosed and monopolized. You shall not be a man even. You shall not own the world; you shall not dare and live after the infinite Law that is in you, and in company with the infinite Beauty which heaven and earth reflect to you in all lovely forms; but you must subordinate your nature to Christ's nature; you must accept our interpretations, and take his portrait as the vulgar draw it.

That is always best which gives me to myself. The sublime is excited in me by the great stoical doctrine, Obey thyself. That which shows God in me, fortifies me. That which shows God out of me, makes me a wart and a wen. There is no longer a necessary reason for my being. Already the long shadows of untimely oblivion creep over me, and I shall decease forever.

The divine bards are the friends of my virtue, of my intellect, of my strength. They admonish me that the gleams which flash across my mind are not mine, but God's; that they had the like, and were not disobedient to the heavenly vision. So I love them. Noble provocations go out from them, inviting me to resist evil; to subdue the world; and to Be. And thus, by his holy thoughts, Jesus serves us, and thus only. To aim to convert a man by miracles, is a profanation of the soul. A true conversion, a true Christ, is now, as always, to be made by the reception of beautiful sentiments. It is true that a great and rich soul, like his, falling among the simple, does so preponderate, that, as his did, it names the world. The world seems to them to exist for him, and they have not yet drunk so deeply of his sense as to see that only by coming again to themselves, or to God in themselves, can they grow forevermore. It is a low benefit to give me something; it is a high benefit to enable me to do somewhat of myself. The time is coming when all men will see that the gift of God to the soul is not a vaunting, overpowering, excluding sanctity, but a sweet, natural goodness, a goodness like thine and mine, and that so invites thine and mine to be and to grow.

The injustice of the vulgar tone of preaching is not less flagrant to Jesus than to the souls which it profanes. The preachers do not see that they make his gospel not glad, and shear him of the locks of beauty and the attributes of heaven. When I see a majestic Epaminodas, or Washington; when I see among my contemporaries a true orator, an upright judge, a dear friend; when I vibrate to the melody and fancy of a poem; I see beauty that is to be desired. And so lovely, and with yet more entire consent of my human being, sounds in my ear the severe music of the bards that have sung of the true god in all ages. Now do not degrade the life and dialogues of Christ out of the circle of this charm, by insulation and peculiarity. Let them lie as they befell, alive and warm, part of human life and of the landscape and of the cheerful day.

2. The second defect of the traditionary and limited way of using the mind of Christ, is a consequence of the first; this, namely; that the Moral Nature, that Law of laws whose revelations introduce greatness–yea, God himself–into the open soul, is not explored as the fountain of the established teaching in society. Men have come to speak of the revelation as somewhat long ago given and done, as if God were dead. The injury to faith throttles the preacher; and the goodliest of institutions becomes an uncertain and inarticulate voice.

It is very certain that it is the effect of conversation with the beauty of the soul, to beget a desire and need to impart to others the same knowledge and love. If utterance is denied, the thought lies like a burden on the man. Always the seer is a sayer. Somehow his dream is told; somehow he publishes it with solemn joy: sometimes with pencil on canvas, sometimes with chisel on stone, sometimes in towers and aisles of granite, his soul's worship is builded; sometimes in anthems of indefinite music; but clearest and most permanent, in words.

The man enamored of this excellency becomes its priest or poet. The office is coeval with the world. But observe the condition, the spiritual limitation of the office. The spirit only can teach; and every man can open his door to these angels, and they shall bring him the gift of tongues. But the man who aims to speak as books enable, as synods use, as the fashion guides, and as interest commands, babbles. Let him hush.

To this holy office you propose to devote yourselves. I wish you may feel your call in throbs of desire and hope. The office is the first in the world. It is of that reality that it cannot suffer the deduction of any falsehood. And it is my duty to say to you that the need was never greater of new revelation than now. From the views I have already expressed, you will infer the sad conviction, which I share, I believe, with numbers, of the universal decay and now almost death of faith in society. The soul is not preached. The Church seems to totter to its fall, almost all life extinct. On this occasion, any complaisance would be criminal which told you, whose hope and commission it is to preach the faith of Christ, that the faith of Christ is preached.

It is time that this ill-suppressed murmur of all thoughtful men against the famine of our churches–this moaning of the heart because it is bereaved of the consolation, the hope, the grandeur that come alone out of the culture of the moral nature,–should be heard through the sleep of indolence, and over the din of routine. This great and perpetual office of the preacher is not discharged. Preaching is the expression of the moral sentiment in application to the duties of life. In how many churches, by how many prophets, tell me, is man made sensible that he is an infinite Soul, that the earth and heavens are passing into his mind; that he is drinking forever the soul of God? Where now sounds the persuasion, that by its very melody imparadises my heart, and so affirms its own origin in heaven? Where shall I hear words such as in elder ages drew men to leave all and follow – father and mother, house and land, wife and child? Where shall I hear these August laws of moral being so pronounced as to fill my ear, and I feel ennobled by the offer of my uttermost action and passion? The test of the true faith, certainly, should be its power to charm and command the soul, as the laws of nature control the activity of the hands, so commanding that we find pleasure and honour in obeying. The faith should blend with the light of rising and of setting suns, with the flying cloud, the singing bird, and the breath of flowers. But now the priest's Sabbath has lost the splendor of nature; it is unlovely; we are glad when it is done; we can make, we do make, even sitting in our pews, a far better, holier, sweeter, for ourselves.

Whenever the pulpit is usurped by a formalist, then is the worshipper defrauded and is disconsolate. We shrink as soon as the prayers begin, which do not uplift, but smite and offend us. We are fain to wrap our cloaks about us, and secure, as best we can, a solitude that hears not. I once heard a preacher who sorely tempted me to say I would go to church no more. Men go, thought I, where they are wont to go, else had no soul entered the temple in the afternoon. A snow-storm was falling around us. The snow-storm was real, the preacher merely spectral, and the eye felt the sad contrast in looking at him, and then out of the window behind him into the beautiful meteor of the snow. He had laughed or wept, was married or in love, had been commended, or cheated, or chagrined. If he had ever lived and acted, we were none the wiser for it. The capital secret of his profession, namely, to convert life into truth, he had not learned. Not one fact in all his experience had he yet imported into his doctrine. This man had ploughed and planted and talked and bought and sold; he had read books; he had eaten and drunken; his head aches, his heart throbs; he smiles and suffers; yet was there not a surmise, a hint, in all the discourse, that he ever lived at all. Not a line did he draw out of real history. The true preacher can be know by this, that he deals out to the people his life – life passed through the fire of thought. But of the bad preacher, it could not be told from his sermon what are of the world he fell in; whether he had a father or a child; whether he was a freeholder or a pauper; whether he was a citizen or a countryman; or any other fact of his biography. It seemed as if their houses were very unentertaining, that they should prefer this thoughtless clamor. It shows that there is a commanding attraction in the moral sentiment, that can lend a faint tint of light to dullness and ignorance coming in its name and place. The good hearer is sure he has been touched sometimes; is sure there is somewhat to be reached, and some word that can reach it. When he listens to these vain words, he comforts himself by their relation to his remembrance of better hours, and so they clatter and echo unchallenged.

I am not ignorant that when we preach unworthily, it is not always quite in vain. There is a good ear, in some men, that draws supplies to virtue out of very indifferent nutriment. There is poetic truth concealed in all the common-places of prayer and of sermons, and though foolishly spoken, they may be wisely heard; for each is some select expression that broke out in a moment of piety from some stricken or jubilant soul, and its excellency made it remembered. The prayers and even the dogmas of our church are like the zodiac of Dendeerah and the astronomical monuments of the Hindoos, wholly insulated from anything now extant in the life and business of the people. They mark the height to which the waters once rose. But this docility is a check upon the mischief from the good and devout. In a large portion of the community, the religious service gives rise to quite other thoughts and emotions. We need not chide the negligent servant. We are struck with pity, rather, at the swift retribution of his sloth. Alas for the unhappy man that is called to stand in the pulpit, and not give bread of life. Everything that befalls accuses him. Would he ask contributions for the missions, foreign or domestic? Instantly his face is suffused with shame, to propose to his parish that they should send money a hundred or a thousand miles, to furnish such poor fare as they have at home and would do well to go the hundred or the thousand miles to escape. Would he urge people to a godly way of living – and can he ask a fellow-creature to come to Sabbath meetings, when he and they all know what is the poor uttermost they can hope for therein? Will he invite them privately to the Lord's Supper? He dares not. If no heart warm this rite, the hollow, dry, creaking formality is too plain than that he can face a man of wit and energy and put the invitation without terror. In the street, what has he to say to the bold village blasphemer? The village blasphemer sees fear in the face, form, and gait of the minister.

Let me not taint the sincerity of this plea by any oversight of the claims of good men. I know and honour the purity and strict conscience of number of the clergy. What life the public worship retains, it owes to the scattered company of pious men, who minister here and there in the churches, and who, sometimes accepting with too great tenderness the tenet of the elders, have not accepted from others, but from their own heart, the genuine impulses of virtue, and so still command our love and awe, to the sanctity of character. Moreover, the exceptions are not so much to be found in a few eminent preachers, as in the better hours, the truer inspirations of all-nay, in the sincere moments of every man. But, with whatever exception, it is still true that tradition characterizes the preaching of this country; that it comes out of the memory, and not out of the soul; that it aims at what is usual, and not at what is necessary and eternal; that thus historical Christianity destroys the power of preaching, by withdrawing it from the exploration of the moral nature of man; where the sublime is, where are the resources of astonishment and power. What a cruel injustice it is to that Law, the joy of the whole earth, which alone can make thought dear and rich; that Law whose fatal sureness the astronomical orbits poorly emulate–that it is travestied and depreciated, that it is behooted and behowled, and not a trait, not a word of it articulated. The pulpit in losing sight of this Law, loses its reason, and gropes after it knows not what. And for want of this culture the soul of the community is sick and faithless. It wants nothing so much as a stern, high, stoical, Christian discipline, to make it know itself and the divinity that speaks through it. Now man is ashamed of himself; he skulks and sneaks through the world, to be tolerated, to be pitied, and scarcely in a thousand years does any man dare to be wise and good, and so draw after him the tears and blessings of his kind.

Certainly there have been periods when, from the inactivity of the intellect on certain truths, a greater faith was possible in names and persons. The Puritans in England and America found in the Christ of the Catholic Church and in the dogmas inherited from Rome, scope for their austere piety and their longings for civil freedom. But their creed is passing away, and none arises in its room. I think no man can go with his thoughts about him into one of our churches, without feeling that what hold the public worship had on men is gone, or going. It has lost its grasp on the affection of the good and the fear of the bad. In the country, neighbourhoods, half parishes are signing off, to use the local term. It is already beginning to indicate character and religion to withdraw from the religious meetings. I have heard a devout person, who prized the Sabbath, say in bitterness of heart. "On Sundays, it seems wicked to go to church." And the motive that holds the best there is now only a hope and a waiting. What was once a mere circumstance, that the best and the worst men in the parish, the poor and the rich, the learned and the ignorant, young and old, should meet one day as fellows in one house, in sign of an equal right in the soul, has come to be a paramount motive for going thither.

My friends, in these two errors, I think, I find the causes of a decaying church and a wasting unbelief. And what greater calamity can fall upon a nation than the loss of worship? Then all things go to decay. Genius leaves the temple to haunt the senate or the market. Literature becomes frivolous. Science is cold. The eye of youth is not lighted by the hope of other worlds, and age is without honour. Society lives to trifles, and when men die we do not mention them.

And now my brothers, you will ask, What in these desponding days can be done by us? The remedy is already declared in the ground of our complaint of the Church. We have contrasted the Church with the Soul. In the soul then let the redemption be sought. Wherever a man comes, there comes revolution. The old is for slaves. When a man comes, all books are legible, all things transparent, all religions are forms. He is religious. Man is the wonder-worker. He is seen amid miracles. All men bless and curse. He faith yea and nay, only. The stationariness of religion; the assumption that the age of inspiration is past, that the Bible is closed; the fear of degrading the character of Jesus by representing him as a man–indicate with sufficient clearness the falsehood of our theology. It is the office of a true teacher to show us that God is, not was; that He speaketh, not spake. The true Christianity–a faith like Christ's in the infinitude of man–is lost. None believeth in the soul of man, but only in some man or person old and departed. Ah me! no man goeth alone. All men go in flocks to this saint or that poet, avoiding the God who seeth in secret. They cannot see in secret; they love to be blind in public. They think society wiser than their soul, and know not that one soul, and their soul, is wiser than the whole world. See how nations and races flit by on the sea of time and leave no ripple to tell where they floated or sunk, and one good soul shall make the name of Moses, or of Zeno, or of Zoroaster, reverend forever. None assayeth the stern ambition to be the Self of the nation and of nature, but each would be an easy secondary to some Christian scheme, or sectarian connection, or some eminent man. Once leave your own knowledge of God, your sentiment, and take secondary knowledge, as St. Paul's, or George Fox's or Swedenborg's, and you get wide from God with every year this secondary form lasts, and if, as now, for centuries–the chasm yawns to that breadth, that men can scarcely be convinced there is in them anything divine.

Let me admonish you, first of all, to go alone; to refuse the good models, even those which are sacred in the imagination of men, and dare to love God without mediator or veil. Friends enough you shall find who will hold up to your emulation Wesleys and Oberlins, Saints and Prophets. Thank God for these good men, but say, "I also am a man." Imitation cannot go above its model. The imitator dooms himself to hopeless mediocrity. The inventor did it because it was natural to him, and so in him it has a charm. In the imitator something else is natural, and he bereaves himself of his own beauty, to come short of another man's.

Yourself a newborn bard of the Holy Ghost, cast behind you all conformity, and acquaint men at first hand with Deity. Look to it first and only, that fashion, custom, authority, pleasure, and money, are nothing to you–are not bandages over your eyes, that you cannot see–but live with the privilege of the immeasurable mind. Not too anxious to visit periodically all families and each family in your parish connection–when you meet one of these men or women, be to them a divine man; be to them thought and virtue; let their timid aspirations find in you a friend; let their trampled instincts be genially tempted out in your atmosphere; let their doubts know that you have doubted, and their wonder feel that you have wondered. By trusting your own heart, you shall gain more confidence in other men. For all our penny-wisdom, for all our soul-destroying slavery to habit, it is not to be doubted that all men have sublime thoughts; that all men value the few real hours of life; they love to be heard; they love to be caught up into the vision of principles. We mark with light in the memory the few interviews we have had, in the dreary years of routine and of sin, with souls that made our souls wiser; that spoke what we thought; that told us what we knew; that gave us leave to be what we inly were. Discharge to men the priestly office, and, present or absent, you shall be followed with their love as by an angel.

And, to this end, let us not aim at common degrees of merit. Can we not leave, to such as love it, the virtue that glitters for the commendation of society, and ourselves pierce the deep solitudes of absolute ability and worth? We easily come up to the standard of goodness in society. Society's praise can be cheaply secured, and almost all men are content with those easy merits; but the instant effect of conversing with God will be to put them away. There are persons who are not actors, not speakers, but influences; persons too great for fame, for display; who disdain eloquence; to whom all we call art and artist seems too nearly allied to show and by-ends, to the exaggeration of the finite and selfish, and loss of the universal. The orators, the poets, the commanders encroach on us only as fair women do, by our allowance and homage. Slight them by preoccupation of mind, slight them, as you can well afford to do, by high and universal aims, and they instantly feel that you have right, and that it is in lower places that they must shine. They also feel your right; for they with you are open to the influx of the all-knowing Spirit, which annihilates before its broad noon the little shades and gradations of intelligence in the compositions we call wiser and wisest.

In such high communion let us study the grand strokes of rectitude: a bold benevolence, and independence of friends, so that not the unjust wishes of those who love us shall impair our freedom, but we shall resist for truth's sake the freest flow of kindness, and appeal to sympathies far in advance; and–what is the highest form in which we know this beautiful element–a certain solidity of merit, that has nothing to do with opinion, and which is so essentially and manifestly virtue, that it is taken for granted that the right, the brave, the generous step will be taken by it, and nobody thinks of commending it. You would compliment a coxcomb doing a good act, but you would not praise an angel. The silence that accepts merit as the most natural thing in the world is the highest applause.

Such souls, when they appear, are the Imperial guard of Virtue, the perpetual reserve, the dictators of fortune. One needs not praise their courage–they are the heart and soul of nature. O my friends, there are resources in us on which we have not drawn. There are men who rise refreshed on hearing a threat; men to whom a crisis which intimidates and paralyzes the majority–demanding not the faculties of prudence and thrift, but comprehension, immovableness, the readiness of sacrifice–comes graceful and beloved as a bride. Napoleon said of Massena, that he was not himself until the battle began to go against him; then, when the dead began to fall in ranks around him, awoke his powers of combination, and he put on terror and victory as a robe. So it is in rugged crises, in unweariable endurance, and in aims which put sympathy out of question, that the angel is shown. But these are heights that we can scarce remember and look upto without contribution and shame. Let us thank God that such things exist.

And now let us do what we can to rekindle the smoldering, nigh-quenched fire on the altar. The evils of the church that now is are manifest. The question returns, what shall we do? I confess, all attempts to project and establish a Cultus with new rites and forms seem to me vain. Faith makes us, and not we it, and faith makes its own forms. All attempts to contrive a system are as cold as the new worship introduced by the French to the goddess of Reason–today, pasteboard and filigree, and ending tomorrow in madness and murder. Rather let the breath of new life be breathed by you through the forms already existing. For if once you are alive, you shall find they shall become plastic and new. The remedy to their deformity is first, soul, and second, soul, and evermore, soul. A whole Popedom of forms one pulsation of virtue can uplift and vivify. Two inestimable advantages Christianity has given us; first the Sabbath, the jubilee of the whole world, whose light dawns welcome alike into the closet of the philosopher, into the garret of toil, and into prison-cells, and everywhere suggests, even to the vile, the dignity of spiritual being. Let it stand forevermore, a temple, which, new love, new faith, new sight shall restore to more than its first splendor to mankind. And secondly, the institution of preaching—

the speech of man to men–essentially the most flexible of all organs, of all forms. What hinders that now, everywhere, in pulpits, in lecture-rooms, in houses, in fields, wherever the invitation of men or your own occasions lead you, you speak the very truth, as your life and conscience teach it, and cheer the waiting, fainting hearts of men with new hope and new revelation?

I look for the hour when that supreme Beauty which ravished the souls of those Eastern men, and chiefly of those Hebrews, and through their lips spoke oracles to all time, shall speak in the West also. The Hebrew and Greek Scriptures contain immortal sentences, that have been bread of life to millions. But they have no epical integrity; are fragmentary; are not shown in their order to the intellect. I look for the new Teacher that shall follow so far those shining laws that he shall see them come full circle; shall see their rounding complete grace, shall see the world to be the mirror of the soul; shall see the identity of the law of gravitation with purity of heart; and shall show that the Ought, that Duty, is one thing with Science, with Beauty, and with Joy.

5

Mother Teresa

A friend of the poor and the unwanted

Introduction

During the early seventies, my wife, the late Madhavi and myself were thrilled when we heard, that a nun from Albania was doing an important work in the slums of Calcutta, and we were wondering how in this materialistic world people have concern for the unwanted and uncared for humans of the streets. We then found it was sister Teresa who (later began to be called Mother Teresa) has been concerned about the lepers, the poor, the unwanted, the rejected and the oppressed. We both were touched by the humanism which was pulsating in the heart of the Mother and felt proud of her. Some years later when her work was recognized all over the world, she received the Nobel Peace Prize at a function at Oslo, Sweden, when the king of Sweden, the Queen, the Princess, the Nobel Laureates, the ambassadors, the diplomats, the Ministers and other distinguished guests – all standing and bowing before Mother Teresa in appreciation of her charitable work. My eyes were filled with moisture to witness the unique scene of the award of the Nobel Peace Prize to a frail Catholic nun which was telecast live while I was at Vienna in 1980. Later, I saw her at close quarters at the Dhaka University in 1984 when Mother came to address the students of Dhaka University after receiving the Golden key of the city of Dhaka from the President of Bangladesh at the Presidential Palace. I was elated to see that God's Grace had descended on her. That was a memorable day for me to get a glimpse of an Angelic personality. I shall always cherish that. Throughout the talk she was appealing to people to give love to the poor.

As days passed, I developed a very great admiration for her and I thought I should write about her work and her achievements in the form of a monograph and started writing subsequently. But then, due to pressure of other important responsibilities, the work could not be completed. But when I heard of her sudden passing away on the 5th September, 1997, I was shaken to my depths. I thought I should complete my write up within the next few days.

I wrote a Tribute to the Mother on the day of her funeral on the 13th of September 1997 for the Press, which I have incorporated in this monograph.

The Mother was great. I wonder whether the Missionaries of Charity would be able to devote the same way as Mother did for the hungry, the unwanted, the rejected and the poor. She had a charisma, and the world recognized her. The running of the Missionaries of Charity was the show of one magnetic force–Mother Teresa. Her words were law, and she commanded the esteem of all people of the globe. Where the Ambassadors and diplomats failed, the Mother succeeded. She had a vision and a mission. I wish each and every one of us understand the spirit of Mother Teresa–'the saint of the gutters' who worked for God, and follow her noble footsteps in wiping out the tears of the millions of unwanted and uncared for, and rejected by the society. May God grant salvation to the Mother, and may the spirit of Mother Teresa guide us all. Amen.

Aligarh
September 17, 1997 **—S.M.B.**

Mother Teresa–Love Personified

A Tribute

Mother Teresa was an apostle of love. She conjured up an image of an angelic entity, healing the wounds of humanity with the loud proclamation to everyone, not to miss the kingdom of God within himself. That kingdom is of love which manifests itself in the whole universe, for, the nature of God is love. Love resolves all differences between man and man, pushes the stage of law behind, pulls the stage of love before, and acts as the moving energy of the entire Creation. Mother Teresa was love personified who drilled into every ear that love is the manifestation of the Divine Absolute in our heart, and that only through love, human soul realized the unity of God. In this world of turmoil Mother Teresa spent her life like a lump of love. The eternal message of the Mother was that 'love purifies the soul from earthly temptations that love is a movement towards the idea of Perfect Beauty, that genuine love comes to fulfil God's design on earth, and that it is only through love, that God is reflected in every other person.' In other words, love and compassion are a part of moral preparation to reflect within man the divinity of God.

Mother, therefore, understood fully the Gospel of love, and taught the lesson of giving, than receiving. In the process, she was

* Published in the Nevhind Times , Pangim.

only adored, but also faced many challenges. She was no humanitarian exploiter. It can only be exclaimed as a proclamation of Jesus by loving the poorest of the poor and unwanted. To the poor and the unwanted the hunger for love was greater than the hunger for bread. 'Love is not a passing sentiment or a feeble emotion, but an attitude of life involving the mind, feeling and will, strong, deep and enduring.' Her passion and compassion on behalf of the poorest, and sickest, reverberated far beyond the squalid Calcutta slumps where her work began. The uncompromising reverence Mother had for human life, is in confirmity of the true Christian Charity which Mother practiced in letter and spirit. This was amazing. One has to kiss a leper, wash his wounds, nourish him like your own child, destroy your sleep to comfort his distress, and suffer his agony as your own.

Mother Teresa was the greatest Christian of her age was greater than all the Popes, pre-eminent leader of the churches and denominations, and Christian theologians and apologists put-together. In the fullness of her life and work, she blazed a trial as a great humanitarian. A true follower of Jesus, her deeds of altruism and charity won her global recognition as a saint of the poor. Despite the highest honours like the Nobel Peace Prize and Bharat Ratna, and other honours conferred on her, she humbled herself by saying 'I am not worthy of it'. For her, no award was big or small. She felt, it was the recognition of the poor and unwanted.

"Others have spoken of the love, but the Mother became the crusading practitioner of this great concept. Others were wanting to cover the journey, but she reached the goal, and showed the world what must be done to make love bubble in soul." Love is like that drop of honey which catches more flies than a gallon of gall 'Love gives you gentleness and friendliness, which are stronger than fury and force.' The mother translated these ideals into practice, led a noble life of service, dedicated herself wholly to relieve the agony of others and kindled a spark of God's mercy in the hearts of all around her.

The Mother's work in Calcutta's slums (which was once the city of despair, became a city of joy), **exemplified the notion**

that when confronted with such Himalayan challenges as traditional poverty, small steps are more effective than monumental anti-poverty programmes, administered by faceless bureaucrates and high priests of global development.

In an age of self-promotion where any work sincerely undertaken, be it social work or educational work or missionary work, blemishes from mean minded sectarian public are not uncommon. Mother Teresa did not care for their comments, nor did she work to seek fame. She felt, that despite economic development, and market forces, there were people whose lives remained mired in the sorry circumstances of their birth. The demographics of the dispossessed kept growing, because the forces of globalization created more victims than beneficiaries. The annual meetings of the World Bank, and the International Monetary Fund debate policies, they lament poverty, and issue grave comments on sustainable development. Better they should study how, one Catholic nun clad in a simple white saree with simple living, did not care much with commissions, conferences, annual reports etc. and, instead, went out simply, into the world to change the lives of millions. She was managing about 600 homes all over the world single handedly, without any bureaucrates, which speaks volume of her administrative capability.

Whenever Mother spoke, the world listened with respect and took notice. Implicit in what the Mother said was also an indictment of the International Development Organisations whose many billion dollars had flattened bureaucrates, but had not lifted the poor from their despair. A nation of nearly one billion people were overwhelmingly poor people and the biggest issue is poverty. That she attracted large crowds and invited great affection than any Indian "Netha" proves eloquent testimony to her unimpeachable integrity, sincerity of purpose, and her deep humility, and her firm faith in God–the qualities that are conspicuously absent in the people governing the world's largest democracy today (viz.) India. In short, noble souls like the Mother are the gifts of God born once in centuries. Will humanity learn the ways of Peace! Such Christianity which mother practiced is needed today, and that infact, is true

Islam. The Western nations pride themselves as Christians, but they never followed the teachings of Jesus or the Gospels in their true spirit. Mother was the zealous follower of Jesus in words, and deeds.

She passed away on 5th of September 1997 at 9.30 p.m. peacefully at the Mother's House when the country was celebrating the Teacher's Day. Mother herself was a Teacher *'Par excellence'*, for, she proclaimed to humanity that the poor must be loved because they have been created by the loving hand of God to love and be loved.

As soon as the news of the death was announced, a wave of tremors seemed to travel though Calcutta where her crusade had begun. That, death caught up Mother Teresa in Calcutta, was her last greetings to the poorest of that city who had embarked with her on one of the most remarkable spiritual and human adventure of this century.

This afternoon, we shall be laying her to rest with full military honours in the presence of world dignitaries from Presidents to Prime Ministers, personal representatives of the Heads of States and Governments from all over the globe, highest dignitary of the Holy Sea representing the Pope at Vatican and in the presence of Governors, Chief Ministers of Indian States and millions of Indians at her 'Mother's Home' in Calcutta which was the nucleus for her grand work of promoting peace in the most fundamental manner by her confirmation of the **inviolability of human dignity.** At this hour of gloom let us all pray together for the departed soul, who brought glory to India's Poor. Her extraordinary spiritual mission and her self-sacrifice and respect for the value of every human life, will, I am sure, continue to inspire the Brothers and Sisters of the Missionaries of Charity to care the poorest of the poor. **There is no example like her in this world.** Let us, therefore, resolve to dedicate ourselves to such noble causes and live up to her expectations which may gladden the soul of the noble Mother who is watching us from the Heavens. That will be our tribute to Revered Mother.

Aligarh
September 13, 1997

—S.M. Bijli

Mother Teresa

(1910–1997 AD)

Bharat Ratna (Star of India)

"Lord make us worthy to serve the poor around the world who live and die in poverty, hunger and disease."

"Once in several centuries, God chooses to send some one who may serve as the connecting link between Him and His children. In an age where compassion for the poor and needy has become an outdated concept, Mother Teresa as she was known the world over, had given in a new meaning and forced a cynical world to acknowledge and honour such a spirit. Wherever pain has to be eased, loneliness solaced, poverty and hunger assuaged–in slumps from New York to Calcutta, in the famine infested wastes of Ethiopia, amidst earthquakes and floods–Wherever human need is most acute, Mother Teresa was there. The most horrible disease according to her was not leprosy now-a-days or T.B. It is a feeling to be unwanted, rejected, abandoned by all."

The citation to confer the honorary degree of Doctor of Human Letters by the Loyola University in the United States in April 1976 read as follows:

"Mother Teresa gives her life for her friends; and her friends are the sick, the injured, the dying and the lonely of our imperfect world. She has brought help to the dearest and least of the bretheren, hers, yours and Christs."

In presenting the Pacem-in-Terris award in April 1976–an award voted by the Catholic inter-racial Council and awarded earlier to Martin Luther King, Bishop O'Keefe told the audience: "I think that in my life time, we shall not have so great a personage with us as we have tonight."

And the President of the World Bank, Robert McNamara declared that "Mother Teresa promotes peace in the most fundamental manner, by her confirmation of the inviolability of human dignity."

Born to Albanian Parents in Skopje in Yugoslavia in 1910 and baptised Agnes Gouxha Bogaxhur, Mother Teresa wanted to be a Missionary at the age of 12. At the age of 18, she joined the Irish branch of the Loreto nuns at Calcutta. At 27, she took her final Vows. Navin Chawla in his book on Mother Teresa Writes:

"She heard a divine call–a call within a call when she was heading for Darjeeling on the 10th September, 1946 for her annual Retreat. As the train passed through a tunnel, she heard a call in her heart. "It was an order" she was to say "I had to abandon the comfort of my convent, give up everything to serve Him and Jesus Christ through the poorest of the poor." She was 35 then, and got Vatican permission to leave the convent and to found a new religious order whose vocation was to serve the poor and dying. She left the Loreto Congregation to work in the slums of Calcutta. Mother Teresa gave the message of love and service to Jesus-in-need, first in one's own home, then in the neighbourhood and the town and then in far away places. She asked everyone specially children to try to see Jesus even when He seemed to be disguised or disfigured by disease."

"Lord make us worthy to serve the poor around the world who live and die in poverty, and hunger". Caring for the dying was only the first step in her crusade in Feb. 1953 followed by others. Then she turned to the thousands of lepers in Calcutta on the land given by the Railways. Mother built a shelter with bricks and mud to house the worst cases of lepers. She visited them each day and provided food, and nourishing the wounds, comforting them with words of love. That was Shantinagar–a few miles away from Calcutta city which was the fulfilment of one of Mother's most cherished dreams: a place that Leprosy victims could call their own; a place where tender love would heal them; a place where they could live and die with dignity. Inspired by her work a number of young women students headed by Sister Agnes entered the fold to strengthen her hands.

"In Titagarh, the Leprosy victims receive generous love. In Shishu Bhavan–a stone's throw from Mother's House, 300 orphans were nurtured with affection. Prem Dan (Abode of Love) off the Eastern bypass in Calcutta sought to remove the loneliness of 300 old ailing. Shanti Dan (Abode of Peace) in Tangra, on the outskirts of the city, drug addicts were rehabilitated by devoted sisters."

"The Nirmal Hriday was the centre close to Mother's heart. Here no one dies lonely. Picked up from the streets and gutters, the dying were truly loved. Mother had once brought in a woman whose feets were half chewed by rats, and a dying man whose wounds were alive with maggots. The Missionary Brothers of Charity took care of the man in Nirmal Hriday, while the sisters looked after women."

Mother Teresa spread God's love by giving whole-hearted free service to the poorest of the poor, irrespective of caste and creed, nationality, race or place. Not only she founded the Missionaries of Charity (sisters) on 7th October 1950, she also founded the Missionary Brothers of Charity on 25th March 1963, and the International Co-workers of Mother Teresa in 1969. She established Slum Schools, Houses for crippled and mentally retarded children; mobile general clinics and centres for the malnourished, mobile clinics and rehabilitation centres for Lepers, drug addicts and alcoholics; night shelters for the homeless and natural family planning guidance and relief work in modern Mumbai and Delhi. Indeed the task was not easy. Mother Teresa was definitely inspired.

Thus the founding of the Missionaries of Charity was the

work of this only one woman Mother Teresa. Meanwhile the world began recognizing the work of Mother Teresa which had gone out from Calcutta to help the poorest of the poor, the suffering, the foresaken, the dying and the disinherited of the earth. Today there are 600 centres all over the world. She set up organisations, schools, orphanages, hospitals, leprosy clinics, night shelters for the homeless, and rescue centres numbering 500, scattered over 100 countries on five continents. 'The greatest poverty is, to feel unwanted, and unloved.' This poverty exists even in affluent countries, She said "There are about 5000 Sisters all over the world and consecrated Brothers, India alone has 350, and more than 4 million lay workers." They work in the slums, the streets, the railway stations. Inspired by the Mother they have dedicated for serving the Poorest of the Poor.

Welcoming the Co-Worker family, Mother Teresa said:

"My gratitude to the Co-Workers is a Prayer that you may each grow in the likeness of Christ and the carriers of God's love. You should be a living example of God's presence in the world....God loves the world through You." She said:

"Just as God sent His Son to proclaim the good news that God loves us and that God loves the world so much. He also gave the Co-Workers and Missionaries of Charity to the World." She reminded the Co-Workers, of the words which heralded the coming of Jesus. "Fear not" "There will be suffering", and more and more people are suffering, I am sure, in every country. There is that terrible fear of nuclear war, that terrible, terrible fear...but such a terrible fear is not for you. We will pray. Prayer cannot fail and not only pray, but put the prayer into a loving action, and also do something for somebody. Dependence on the providence of God for the work with the poor was the clear and only Course."

Trust in the future, as with everything else, was part of her trust in the profound in-scrutable designs of providence.

It is an accident, Mother chose India to be her home–the land of saints and sages, land of Buddha and Mahavira, Chishtis and Sufis, and Nanak and St. Xavier. Their impact along with the Christian Gospel inspired Mother Teresa. The Mother was fascinated by the moral teachings of the Jains. "My contemplation" of Mahavira appealed to her most.

"May I never cause pain to any living being,
May I never utter untruth,
And may I never covet the wealth or wife of another.
May I never drink the nectar of contentment...
May there be mutual love in the World
May delusion dwell at a distance...
May all understand the Laws of Truth and
joyfully sorrow and sufferings endure.
Om Shanti; Om Shanti; Om Shanti;
Peace, Peace and Peace."

24th Thirthankara.

She said 'Mahavira had shown the path to perfection through right knowledge, right vision, right conduct as the three crown jewels of Spirituality; and the Christian Gospels say:

"If you do not love your brother whom you see, how can you love God whom you do not see." Words and flesh, ideas and spirit which is every one and the same in all nations and periods of history. "Let our prayer be born of the spirit and not mere flesh and blood." This was the central doctrine of Christian theology, and mother turned up to that doctrine in its true and practical spirit and pulled all others to shame when they have not lived up to the teachings of Jesus. When Saint Thomas Aquinas (1225-1274) was mentally worried as he looked around and saw people scarcely recognizing the faith of Christianity in view of the rites and rituals in which they were involved, and watching the great processions of the Bishops in their scarlet robes, and the pompous titles by which they addressed one another, St. Thomas Aquinas asked unto himself "was this the humble religion of Christ?" He felt that "the entire ceremonial of the Church, with its relics and symbols had become a mere external show. The church had been transformed from merely a spiritual into an ecclesiastical order. Was this what the Fathers of the early Christian Community had envisaged?"

"Poor, unwilling blunderers, indeed, are the men who

undermine and pervert the very principles of their Gospel. The Christian eye had become so eager to behold Jesus in the flesh that the Christian heart had forgotten to see Christ in the spirit. Men blessed the dead bones of the saints, but they failed to understand their living souls. It was time to bring men back to the true ethics of Christianity" said Aquinas. Some voices had called in accents of love, others in tones of wisdom, and Thomas Aquinas came forward to combine the two. He decided to weave the sayings of the Holy Fathers and the scriptures into one vast philosophical system to embrace intellectual and moral and theological life of the Catholic world. "Had not Saint Socrates, St. Plato, St. Buddha and St. Confucious done the same for their Pagan World?" Therefore, St. Thomas Aquinas composed the *'Summa Theologica'* (the summary of the word of God through the mouth of a philosopher) the monumental hand book of ethics, religion and metaphysics. He was a follower of the God intoxicated Sufi philosopher Al-Ghazali. The existence of God is affirmed not as an act of faith but as a fact of reason.

The entire social and moral philosophy of the scripture is expounded in a series of logical propositions that remind one of the treatment of that later philosophy of faith, Spinoza's Ethics. "The hand work of the Lord is a sensible fact. Who else but the Lord could have taken the nameless chaos of substance and moulded into a meaning and a form?"

Mother Teresa in the twentieth century thrilled the soul of the great Saint Thomas Aquinas of the 13th century with joy. She understood well the true spirit of the Christianity and **realised that only by serving the poor with joy she could serve the Lord. She had a vision and indeed she was inspired.**

She was also influenced by the Parsies belief in the final judgement similar to that of Muslims, the Jews and Christians. Prophet Zarathustra gave the world a message of love, four thousand years ago–a message that spells out: "Love thy fellowmen for thou art thy brother's keeper; Love him with good thoughts, good words and good deeds *(Hukt, Howarshat and Humat)*; love little children, for, they are innocent of the earth; care for all those that are sick suffering and in need." Be it as it may.

In response to an invitation of the Diocesan Council of Catholic Women at Pennyslvania Mother Teresa said: **"Today, talking about the poor is in fashion. Knowing and loving and serving the poor is quite another matter. "The work you do is His gift to you. The pass word of the early Christian was joy. Serve the Lord, therefore, with joy."**

She wrote to all Co-Workers to pray. Mother Teresa said: "I would like the Fifteenth Chapter of St. John. (on the vine and the branches) to become our life." Reverting to one of her favourite quotations from the scripture, she wrote to all Co-Workers.

"Let us become a true and faithful branch of the vine Jesus, by accepting Him in our lives as it pleases Him to come."

as the truth - to be told
as the life - to be lived
as the light - to be lighted
as the love - to be loved
as the way - to be walked
as the joy - to be given
as the peace - to be spread
as the sacrifice - to be offered in our families and with our close neighbours as well as far away neighbours.

Every house of the Missionaries of Charity all over the World had its special character as the sisters shaped their programme to the needs of the people.

"If in coming face to face with God we come closer to Him in our lives, then we were converting. We become better Hindus, better Muslims and better whatever we are."

"Shine through me" said Newman's prayers, "and be so in me that every soul I come in contact with, may feel thy presence in my soul."

"Let them look up and see no longer me—but only Thee, O Lord

Stay with me and when I shall begin to shine as Thou dost--
so to shine
as to be a Light to others,
The Light, O Lord, will be all from Thee;
None of it will be mine,
It will be Thou shining through me."

Mother was a dazzling candle of the world and was a symbol of love and affection.

Mother Teresa was a gift of God to Calcutta. She drew attention to poverties of mankind both spiritual and temporal; and in her humble way tried to meet them. Her name had become synonymous with the work of the poor, the rejected and the dying. Mother's sunshine smile enveloped everyone in its warmth strengthening their ties with Jesus she and her sisters thrive on. Mother Teresa was very grateful to the Co-Workers and in a prayer that "You may each grow in the likeness of Christ and the carriers of God's Love. You should be a living example of God's presence in the world...God loves the world through you."

To a packed congregation at St. James Church in Piccadilly, the heart of London, Mother Teresa recited the following prayer:

"Lead me from death to life,
from falsehood to truth,
Lead me from despair to hope,
from fear to trust,
Lead me from hate to love,
from war to peace,
Let peace fill our hearts, our world
our Universe."

This prayer was recommended by Mother Teresa to all the Co-Workers all over the world.

Honours Conferred

Honours and recognition of her work came from all over the world:

The Indian Government chose Mother Teresa for the 'Padma

Shri' award in Sept. 1962. At the Presidential Palace (Rashtrapati Bhavan) when Mother Teresa entered the glittering Durbar Hall with its painted ceilings and all the pomp and panoply that attend such functions—the military on parade and the guards on duty, all dressed in splendid colours, a band in attendance, she walked up just as she is every day, received the award as she would have received a dying man or picked up a child, but the Durbar Hall went mad. The stumping and clapping and the cheering were absolutely spontaneous. The philosopher President of India Dr. Radhakrishnan who presented the award was in tears when he handed over the 'Padam Shri' award to Mother Teresa.

She received the Ramon Magsay-say award in 1962. Also Pope John XXIII Peace Prize of $ 25,000 in Rome in 1971 and the Mater et Magistra Medal by the third order of St. Francis in 1974. She received the Balzan International Foundation Prize provided for, in the will of Angelina Balzan Danieli (The prize was given only to those who promoted initiatives of peace and humanitarianism and brotherhood among people, and brought to the work an amount equal to $ 3,25,000).

Yet another—the Templeton Foundation Prize was presented by Prince Phillip at Cambridge, England in 1973.

The Discovery Medal was awarded in June 1981 at a special convocation at Marquette University at Milwaukee, Wisconsin.

The Kennedy International award was conferred on her in 1971.

The prize of the good Samaritan Boston 1971. The Angel of Charity Award in 1972, the first Albert Schewitzer International Prize was awarded in 1975.

Queen Elizabeth honoured her with the Order of the British Empire in 1978.

The Jawaharlal Nehru Award for International Understanding was presented to her in 1972.

The citation read

Some day perhaps mankind will devise satisfactory solutions for every human predicament. But as long as compassion counts for something in human condition, the hope of defeated men everywhere, despairing men at the end of their tether, will rest on a chosen few whom the giving is all. "One such messenger of mercy is Mother Teresa."

The award carries a cash prize of one million Indian rupees which was handed over by the President of India at the special Investiture ceremony at the Rashtapati Bhavan at New Delhi.

And – The Nobel Peace Prize

The Norwegian Nobel Committee awarded the Nobel Peace Prize to Mother Teresa in 1979.

The *Aula Magna* of the Oslo University was filled with academics, diplomats, politicians, members of the armed forces in full uniform, and an immense press corps, she received what has been termed the Ultimate accolade–the Nobel Peace Prize. Navin Chawla describes the scene as follows:

As she was led to the stage by the Chairman of the Norwegian Nobel Committee, Professor John Sannes awaited her. All stood at the entrance, King Olave V, Crown Prince Herald and Crown Princess Sonja. A symphony orchestra placed on the stage played Greig's "Gratitude" and multicoloured bouquets of flowers shone under the brilliant chandeliers. In a powerfully worded address in English, Professor Sannes began:

"Your Majesty, Your Royal Highnesses, Your Excellencies, Ladies and Gentlemen."

"The Norwegian Nobel Committee awarded the Peace Prize for 1979 to Mother Teresa."

The citation read as follows:

"The year 1979 has not been a year of Peace. Disputes and conflicts between nations, peoples and ideologies, have been conducted with all the accompanying extremes of inhumanity and cruelty. We have witnessed wars, the restrained Violence; we have witnessed fanaticism hand in hand with cynicism; we have witnessed contempts for human life and dignity... We are faced with new and overwhelming floods of refugees.

Not without reason, the word genocide has been on many lips. In many countries, completely innocent people have been the victims of acts of terror. In this year, moreover, we recalled the way in which an entire ethnic group was virtually exterminated in Europe only a generation ago. The Holocaust film series has shaken us, not only as an evil memory from our own not-too-distant past, but as we consider the world of 1979, not one of us can be certain, that the like of which may not recur in future."

"The Norwegian Nobel Committee has considered it right and appropriate, precisely in this year, in their choice of Mother Teresa, to remind the world of the words spoken by Fridtjob Nansen."

"Love of one's neighbour is realistic policy. As a description of Mother Teresa's life's work, we might select the slogan that a previous Nobel Peace Prize Laureate, Albert Schweitzer adopted as the leitmotif for his work: 'Veneration for life.' Mother Teresa's work for the poor was performed without condescension and as a witness to the dignity of every person. Her work was done in such a way as to build bridges across the great gulfs that separate parts of the human family..."

"In awarding the Nobel Prize for 1979 to Mother Teresa, the committee has posed a focal question that we encounter along these paths: Can any political, social or intellectual feat of engineering, on the international or on the national plane, however, effective and national, however idealistic and principled its protagonists may be, give us anything but a house built on the foundation of sand, unless the spirit of Mother Teresa inspires the builders and takes its dwelling in their building?"

"The sisters with serene ways, their sarees, their knowledge of local languages... have come to symbolize not only the best in Christian Charity, but also the best in Indian culture and civilisation from Buddha to Gandhi."

"Mother Teresa's work in the world as she finds it, in the slums of Calcutta and other towns and cities. But she makes no distinction between poor and rich persons, between poor and rich countries. Politics has never been the concern, but economic, social, and political work with these sane aims, are in complete harmony with her own life's work."

"We would like to remind this international audience that, help on the international level can only serve the cause of Peace if it does not offend the self-respect of poor nations and we urge that such help from the rich countries be given in the spirit of Mother Teresa."

"There would be no better way of describing the intentions that motivated the decision of the Norwegian Nobel Committee than the comment of the President of the World Bank, Robert McNamara when he declared "Mother Teresa deserves Nobel Peace Prize because she promotes peace in the most fundamental manner by her confirmation of the inviolability of human dignity."

The Gold Peace medal and diploma representing the Prize and its gift of over U.S. $ 1,90,000 were placed in Mother Teresa's hand and she was left alone in the spotlight before the microphones on the impressive rostrum.

While accepting the Nobel Prize, Mother Teresa asked everyone to join her Prayer. The prayer already distributed to everyone in the Aula Magna, including the Press was the Peace prayer attributed to everyone's Saint Francis, the poor man of Assisi. About 800 voices in toned in Unison:

"Lord make me a channel of peace, where there is hatred, let me sow love; where there is injury, pardon... where there is despair, hope...; Grant that I may not so much seek to be consoled as to console; to be loved as to love; for it is in giving that we receive; it is in pardoning that we are pardoned; and it is in dying that we are born to eternal life."

Bharat Ratna (Star of India)

If Mother Teresa thought that the days of public ceremony were behind her as she left Oslo, she was mistaken. The jury constituted to select a person for the highest civilian award of India for 1980 were unanimous in their view, when they opined that there was no one more deserving for the highest award 'Bharat Ratna' than Mother Teresa. India was, therefore getting ready to honour her with its highest civilian award–The Bharat Ratna (The Star of India). To the Strains of The Indian National Anthem at a special investiture ceremony at the Presidential Palace—The Rashtrapati Bhavan in New Delhi in the presence of the Prime Minister Mrs. Indira Gandhi, Members of the Cabinet, Diplomats, high military and civil officials and the top dignitaries, Mother Teresa stepped upto the dais to be invested with the ultimate honour of her adopted country by the President of India. The President Neelam Sanjeeva Reddy told the audience "She embodies in herself, compassion and love of humanity as few in history have done.... Her entire life has been a personification of service and compassion. These are the imperatives of human existence which are generally affirmed in words but denied in actions."

The then Prime Minister Mrs. Indira Gandhi congratulating her said "To meet her is to feel utterly humble, to sense the power of tenderness and strength of love."

The strength of love taught and practiced by Mother Teresa and the Missionaries of Charity could be seen in the works of Mercy, since Mercy is only love under the aspect of need, love going out to meet the needs of the person loved. The work of Mercy, feeding the hungry, clothing the naked, sheltering the shelterless, interrupted or reversed by every war, were being recognized as works of peace. The ultimate accolade – the Nobel Peace Prize to Mother Teresa awakened many to realise that works of Mercy might be the truest undergirding of peace, to be reversed only at humanity's peril.

The Harvard University at Cambridge (Massachussettes) conferred an Honorary Doctorate of Law in 1982. Earlier Honorary Doctorates were conferred by St. Francis Xavier University Antigonish, Nova Scotia, Canada in 1974.

The Cambridge University (England) founded 1100 A.D. conferred the degree of Doctor of Divinity *(honoris Causa)* in June 1971. While presenting Mother Teresa to the Chancellor of Cambridge University, the orator of the University said:

"The reverend Mother whom we are delighted to see among us would reply, if you inquired about her career, that it was of no importance. I present to you one who is not the least among the hand maids of the Lord, the Reverend Mother Teresa–Founder and leader of the congregation of the Missionaries of Charity."

The Vishwabharati University at Shanti-Niketan founded by Nobel Laureate Rabindranath Tagore conferred on her the honorary degree—*Deshikottama*, for contribution to suffering humanity.

Santiago University conferred the degree of Doctor of Divinity *(honoris Causa)* on Mother Teresa. Doctor of Laws *(honoris Causa)* by the Madras University in 1984. The President of Bangladesh presented the Golden Key of the City of Dhaka to Mother Teresa in 1985.

The Honorary Doctorate from the University of Alberta in Edmonton, Canada was accompanied by a visit to the town of St. Paul where it seemed as if every resident of the town was present at the ceremony of the presentation of a gift by Bishop Raymond Roy – a large amount of $ 9,25,000 all collected by the people of this small town of St. Paul.

At the town of Sydney (Nova Scotia) in 1974, two Indian Medical men came to cheer Mother Teresa after the speech – One of them Dr. M.M. Chauhan, a medical practitioner who gave all his energies to his practice. Some years later Dr. Chauhan a bachelor and a devout Hindu died bequeathing his entire estate to the work of Mother Teresa. It was nearly $ 5,00,000.

Awards, distinctions and prizes never altered her humility. She always greeted these honours in the name of the poor of the world.

The President of U.S. awarded the medal of freedom in the name of God and the Poor who are being recognized and wanted in1985. The Mother replied Personally she was unworthy.

She received the Soviet Land Nehru award in 1990 at a special function at New Delhi.

Albania's Golden Honours of the Nation in 1991.

Bharat Ki Suputri title in 1992.

The Rajeev Gandhi *Sadbhavana* Award in 1993.

In February 1994 the U.S. Congress passed a legislation to give Mother Teresa the Congressional Gold Medal–the highest honour the U.S. Congress can bestow on a civilian.

In November 1994 she became only the fifth non-American to receive honorary citizenship.

The Mother transcended all religions in her purity of representing the work of God. It was the power of love which made the Mother such an extra-ordinary person. When someone asked that there is an allegation that she converts people to her faith, she replied promptly 'yes' "I convert people to become better Hindus, better Muslims, and better Protestants." The bodies of the inmates who die at Kalighat and who were not known to be Christians, Muslims or Parsis were invariably cremated, and others were handed over to the people of their respective faiths to dispose off. Thus, she transcended her religion in reaching over to people of all faiths and the faithless besides. She followed Jesus in essence and absorbed his spirits in her.

She was remarkably tolerant to those who did not believe her passions about her faith. She was not only pious but also delightfully practical. Her charisma appealed to something very basic in us all, the desire to reach out goodness. She always spoke of loving, caring and sharing.

When some sections of the Indian Society, specially the Vishwa Hindu Parishad and the B.J.P. were biased about the work that the Mother was engaged in, she said "while you go on discussing causes and explanations, I will kneel besides the poorest of the poor and attend to their needs. The beggar, the leper and the victim of race do not need discussions and theories.... They need love. The hungry can not wait for the rest of the world to come up with a proper answer. They are without constituency and ideologies." She was a genius of practicability. She never turned down anyone who was poor, and never refused a child–Hindu, Muslim, Christian or whomever be.

Swami Vivekananda once said that "there is a howling cry that we are poor, but how many charitable institutions are there for the well being of the poor? How many people really weep for the sorrows and sufferings of the poor in India? I consider that the great national sin is the neglect of the masses, and that is one of the causes of our downfall." In India there are two great evils. "Trampling on the women and grinding the poor through caste restrictions." he wrote in one of his letters. "No religion on earth preaches the dignity of humanity in such a lofty strain as Hinduism, and no religion on earth treads upon the necks of the poor and the low in such a fashion as Hinduism." "We speak of many things parrot-like, but never do them; speaking and not doing has become a habit with us–we are lazy, we can not work, we can not combine, we do not love each other; we are intensely selfish, not three of us can come together, without being jealous of each other." As against such lack of organisational ability, Swami Vivekananda also believed that no amount of politics would be of any avail until the masses were educated, well fed, and well cared for. And, therefore, he made a beginning in this direction by giving shape to the Ramakrishna Mission at a meeting held at Balaram Mandir on May 1, 1897 to carry out the social and welfare activities. Vivekananda said:

> **"India is restless with the thought of how to face the hunger... First of all, you must remove the evil of hunger and starvation, this constant anxiety for bare existence, from those to whom you want to preach religion... First bread, and then religion." Therefore, Swami Vivekananda advised the workers, "You must renounce everything. You must not seek comfort or pleasure for yourself. You must look upon gold as object of lust, as poison, name and fame as filth, wordly glory as terrible hell."** Let the Vishwa Hindu Parishad and B.J.P. and all those who are habitual in accusing others and tell the people they are the only puritans in the world, search their hearts and conscience before casting aspersions on others. Their conscience would speak for itself. Let them do research on what the great Swami Vivekananda had said, and learn from his work, the concept of humanism.

The Mother was very appreciative of the Swami's philosophical thoughts, and with love and admiration she followed, in the context of India's misery and poverty of the poorest of the poor, and selflessly devoted to do whatever that was possible for her. He faith and selfless practical gifts were able to move mountains of insensitivity and uncaring not only in India but also around the world. She, therefore, lived for God. As long as the order she founded continue to work for the poorest of the poor, the Mother's legacy will endure.

As an administrator of the Missionaries of Charity, she excelled the bureaucrates. What a great administrator she was without bureaucrates and civil servants to run about 600 homes with 4000 Sisters and Brothers of Charity all over the world spread in Asia, Africa, Europe, and Latin America. She exemplified the notion that when confronted with such Himalayan challenges as traditional poverty, small steps are more effective, than monumental anti-poverty programmes administered by faceless bureaucrates and high priest of global development. The annual meetings of the World Bank and IMF only interested in debating policies and lamenting poverty to issue comments on sustainable development. It would be fine, if they learn how a humble Catholic nun with simple living, did not care for commissions and conferences and annual reports etc., and instead, went out simply into the world to change the lives of millions.

For her, no award was too big or too small. There were many to whom her touch transformed. She turned Calcutta from a city of despair to the city of joy. She touched the lives of millions–the poor, the naked, the hungry, and the unwanted through love. Such was her influence on the people. Her extra-ordinary spiritual mission, self-sacrifice and respect to the value of every human life, will I hope continue to inspire every one of the Missionaries of Charity to care for the poorest of the poor. There is no example like her in this world.

Sudden Passing Away of Mother

The news of the tragic death of Princess Dianna on the 3rd of September, 1997 gave a great shock to her. She was terribly impressed by the princess who joined her in ameliorating the distress of the poor as she met her last on the 18th of June 1997 at the Missionaries of Charity at New York. She prayed for the soul of Dianna at the Chapel and was feeble and in poor health to travel to London to attend her funeral. The next day of Princess Dianna's funeral on the 5th of September, 1997, the Mother passed away silently at 9.40 p.m. at her Mother's Home at Calcutta, when the country was celebrating the Teacher's Day. "I can't breath any more" were the last words of the Mother before she fell back on her bed to die. In a twinkling of an eye, the Mother was no more. The greatest healer of pain and suffering has left the world. I firmly believe, the Mother was a teacher *par-excellence* because she taught the world to love and be loved. News of her death spread like a wildfire throughout Calcutta and there was gloom in the 'city of joy', and all over India and abroad. "Bad news travels more quickly than good" and the world television flashed the news, making the people of the globe grief stricken.

The death of the Mother seems to be the end of the old order in the Missionaries of Charity which was founded and spearheaded by a simple frail, charismatic figure about 50 years ago. The funds flowed out in steady stream so long as Mother Teresa was alive. Instead of an organisation that revolved around one person, whose word was law. To the Mother, time had its importance. She used to say it several times that "time is the most important in one's life, but never think of how much, but how". The quality of time spent is always paramount for her. She has sown the world over, the seeds of love and affection. It has now borne crop. Mother Teresa might have done more to fight the poverty of the world. She was the Christian of her age. In the International popular reckoning, this Catholic nun clad in a simple white saree, small, frail, bent and gnarled was greater than the Pope, pre-eminent leaders of the church and denominations, and Christian theologians and apologists put together.

Condolence messages started pouring in from the heads of States and the Government all over the world and the President of India and Prime Minister left immediately on hearing the news of her demise for Calcutta from Delhi, to pay their respects to Mother.

As a rare gesture of affection and deep regard to her gracious personality, the Government of India declared a state mourning on the 6th of September 1997 and flags flew half mast throughout the country. The Government of India further accorded a state funeral to Mother, which is a rare gesture for a civilian, on the 13th of September, 1977 with full military honours. In death, as in life, the mother drew a following, from all, irrespective of caste, religion and creed, colour and sex. Her deeds of altruism and charity which sprang from the very core of Jesus was a practical example of the Christian charity as proclaimed by Jesus. People whether they are Christians or Muslims, or Hindus preached and pretend to be followers of their religions, but never practiced them in their true spirit. The Mother practiced as per the gospels. She was, therefore, a true Christian, and her acts of service was nothing but **Islamic through and through.** She once said, "We are called upon not to be successful, but to be faithful," She lived for her God.

It is Mother's love which brought the dignitaries of the world for her funeral. Among the admirers were the heads of state and government and other dignitaries who came to attend the funeral ceremony. Albanian President Rexhep Mejdani, Italian President Oscar Luigi Scalfaro, Ghanian President Jerry Rawlings and Bangladesh Prime Minister Sheikh Hasina Wajed were present. Queen Fabiola of Belgium, Queen Noor of Jordan and Queen Sofiya of Spain were there too. The Duchess of Kent, Katharine Luch, represented the British Government. First Lady Hillary Clinton represented the U.S. Government, while French President Jacques Chirac's wife Bernadette Chodron de Courcel represented her country. The First Ladies of Canada and Poland were also present. Representatives of 46 other countries, including Pakistan, Albania, Germany, Norway, Australia, Sweden, Mexico, Brazil, Switzerland and Austria attended the funeral. President K.R. Narayanan, Prime Minister I.K. Gujral, Defence Minister Mulayam Singh and Bharatiya Janata Party leader and former Prime Minister Atal Behari Vajpayee placed wreaths on the body. Millions of people thronged to have a last glimpse of the Mother with flowers and wreaths. Calcutta's farewell to Mother Teresa was a lofty tribute to a life of selfless service. Army officers of the rank of Major-General and Brigadier carried the coffin from the church and placed it on the gun carriage. The procession moved through the historic thorough fares of the city – and reached the Netaji Indoor Stadium. After a three-hour ceremony, attended by representatives of governments and people from around the world, the cortage made its final journey from the Indoor Stadium to 'Mother's House. Army pall-bearers lifted the white coffin from the gun carriage and entered Mother's House. Millions of people bade farewell – it was a tearful farewell. The neighbours near the Mother's House said "My God, what Mother has done is a miracle." The Jawans of the 14th Gorkha Brigade, who lined the road outside Mother's House, reversed arms and bowed their heads. Three volleys from 14 rifles were fired by the Gorkhas in salute, while four buglers sounded the Last Post, bringing to a ceremonial end, a chapter in the history of the Missionaries of Charity. She was *'Par-excellence.'*

"There rest thy feet where live
the poorest, the lowliest, and the lost."

—*Tagore.*

List of Readings

1. Biswas, Soutik : 'A quite presence', *Outlook,* Sept. 29, 1997, Vol. III, No. 40.

2. Chaudhry, Kalyan and Parvathi Menon : For the poorest of the poor, 10-12 (Mother Teresa), *Front Line,* Oct. 3, 1997, pp. 4-9, The Hindu Publication.

3. Chawla, Navin : *Mother Teresa, A Biography.*

4. Chawla, Navin : The Magic of Faith, *The Week,* Sept. 21, 1997, pp. 42-43, Vol. 15, No. 40, Manorama Publication.

5. Chawla, Navin : An Enduring Legacy (Mother Teresa), *Front Line,* Oct. 3, 1997, Vol. 14, No. 19, pp. 10-13, The Hindu Publication.

6. Ganguly, Tapash : A Life of Compassion, *The Week,* Sept. 21, 1997, Manorama Publication, Vol. 15, No. 40.

7. Gupta, Pranay : One Hovel at a Time (Mother Teresa), *News Week,* New York, Sept. 15, 1997, p. 6, Vol. CXXX, No. 11.

8. Lapierre, Dominique : The Fourth Vow, (Mother Teresa), *The Week,* Sept. 21, 1997, pp. 44-46, Vol. 15, No. 40.

9. Menon, Parvathi : A Life of Selfless Caring, *Front Line,* The Hindu Publication, Oct. 3, 1997, pp. 13-16.

10. Menon, Parvathi : Mother Teresa of Calcutta, *Front Line,* The Hindu Publication, Oct. 3, 1997, Vol. 14, No. 19, pp. 17-20.

11. Sundaram, Laurance, V. : In the Service of the Poor, *Front Line,* The Hindu Publication, Oct. 3, 1997, p. 24, Vol. 14, No. 19.

12. Uthup, Usha : Hotline to God, (Mother Teresa), *The Week,* Manorama Publication, Sept. 21, 1997, p. 46, Vol. 15, No. 40.

13. Woodward, Kenneth K. : Little Sister of the Poor, (Mother Teresa), *News Week,* New York, Sept. 15, 1997, Vol. CXXX, No. 11.

14. Encyclopaedia Britanica :

❑❑❑

Index

B

❑❑❑